RALPH J. SABOCK, Ph.D.   The Pennsylvania State University
University Park, Pennsylvania

SECOND EDITION

THE COACH

1979

W. B. SAUNDERS COMPANY   Philadelphia   London   Toronto

W. B. Saunders Company: West Washington Square
Philadelphia, PA   19105

1 St. Anne's Road
Eastbourne, East Sussex BN21 3UN, England

1 Goldthorne Avenue
Toronto, Ontario M8Z 5T9, Canada

Library of Congress Cataloging in Publication Data

Sabock, Ralph J

The coach.

Bibliography: p.

Includes index.

1. Coaching (Athletics)   2. Coaching (Athletics)—
  Vocational guidance.   I. Title

GV711.S22 1979   796′.077   79–1522

ISBN 0–7216–7891–2

The Coach   ISBN 0-7216-7891-2

Last digit is the print number: 9   8   7   6   5   4   3   2   1

To my wife EULA,
daughter ANN, *and son* MIKE

PREFACE

This book was written primarily for young men and women who are preparing to become athletic coaches. I do not believe that anyone can learn to be a coach solely by reading a book. But I do believe people can learn a great deal *about* coaching, and everything the profession entails, by reading this book. Therefore, the purpose of this book is to provide some insight into the coaching profession and to examine the many facets involved in this field of endeavor. In short, this is an attempt to describe high school coaching to those who are about to enter the profession.

It makes little difference what sport the reader coaches – the material in this book is applicable to any coach. Naturally, the relevance of each chapter will be determined by the situation the reader is involved in; some flexibility may therefore be necessary in applying the principles presented.

There is no attempt in this book to present idealized situations or to give a distorted view of a "fun-and-games" atmosphere in the coaching profession. This book is intended to be as realistic as the author's biases will allow. It is an exciting life, to be sure, but it is also a demanding one, and not without unhappy moments occasionally.

Coaching is not mechanical, nor is it all X's and O's on a piece of paper. It is a life of dealing with people, all kinds of people – adults, youngsters, fellow teachers, pleasant people, not-so-pleasant people, friendly people, antagonistic people, and above all, parents. This is one of the main aspects of the profession which sets it apart from most other professions and occupations. We are not dealing with a product which has a price tag attached when it comes off an assembly line. Rather we are dealing with the most complex thing on earth – human beings – each with his or her own hopes, dreams and goals in life.

Coaches who assume they will achieve a high degree of success because of their great knowledge of the intricacies of a game or because they themselves were outstanding performers are probably due for a real shock. It really doesn't take any super intellect to figure out how to score points in a game. But that is only a minute part of coaching. We are in the people business. It may be that the most crucial pre-

v

requisite of successful coaching is the ability to work with people rather than with the mechanics of a game.

It matters little how much knowledge a teacher possesses. The crucial element lies in how much and how well an individual can teach what he or she knows, and without an understanding of youngsters and empathy for them, the mechanical teacher faces severe limitations. This is especially true for teachers of athletics, a field in which human emotions and personal relationships are involved to such a high degree—more so than in any other single situation in a public school.

Consequently, no effort is made here to discuss the techniques and mechanics of coaching a specific sport. The idea is rather to provide some insight into many of the intangibles of coaching that up till now could only be learned through the trial and error of experience, but are nonetheless critical in the coaching profession, particularly for the neophyte.

There are no definite answers to many of the problems confronting high school coaches because the situation frequently dictates what an individual can or cannot do. It is hoped that this book will cause each reader to evaluate and reevaluate his or her beliefs about the role of a coach, methods of coaching athletic teams and the role of athletics in the school community, and that it will help a young coach to look at his or her job from a point of view other than the scoreboard, in order to formulate a personal philosophy of coaching that is based on sound principles of education and high ethical standards.

If I can supply you with a thought,
You may remember it or you may not.
But if I can make you think a thought
  for yourself,
I have indeed added to your stature.

Elbert Hubbard

RALPH J. SABOCK

ACKNOWLEDGMENTS

Traditionally, coaches have been more than willing to share their ideas and thoughts with their fellow coaches. As a result, every coach would be hard pressed to be able to identify and separate personal ideas from those learned from others. And so it is with the author.

I have learned something from every coach I've ever been associated with. I have also learned something from every coaching clinic I ever attended. But the greatest lessons of all were those learned while coaching high school athletes.

Specifically, the coaches I have had the privilege of knowing and who have helped shape many of my ideas as set forth in this book are Ed Sherman, Woody Hayes, Gene Coleman, Jim Burson, Roger Campbell, Dick Taylor, Jeff Green, Roger Pinnicks, Roger Sherman, George Mirka, Lester Baum, Dave Crockett, Warren Crouch, and Sterling Apthorp. A special acknowledgment is due a real gentleman, the late Dow Nelson, and also the late Frank Welling, Worthington High School, Class of 1903, whose loyalty, enthusiasm, and concern for youngsters were a great source of inspiration for all of us who had the privilege of knowing him.

I would like to express my appreciation also to my students in P.E. 460, Coaching Methods, for their ideas and their willingness to challenge my thoughts and beliefs. My thanks go also to the many individuals who took time to speak to these students about various aspects of coaching, such as Dick Anderson of Penn State, who added to our understanding of the recruiting process; Judy Anderson, who provided insight into the coaching of girls' athletic teams, as well as offering many valuable comments regarding the revision of this book; and Bob Carroll for his assistance in this revision.

The chapter on the coach's family is by and large a contribution of my wife, Eula, based on our exciting years as a coaching family in which she played an important role.

My sincere thanks go to coach Bob Nastase for writing the material on coaching in the inner-city; and also to Nancy Pautz for her comments on coaching inner-city youth.

The photographers were Dave Shelly, Laurie Usher, Dick Brown, Jean Dixon, and Ken Kasper.

Finally, my heartfelt appreciation to the many fine young people it has been my privilege to teach and coach.

R.J.S.

CONTENTS

1 NATURE OF THE PROFESSION   2

Security; financial aspects; life of a coach; salary scales;
applying for a coaching position; types of coaches; points of
decision; special relationships; typical working day;
emotional tension; critics.

2 THE ROLES OF A HEAD COACH   52

Teacher; disciplinarian; salesperson; public relations;
guidance counselor; diplomat; organizer; example; detective;
psychologist; judge and jury; leader; mother/father figure;
dictator; politician; actor; director; fund raiser; field
general; citizen of the community; equipment manager;
trainer; citizen of the school; the inner-city coach.

3 THE ASSISTANT COACH   80

Accepting a job as assistant coach; hiring an assistant
coach; the nature of the position; the roles and responsibilities of an assistant coach.

4 THE COACH'S FAMILY   94

Effects of coaching on a family; the married female
coach; the married male coach.

5 QUALITIES OF A GOOD COACH   116

Emulating *versus* imitating; transparent realism; reasoning;
interest in individuals; respect; motivation; peaks and
valleys; dedication; discipline; identification of goals;
recognizing talent; utilizing available talent; enthusiasm;
desire to win; willingness to work; knowledge of sport;
dislike for mediocrity; understanding boys and girls;
reasons youngsters participate in sport; factors that make a
difference between winning and losing; pride; organization;
language; morals; honesty; dignity; courage of convictions;
ethics; good judgment; consistency; fairness; imagination;
humor.

6 OFF SEASON PREPARATION – A KEY TO SUCCESS   148

Philosophy; style of play; coaches' clinic; staff organization; equipment issue; holiday practice; classroom; mouthpieces; physicals; parent involvement; managers; publicity writer; student trainer; statistician; correspondence to players and parents; notebooks; checklist; custodians; practice contests; initial team meeting; senioritis; team clinic; budget; purchasing equipment; banquets; team captains; films; booster clubs; publicity pictures; seniors' evaluation form.

7 PRE-SEASON STAFF PLANNING   188

Agenda coaches' clinic; coaches' assignments; practice procedures; acclimatization; training rules; discipline; conduct of players and coaches; coaches' appearance; drills; travel conduct; practice plans; scouting; cutting; evaluation of personnel; depth charts; master schedule; pre game–post game; pep rallies; awards; agenda team meeting; thirty rules for getting things done through people.

8 THE RECRUITING PROCESS   222

Nature of recruiting; roles of a college recruiter; seniors' questionnaire; high school coaches' responsibilities; recruiting guidelines in a school; high school coaches' assistance to college recruiters, bird dogs, and front liners financial aid; scholarships.

9 ETHICS IN COACHING   238

Ethics defined; spirit of the game; teaching honesty; competition; examples of situations in sport involving ethics; professional ethics.

10 ISSUES AND PROBLEMS   260

Issues: Drugs; elimination of sports; politics in sport, religion in sport; girls' athletics; winning; junior high athletes; little leagues; all-star teams; all-star games; polls; excusing athletes from physical education classes; soliciting funds.

Problems: Results of coaches' questionnaire; legal liability; crowd control; pregnancy and marriage; coaching your own child; misconduct and discipline; conclusion.

APPENDIX   289

Sources of official rules
Scheduling tournaments
Averages

BIBLIOGRAPHY   301

INDEX   306

THE
COACH

CHAPTER 1

Photo by Patrick Little.

1
NATURE OF THE PROFESSION

Life is no brief candle for me. It is a sort of splendid torch which I have got hold of for a moment, and I want to make it burn as brightly as possible before handing it on to future generations.

George Bernard Shaw

There is no question that one of the most important decisions you will ever make in this world is your choice of a profession and what you intend to do with your life. For some individuals this is no problem, because they have already committed themselves to becoming teachers and coaches. As a result, everything they do is geared toward reaching this goal.

On the other hand, there are many college students, including some of the ones reading this book, who really are not sure what they want to be. As a result, many of the courses they take in college have little or no meaning to them because of the lack of career goals.

Coaching is an exciting occupation — there is no doubt about that — but only for those who are dedicated and who enjoy it. For others, coaching is simply a lot of hard work, and time-consuming at that. There doesn't seem to be any middle ground. This is not a "ho hum" profession to be entered into on a whim. Rather, it is one to prepare for because you really want to be a coach more than anything else.

If an informal survey were taken among a group of prospective coaches as to their reasons for choosing coaching as a career, the answers would probably be:

1. I like sports.
2. Since I enjoy playing the game, coaching will allow me to keep in close touch with something I really enjoy.

3. I liked my high school coach so I decided to become a coach too.
4. I want to become a college coach someday.
5. I needed to declare a major; and since I enjoy athletics, I decided to try physical education and coaching.
6. Prestige.
7. I think I would enjoy the excitement and glamour associated with coaching.
8. Extra money that you get paid for coaching.
9. I like working with boys and girls.
10. I want to teach boys and girls to learn to enjoy the game.

No doubt there are other reasons that could be added to the list, but the reasons just given would probably be mentioned most frequently. Whether or not each of the reasons is sound will not be discussed here, but everything that follows in this book should help you to determine the appropriateness of the factor or factors which influenced your decision to prepare for a coaching career.

Several points ought to be clarified, however, before progressing. The first is that athletic success and enjoyment, through participation, does not necessarily mean that one will experience success and enjoyment in coaching. The former does not necessarily guarantee the latter; participating in athletics and coaching an athletic team are poles apart. Participating in a sport and coaching that sport are two entirely different experiences. This is due in part to the degree of individual commitment and personal responsibility for the overall success of the team. Many coaches enter the profession because of this early interest in athletics, and while the reasoning is basically sound, it may be that additional insight into their true motives and a greater knowledge of the profession are needed in this case.

The second point that needs to be clarified is that money, glamour, and fame come to relatively few coaches, and even then are usually short-lived. The average sports fan and school administrator have notoriously short memories where coaches' past records and accomplishments are concerned. Coaches rarely have much of an opportunity to rest on their laurels. A winning team last season sometimes makes little difference to fans if the current season is going badly. What happened yesterday is history, and in the eyes of the fans it is the present that counts.

This concept is illustrated by a speech from the movie *Patton*. With a little imagination, you can also visualize the coach returning to town after that big win.

For over a thousand years, Roman conquerors returning from the wars enjoyed the honor of the triumph, the tumultous parade. In the procession came trumpeters and musicians and strange animals from the conquered territory with carts laden with treasure and captured armaments. The conqueror rode in a triumphal chariot with the day's prisoners walking in chains before him. Sometimes his children robed in white stood with him in the chariot or rode the trace horses. A slave stood behind the conqueror holding a golden crown and whispering in his ear the warning — that all glory is fleeting.

As far as the financial rewards of coaching are concerned, any extra pay received for coaching rarely, if ever, adequately compensates a coach for the time actually spent throughout the year in guiding and developing a team. Many coaches have taken the amount of this extra salary and compared it with the time involved in coaching only to find that, when the pay is broken down into an hourly rate, they are being paid as little as 30 cents an hour. Financial security is not inherent in coaching high school athletic teams.

The third point that should be clarified at the outset is that in most public school situations coaches are hired with the understanding that their first responsibility is to teach a full day of classes every day of the week, and the coaching responsibilities are to be fulfilled over and beyond this. Naturally, there are exceptions, but prospective coaches need to be aware that if it is the love of athletics that leads one into the profession, it is also necessary to have a similar feeling toward teaching classes as well.

The salary structure should give coaches a good idea about the relationship between their daily teaching responsibilities and coaching. If the beginning salary is $10,000 and the coaching salary is $1000, coaches are being paid ten times as much to teach classes as they are to coach, which is precisely the way most school principals look at the two assignments.

To further illustrate this point, let us compare a sport season that lasts three months for approximately two-and-a-half hours a day, involving some 10 to 100 athletes, to a nine-month school year seven-and-a-half hours per day, with anywhere from 100 to 250 students involved each day. It is not difficult to understand where a coach's primary responsibility lies, in the eyes of the administration at least. It may be that it is precisely this situation that causes school administrators to state that "First we hire teachers and then we hire coaches." Generally speaking, this is not an insinuation that coaches are not teachers, but rather it is an emphasis on a coach's first responsibility — the daily teaching schedule, not an extracurricular activity. This is not an exception, but the rule, and prospective coaches need to be aware of this to avoid accepting a position with the false assumption that they will be a coach, period. It just isn't that way in most high schools.

The final point that needs to be clarified and elaborated upon is the fact that coaching is many things above and beyond actually coaching a team, regardless of the level or situation in which a coach works. A high school coach wears many hats during the entire school year because of this unique role in the school community and because of the special relationship that normally exists between coach and athlete (Chapter 2). It is important that beginning coaches, especially, become aware of this fact and begin to develop an understanding of these various roles and responsibilities.

One of the first concerns everyone has upon entering a new profession is job security. Security in the coaching profession can be described simply as the odds against getting fired. Those who are in the profession are well aware of the fact that this is always a distinct possibility in the life of a coach and is not necessarily confined to college coaches or to coaches of professional teams.

Security in coaching lies in three broad areas. First, and foremost, coaches must rely a great deal on their own ability, regardless of the number of assistants on the staff. This ability covers a multitude of competencies, but in the final analysis it all comes down to the coach's ability to prepare youngsters to play the game well.

Second, the head coach must have complete faith in the players on the team and in the coaching staff — faith that the athletes will perform in the excitement of competition the way they have been taught in practice, and faith that the assistant coaches are dedicated enough and possess enough knowledge to do an outstanding job of teaching the skills and attitudes necessary for excellence in an athlete. A coach wins with the right kind of people properly led.

Faith in young boys or girls is an absolute must among coaches. There is no other way to describe or illustrate this fact than to point out that coaches entrust their professional careers to 16- or 17-year-old youngsters playing a game. Salespeople must have complete faith only in themselves and their ability to sell a product; an architect must have complete confidence in his own ability to create; a musician must have faith in herself to play well; but coaching is unique in that coaches are evaluated not by how they themselves perform, but by how well others perform as a result of their teaching. Men and women who choose to coach as a way of earning their living have their career in "the hands of God and 16-year-old youngsters," as some coaches have put it. This takes faith. Coaches who aspire to move on to the "big time" on the basis of their won-lost record must bear this in mind.

This single factor, more than any other, is probably the greatest difference between a coach's approach to a season or a game and that of the young athletes. To the athletes a game is to be played and enjoyed. To ambitious coaches it is their way of life and their future. This difference varies in direct proportion to the level of ambition a coach has, which in turn can become a potential trouble spot in the relationship between a coach and a team.

Third, coaches must recognize the importance of cooperating with the administration of the school. This will be discussed in greater detail later in this chapter, but basically it means that coaches should remember that their sport is in reality a relatively small part of the total school program and they should not expect the school administrators to adjust the school program solely to suit the needs of an athletic team. Schools can exist without sport, but sport on the secondary level could never exist without the schools.

THE LIFE OF A HIGH SCHOOL COACH

Coaching on the high school level could be described in almost any way except dull. Coaching can be a truly exciting way to earn a living, in that every day brings new challenges. Dealing with teenagers who are predictably unpredictable is in itself enough to insure that the life of a coach will not be a boring one. Associating with high school athletes, watching them grow as athletes and as young adults, and sharing the ecstasy of triumph or the unhappiness of defeat is one of the aspects of coaching that sets it apart from any other teaching position in a school. Coaches who are so eager to "climb the ladder" to bigger and better jobs that they fail to be aware of these aspects are to be pitied, for they have missed some of the most satisfactory experiences in the profession — associating with young athletes.

The competition surrounding every phase of a sports season is another factor that insures that coaching will not become monotonous. Until a season ends, one contest is no sooner over, than a coach's thoughts are immediately directed to the next opponent. A coach rarely has much time to savor a team victory or an individual athlete's victory until the last game or match has been played. The presence of another opponent on the schedule keeps reminding coaches that what happened yesterday makes little difference today in competitive athletics. This is also a lesson youngsters should learn. The newspaper that praised them, the coach or the team yesterday, is in someone's trash container today.

As in every profession, there are times when frustration enters the picture. There are many things that can cause this feeling for coaches, but generally the primary cause is the impatience coaches sometimes feel in accomplishing their chief goal in the sports they coach. Usually this means having a winning team and the opportunity to organize the entire program in such a way that winning teams become the rule rather than the exception.

Photo courtesy of Brett Senior.

Some of this frustration will be directed toward the administrators of the school, if they don't give a coach a free hand in organizing the program the way the coach thinks best. Their unwillingness or inability to grant every request the coach makes in order to develop and expand a program also breeds frustration. When this occurs, coaches sometimes assume that the administrators just don't care and are "sitting on them and the program." There are situations where this is true, but there are many others where this is not true at all and coaches, through their narrow point of view, might be making a false assumption.

Normally, it takes time to develop a good program, and it might be several years before a varsity team attains the goals a coach has set for a program. In the meantime, a team might be losing games, and this often compounds the feeling. Losing is particularly frustrating when a team comes out on the short end of the score in a game they should have won. When coaches allow frustration to grow, and begin to dwell on it, this can affect them to the point where they hamper their effectiveness as coaches without realizing it.

One Day at a Time

"There are two days in every week about which we should not worry, two days which should be kept free from fear and apprehension.

"One of these days is *Yesterday*, with its mistakes and cares, its faults and blunders, its aches and pains. Yesterday has passed forever beyond our control. All the money in the world cannot bring back yesterday. We cannot undo a single act we performed; we cannot erase a single word said — 'Yesterday Is Gone!'

"The other day we should not worry about is *Tomorrow* with its possible burdens, its large promise and poor performance. Tomorrow is also beyond our immediate control. Tomorrow's sun will rise, either in splendor or behind a mask of clouds — but it will *rise*. Until it does we have no stake in tomorrow, for it is yet unborn.

"This leaves only one today — *Today!* Any man can fight the battle of just one day. It is only when you and I have the burdens in these two awful eternities — *Yesterday* and *Tomorrow* — that we break down."[1]

On the other hand, coaching can be a very rewarding experience — rewarding, not in strictly financial terms, but in ways that cannot be weighed or measured. Granted, rewards of this type do not pay the bills or put food on the table, but they do create a special atmosphere that makes coaching so much more than a job. It is this aspect that helps coaches avoid the feeling of going to work when it is time for practice. When practice becomes a chore, it is time for a coach to consider another occupation. These rewards are really the inner satisfaction coaches feel from teaching youngsters, being able to share an important part of their young lives and seeing some concrete evidence occasionally that these youngsters learned something worthwhile because of

---

[1]Compliments of LSU Basketball.

their teacher. Sometimes a coach will find this out years after an athlete has graduated, or that coach may never know for sure how much of an impact he or she had on a youngster. The impact that coaches make on a youngster's life remains largely a mystery. There is no way to measure this, but coaches receive enough feedback from athletes and parents from time to time, to know that they can, and do, make lasting impressions on the attitudes of young people through athletics.

The life of a coach can also be traumatic. This is especially true when an athlete suffers a serious injury. When we care about people, what happens to them also happens to us, and seeing a youngster get hurt cannot be shrugged off easily. Another factor in coaching that can be traumatic occurs when a barrage of criticism is directed at the coach. Every coach has to learn how to cope with criticism, but it can be painful, nevertheless, especially when it gets to the point where it upsets the coach's family.

Every prospective coach should be well aware of the fact that coaching is an extremely demanding occupation. It is demanding on a coach's time, energy, family life, and physical well-being, and eventually it does take its toll. It is a rare individual who has been a head coach in a high school for more than 15 years and still has the enthusiasm necessary to do the job well. This is particularly true of the people involved in the "pressure sports," which vary from one part of the country to another but are generally the sports that draw the largest crowds and create the greatest interest in a community.

Photo by Laurie Usher.

When coaches are completely dedicated to a sport they automatically become thoroughly involved mentally, physically, and emotionally, becoming totally committed to this responsibility. When this occurs, coaches' lives can assume some of the feelings of living in a "pressure cooker" world because of the stress coaches create for themselves. There are communities where pressure already exists for coaches to win, and if they don't, they lose their job. This is not unheard of in high school coaching; however, this normally occurs to coaches of the high community interest teams.

There are situations in which a coach even helps create the pressure. For example, if a coach accepts a position in a school where the athletic teams have not been very successful, that coach's first goal is to get them winning and to create interest in the school and community. At first, each victory is appreciated and enjoyed by the community. But if after a few years the coach has gotten the program to the point where winning seasons become the rule rather than the exception, the attitude of the community changes from appreciation of a win to the expectation of a win. And so it becomes a vicious cycle. Regardless of the community or part of the country, everyone loves a winner. When they get a taste of winning teams, the fans become "addicted" to it, and begin expecting the team to win all the time, which in turn puts more pressure on the coach to keep on winning. The coach soon learns that, in spite of past accomplishments, one bad season and the pressure mounts as people begin to wonder if the game has passed this coach by. As was mentioned earlier, sports fans have notoriously short memories when winning and losing enter the picture, and this is another reason coaches often feel as though the world of coaching takes place in this "pressure cooker," at least during the season.

If coaches' salaries were extremely high it might be easier to live with some of these points, but as a general rule, the salary of a coach is low in relation to the demands of the position. To a beginning coach, $150 to $2000 extra pay for coaching seems like a great deal of money, but when divided throughout twelve months, minus various deductions, this extra allowance for coaching is almost insignificant. There are school districts in various parts of the country, moreover, which do not pay coaches anything extra for this responsibility. Instead, they offer release time during the day in which the coach has no teaching responsibilities. In theory, this sounds reasonable, but in actuality, the coach is frequently found monitoring a study hall, substituting for a teacher who is absent, or filling in for another coach who had to leave school early for a game.

Extra pay for extracurricular activities has long been a source of irritation among high school faculties, particularly where coaches are concerned. One school of thought opposes any extra compensation for additional responsibilities — these are usually the teachers who are not involved in any extracurricular activities. Their argument is that they work after school, too, grading papers and preparing lessons for the next day and they don't get extra pay for that, so why should a coach get extra pay. Most of the criticism is directed at the coaches simply because, if school policy dictates additional pay for after-school activities, the coaches normally receive much more than anyone else, such as the band director or yearbook advisor, for example. This single item provides a great deal of fuel for the faculty critics of the role of athletics in a public school and it is not unusual for coaches to find themselves being challenged over this point by a group of fellow teachers in the lounge or school cafeteria from time to time. Trying to justify extra compensation to teachers who already have their minds made up is not an easy thing to do.

At any rate, financial security is not one of the absolutes in coaching, and people who accept coaching positions primarily for the extra salary are making a serious mistake. An allowance of $1000 for coaching breaks down to about $83 a month. When all the deductions are taken out, this might make a difference of $60 a month in a coach's paycheck. Certainly this will help pay the bills, but it won't alter a coach's style of living very much, and it is questionable whether this is adequate compensation for what a coach really does during a season or what the season does to the individual coach and the family.

Salaries for coaching should be based on a carefully thought-out formula. A sample of factors that could affect coaching salaries is:

1. total hours involved after school
2. week-end and vacation time involved
3. number of students involved
4. experience
5. pressure
6. travel supervision
7. indoor/outdoor
8. total responsibilities, equipment, funds, facilities
9. injury risk

A point value is given to each item and a dollar allotment per point determines the salary in a system of this sort. In some schools, the coaching salary is based on a percentage of the teaching salary.

All of these aspects of a coach's daily life have an impact on his or her family, whether the coach wants them to or not. If the impact doesn't come from a coach's discussions of these things with the family, the coach transmits problems, tensions or pleasure with the job simply by his or her frame of mind and conduct around home.

The wife or husband of a coach also gets feedback from another source, and that is the critic in the stands, who can be really quite vicious. Of course they hear compliments, too, not only in the stands but also from parents who write, call, or simply meet them in the local stores. But one of the strange things about people seems to be that criticism is voiced more easily and more frequently than are compliments. It seems that when people are relatively satisfied they often remain silent, while the unhappy few really sound off. Consequently, it becomes important for a coach's spouse to develop a "thick skin" in order to survive this sometimes unpleasant "world of the grandstand." People sometimes say things around a coach's spouse that they would never have the courage to say to the coach's face. Consequently, the coach's husband or wife is often aware of things, people, and attitudes that the coach is never aware of, being oblivious to this on the sidelines. Therefore, wives and husbands are subjected to, or experience, a different kind of pressure. Normally, this kind of unpleasantness occurs in direct proportion to the numbers on the scoreboard and the won-lost record. Winning seems to be the primary preventive measure for the vocal abuse directed at a coach from the grandstands.

A coach's children have special experiences, too, because Dad or Mom is a coach. They not only hear good and bad things in the stands, but they also hear the same kinds of things from classmates at school. Because one of their parents is a coach, and possibly well known in the community, the children sometimes share in the special role their father or mother holds in the community. Their friends are happy to associate with the coach's son or daughter and may even be a little envious of them. When the team ends up on the short end of a score, particularly in the bigger spectator sports, some of the other students in the school take this opportunity to "cut the coach's sons or daughters down to size" by telling them what a lousy coach their mom or dad is. Children can be very nasty or cruel to one another, and more than one coach's child has come home from school in tears from the abuse of other children in school when the team lost. But when the team is winning, everyone wants to be that child's friend. This is not so strange, because the same thing happens to the coach.

One temptation a coach should treat with caution is allowing a small son or daughter to dress up like a cheerleader and show off at a game with the school cheerleaders, or allowing a child to show off on the sidelines during a game. This might seem cute to the coach, but it tends to give small children a false impression of their importance, it can cause criticism from their classmates and spectators, and it can turn these youngsters into "coaching brats." Their showing off during a game can detract from the cheerleaders or the game, and this is unwise. This temptation should be avoided.

Obviously, a coach's family cannot escape being affected by the coach's position and involvement in athletics. Because of this, the family can be drawn together in a closeness that is unshakable. On the other hand, families have been broken up because a wife or husband cannot cope with all these aspects of a coach's life, which in turn breed other problems until there seems no other way out. The coach's family is discussed in greater detail in Chapter 4.

APPLYING FOR A COACHING POSITION

Coaching is seldom a life-long profession in that most people quit coaching long before they retire from the teaching profession. Coaching can also be a nomadic existence when a coach is eager to advance to bigger and better jobs, including advancing to the collegiate level. Unless an ambitious male coach is very lucky, he will probably make up to six moves before he finally reaches the position he thinks he wants. This is not quite the case with women coaches. For one thing, women's interscholastic and intercollegiate sports are on the increase and qualified women coaches are in great demand. If a female high school coach wants to get into college coaching, she needs first to earn a master's degree, and then begin applying at various colleges and, as a rule, many opportunities will follow.

The male coach does not find it quite so easy, primarily because of the intense competition for college coaching jobs. High school coaches who apply for head coaching positions in larger school systems frequently find themselves competing with applicants who are presently coaching in colleges. This occurs for several reasons. Some assistant college coaches become disillusioned with high-powered collegiate athletics; they dislike recruiting; they are anxious to become a head coach if they have not had this previous experience; the high school salary might be better than that of a college (which is not unusual); and the athletic program at a large high school might be a better one in which to work than a small independent college with limited financial support.

At any rate, when and if a high school coach applies for another coaching position, there is one principle that should never be violated: under no circumstances should an application be made for a specific position until it has been officially declared open. Sometimes young, eager coaches, hear, via the grapevine, that a certain coach is thinking about leaving a position, whereupon they immediately contact the superintendent of schools to apply for the position. In most cases the superintendent has no idea of what is going on, and it puts the current coach in a delicate position. This whole situation is one of professional ethics that should not be violated.

Another situation a coach should not be a party to is one in which a school board member, booster club member, or school administrator makes inquiries as to whether or not she or he would be interested in a head job at their school because they are thinking about getting rid of the present coach. The only small detail in this situation is that the individual they are thinking about removing hasn't been told yet. Clandestine meetings like this are to be condemned, but they do happen. Coaches who allow themselves to be drawn into a messy situation like this usually do so because they have no personal ethics, are in great need of a job, or suffer from an inflated ego because a school came after them and they see themselves as the savior of a bad situation. Sometimes these circumstances become full-fledged emotional issues in a community, and the prospective new coach can suffer in the process because of the part played in the "behind the door" negotiations that took place. The old saying about there being honor among thieves does not always apply to some school administrators and members of the coaching profession, unfortunately.

In a normal situation, when an individual applies for a coaching position, there are several things that the applicant should keep in mind: (1) be honest; (2) the interviewing person or persons will be sizing up the applicant to see if the applicant will fit in the particular situation available; (3) the applicant should have a list of questions to ask about the school and community; and finally, (4) every prospective coach should be aware that searching for a coaching position in the present tight job market is an aggressive, time-consuming, costly, and often frustrating experience.

On the other hand, in many schools, the need for female coaches is so desperate that women teachers of subjects other than physical education are being hired and assigned coaching responsibilities with little or no regard to their competencies — or interest, for that matter. Normally, there are a number of former athletes among the men on a given faculty who have some interest in coaching. But it seems that very few women, outside of physical educators, have this kind of background and interest at present.

Regardless of how attractive a situation might appear on the surface, it is a mistake not to ask pertinent questions that are important to the applicant personally. It is important that the situation be one to which an individual can adjust without sacrificing personal beliefs about principles of teaching and one in which that individual can be relatively happy. The kinds of questions an applicant might ask include:

1. How did this opening occur?
2. Is there unrest on the staff because of this vacancy and the way it came about?
3. If the position is head coach, are the assistants presently on the staff being considered for the job?
4. What is the attitude of the administration toward the athletic program?
5. Is the administration interested in excellence in the athletic program?
6. Does the head coach have an opportunity to sit in on interviews with prospective assistants, and is his or her opinion considered?
7. Will the head coach have the responsibility of organizing a particular sport in every grade level in which it exists?
8. What is the role of junior high athletics (if there are any)?
9. What is the relationship between girls' sports teams and boys' sports teams?
10. How are facilities shared by boys' and girls' interscholastic teams?
11. What are the teaching responsibilities?
12. Do coaches get any release time?
13. What is the school policy concerning attendance at coaching clinics?

14. What type of community is this?
15. Are there educational opportunities nearby for graduate school?
16. What is the housing situation?
17. Are there opportunities for summer employment?
18. Are there fringe benefits provided by the school?
19. What is the discipline like in the school?
20. What is the salary scale?

Naturally, every applicant for every position isn't necessarily interested in asking these same questions. What is asked by the applicant will be determined by the circumstances of the moment and the position, but a true interview is a reciprocal exercise.

Some of the questions a school official or school board might ask would be based on problems they have had in their athletic program, or on current problems the school might be faced with. An applicant can learn much about the job if he or she listens carefully to the kind of questions that are being asked. Some of the interview questions an applicant might face are as follows:

1. Tell us about your background.
2. Why do you think you would like to coach at this particular school?
3. Do you drink or smoke?
4. Are you married?
5. How do you see athletics in relation to the total school community?
6. What are your ideas on training rules?
7. What are your ideas concerning discipline?
8. What is your attitude toward winning and losing?
9. What kind of offense and defense would you use?
10. How do you see your role in the school and community?
11. Do you believe in cutting youngsters from a team?
12. What are your feelings about the personal appearance of the youngsters on your team?
13. Give a general outline of the way you would organize this program, 7th grade through 12th.
14. How do you see the relationship between boys' and girls' athletics?
15. How do you see the relationship between varsity sports and the junior high program?
16. In your opinion, what are the three or four most important criteria for developing a sound program?
17. What would you do if your best athlete violated a rule that called for dismissal from the team?
18. What do you think about the idea of another teacher in the school disciplining an athlete by not allowing him to compete in a regularly scheduled game?
19. Why should we hire you?
20. Why are you interested in leaving your present position?

As in the case with the list of questions a coach might ask, this list, too, is not all-inclusive, because the situation will dictate the questions and concerns of the employing officials. The important consideration for a new coach is to be aware of the general line that questions often follow, and give these a lot of thought prior to the interview. Again, it is important enough to repeat the necessity of being honest. If a school board likes what an applicant says and believes in, they will hire this individual; if they don't like what is said, the applicant is better off not getting the job because he or she would probably be unhappy with it. An applicant who tries to guess what an interviewing body wants to hear will probably fail in the interview. When people ask for an opinion, the prospective coach is obliged to give one, but should take care not to be dogmatic or indecisive. The trick is to state a belief or an opinion, without making it seem like either a declaration or an apology.

TYPES OF COACHES

This discussion examines five basic categories of coaches. These are generalities in that individual coaches might fit more than one of these in varying degrees.

Idealists are those who thoroughly enjoy coaching and have deep convictions concerning the values of athletics and fair competition. These individuals are more concerned with teaching youngsters positive values than they are in poring over the rule book to see how they can bend a rule to give their team an advantage over an opponent. These people believe that a coach should be much more than a teacher of skills, and they are less apt to manipulate youngsters to further their own ambitions. To these people, winning or losing is not the beginning and end of the world.

Rolling stones are coaches who simply move from school to school, without any apparent goals in sight. They never seem to be satisfied with their present position, because the one in another town always looks better. Sometimes coaches become wanderers because they never learn, or are unwilling to learn, how to become a part of the school community and are forced to move. These people seem to be constantly searching for that "better job," even though they would be hard-pressed to describe it.

Climbers are those whose only goal in life is to reach the top in the coaching profession. These are the coaches who will do anything to win and to whom ethics is only a word in the dictionary. Their belief is that a winning record is the only way to the top, and to them the end justifies the means. Unfortunately for them, their reputation often precedes their applications for bigger and better jobs, and that prized position rarely comes to them. These are the coaches who use schools and youngsters for their own benefit and often create a lot of hard feelings in a school because to them the only thing that matters is their team, and everything else is secondary. After they have gotten every-thing out of the situation they can, they discard it and move on, sometimes leaving a lot of wounds behind for someone else to heal.

Ambitious coaches could be described as a combination of the three already listed, but the difference is in the degree of each charac-teristic. These coaches know what their goal is, and everything they do is predicated on reaching that goal. Am ambitious coach must be an opportunist, to be ready to make a move when the situation presents itself, rather than waiting for a situation to fit a personal timetable.

Hangers-on are the long-time coaches who continue to coach be-cause they thrive on the ego recharge the title of coach provides them. They are afraid to give up the position for fear they will miss playing the role. Deep inside they know they don't enjoy all the aspects of the position anymore, but they hang on to the job anyway because they have been coaches so long. They don't know what it would be like not to be one. They realize, too, that once they retire from coaching, it is usually very difficult to get back in even if they want to. There is no question that the withdrawal pains are real, and it usually takes some time before they disappear completely, if in fact they ever do.

POINTS OF DECISION

Regardless of the kind of coach an individual is, there will be opportunities throughout a career which become "points of decision," or "crossroads," in this profession. Sometimes these opportunities occur by design, but frequently they present themselves when a coach least expects them. Most young coaches, in all their eagerness and enthusiasm for competitive athletics, enter into the profession with the idea that they will coach forever, and as a result, they frequently fail to consider other possibilities in the profession or alternatives, especially if their coaching situation is a satisfactory one. They are also unaware that the emotional and physical price of coaching is quite different at age 50, for example, than it is at 21. Consequently, when other profes-sional opportunities are offered, decisions are often made on the spur of the moment, without benefit of planning for the future.

It is not an easy task for most people to look ahead five, ten, or twenty years and decide where they want to be or what they want to be doing. While this seems impossible, a young coach should make every effort to consider several possibilities, merely as alternatives for the future and this should be done after two or three years of teaching and coaching. This at least would provide some sense of direction at the beginning of a coaching career, which in turn can always be reevaluat-ed at a later time, according to necessity or circumstances. The impor-tant thing about looking ahead and setting goals is that individuals can begin preparing themselves for several possibilities, so that when and if an opportunity does come along that seems attractive, they will be ready to take it. Sometimes, these opportunities present themselves only once, and a decision must be made quickly, because tomorrow might be too late.

Another consideration in this regard is that, owing to circumstances beyond our control, a person might arrive at one of these crossroads in an unpleasant way. This, in turn, makes the decision-making process more difficult because of emotional factors.

When one door closes; another opens; but we often look so long and so regretfully upon the closed door that we do not see the one which has opened for us.

Alexander Graham Bell

The chart on the opposite page illustrates the possibilities every coach or prospective coach should be aware of, beginning with undergraduate students, and continuing through various stages throughout an individual's productive working years.

The remainder of this section then, is an attempt to elaborate on these possibilities, and to provide some basis for decisions a person might make, or at least consider.

At the conclusion of undergraduate school there are basically five directions a physical education major can go. An individual could go to graduate school, become a head coach in a high school, become an assistant coach in a high school, take a job in some related field, or take a job in a totally unrelated field.

Positions in related fields involve such things as youth work, athletic equipment sales, sports camps, and recreation centers. Non-related fields include sales, insurance, and management trainee programs, to mention just a few.

If an individual chooses not to pursue these two areas, the next choice might be to attend graduate school. Even though a Master's degree is normally a requirement for getting into college coaching, a false assumption many young coaches make is that attending graduate school will guarantee them a college coaching position, or at least a head job in a high school. This is not necessarily true. There are too many coaches today who have advanced degrees, plus coaching experience, who are applying for these same jobs. Consequently, the competition is fierce.

Another factor to consider is that earning a Master's degree automatically places an individual on a higher salary scale in a public school system. This can be a disadvantage when applying for a high school position. Some school administrators are more apt to employ teachers with Bachelor's degrees only, because these teachers cost less than those with advanced degrees. It is simply a matter of economics.

The main advantage in going directly into graduate school prior to teaching is that a person can complete another year of schooling before being overwhelmed with teaching and coaching responsibilities, or perhaps family responsibilities. The main disadvantage in entering

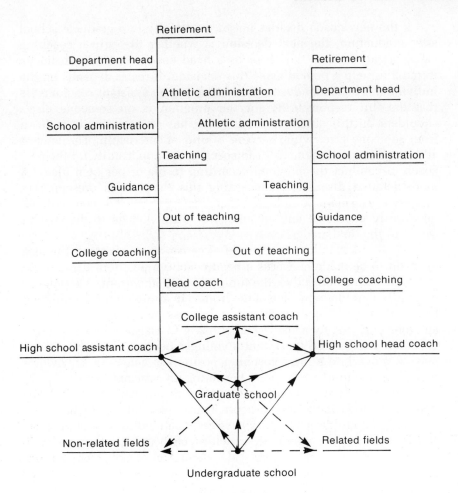

Retirement

Department head

Athletic administration

Retirement

Athletic administration

Department head

School administration

Teaching

School administration

Guidance

Teaching

Out of teaching

Guidance

College coaching

Out of teaching

Head coach

College coaching

College assistant coach

High school assistant coach

High school head coach

Graduate school

Non-related fields

Related fields

Undergraduate school

Five possible directions:

1. High school assistant
2. Graduate school
3. High school head coach
4. Related fields
5. Non-related fields

graduate school immediately upon completion of undergraduate work is that there is a tremendous lack of perspective from which to view the various courses. Without actual teaching experience, the values a graduate student receives from the course work are neither as great nor as meaningful as they could otherwise be. The important thing is that a coach eventually obtains an advanced degree, whatever the timing.

At the conclusion of graduate school, a person has five choices once again. These are the same choices that existed out of undergraduate school, with one exception; and that is, the choice of graduate school is replaced by the possibility of going into college coaching.

If the new coach decides not to go directly into graduate school after graduation, the next decision is whether to begin a coaching career as an assistant coach or as a head coach. There is no magic formula to help a person make this decision; it really depends on the individual. The chief advantage of becoming an assistant coach first is that the full responsibility for the program is on someone else's shoulders. In this situation, an assistant has an opportunity to learn from someone else, while serving a kind of internship. The biggest advantage in starting out as head coach is the opportunity for the new coach to conduct the program according to his or her own ideas. A more detailed discussion concerning this decision is presented in Chapter 3. The main point here is that whatever choice is made will not necessarily guarantee any advantage or disadvantage to the coach's career in the final analysis.

When a person begins a coaching career as an assistant, the next decision to be made concerns a head coaching position. If this is an individual's next objective, the timing is very important. A coach can be an assistant too long. One of the ironies in applying for a head job is being eliminated from consideration because of a lack of experience, and then applying for a head job after being an assistant for six or seven years, only to be told they want a younger person. The ideal time to make a move into a head coaching position is generally somewhere between three to five years after becoming an assistant.

A coach may stay at one location too long and get too comfortable, thereby making a move very difficult. This is especially apt to happen if the coach has children, and they have begun attending school. Another consideration is the ease with which a coach can get trapped by finances. Working up on a salary scale, and a summer job, make it much easier to stay put. A move might mean a cut in overall income. It often comes as a surprise when coaches discover that frequently the salary scale in public schools is higher than it is in many colleges. For an experienced high school coach who has a Master's degree, it would not be unusual to be offered an assistant coaching position in a college for several thousand dollars less than the former high school salary.

Regardless of the decision made at this crossroad in an individual's career, the next decision to be made concerns a coaching position on the college level. Contrary to common belief, it is not mandatory to be a high school head coach in order to make the move into college coaching. Assistant coaches on the high school level can and do become college coaches, usually because someone on the college staff knows them personally, and offers them this opportunity. Without any question, this is the surest way into college coaching for a high school assistant. The old cliché, "It's not what you know but who you know," is a matter of fact in this circumstance.

Another possibility for an assistant coach is to become a graduate coaching assistant at a college, while working toward a Master's degree with the hope that a good enough impression can be made on the head coach to be offered a permanent position. There is always the possibility, too, that if the head coach is impressed and an opening does not exist on the staff, the head coach will recommend this graduate assistant to a coach in another college. With the number of men working on advanced degrees at present, the odds against a man getting into college coaching this way are great, but the possibility always exists.

As far as women coaches are concerned, the picture is quite different. Generally speaking, the demand on the college level is still greater than the supply of qualified women coaches. The master's degree is still desirable, but because of the need, women can become college coaches if they have begun working toward a degree, or will, once they become part of a college faculty. With the increase in women's intercollegiate athletic teams, there are many opportunities available for women coaches whose ambition it is to become a college coach. This often means moving to another location. If the female coach is single, this is usually no real obstacle. If she is married, this presents other problems. Generally, this problem does not appear to be as great for married male coaches, at least for those whose spouses are not employed outside the home.

For the head coach in high school who wants to become a college coach, there are certain considerations that do not apply to an assistant. First of all, the most difficult step for any high school coach is getting that first college job. This means that in most instances an individual cannot be too choosy, and that individual must be ready to make the move when the opportunity presents itself. It may be that taking a particular college job will mean a cut in pay. It may be, too, that the particular job that has been offered is not the most attractive one, but a high school coach should remember that once on the college level it is much easier to move to other college coaching jobs than it ever is from high school to college. Consequently, the first college position might have to be accepted as a steppingstone to the kind of college coaching a person is looking forward to.

While it is virtually impossible for a high school assistant to move directly to a head coaching position in a college, it is possible for a head coach to do so. This is not as common as it was in the years prior to and during World War II, but it can and does happen occasionally.

The second consideration specific to the high school head coach is the won-lost record. There is little doubt that championship teams attract attention to the coach. The implication in this statement is that a winning team is a coach's ticket to college coaching, but this is not necessarily true. There are literally thousands of ambitious high school coaches whose teams are winners, any one of whom is probably just as qualified to coach in college as the next coach. The deciding factor more often than not is knowing the right people (a head college coach), and in being in the right place at the right time.

> . . . the swiftest person does not always win the race, nor the strongest man the battle, . . . and skillful men are not necessarily famous; but it is all by chance, by happening to be at the right place at the right time.
>
> *Ecclesiastes* 9:11

Oliver Wendell Holmes wasn't necessarily talking about coaches when he made the statement, "great places make great men," but it is very appropriate. The implication for coaching is that coaches sometimes are successful because of the situation they are in and not necessarily because of their own talent. To an ambitious coach this statement is of extreme importance. There are school situations in which the best coach in the nation would have difficulty being a consistent winner, because of the smallness of the school, the attitude of the community and school toward a specific sport or toward sports in general, the strength of the competition within the league, and the kind of community the athletes live in.

For example, a coach in a relatively small school in an affluent community, who has to compete with schools that are bigger, operate under a philosophy geared solely to winning, and are blessed with talented athletes who grew up in a tough community, is going to have difficulty winning consistently, regardless of how knowledgeable he or she is.

Photo courtesy of The Pennsylvania State University Still Photography Services.

On the other hand, if a coach is in the largest school in the league with a weak schedule, an abundance of talented athletes and the opportunity to organize the program to provide the greatest opportunities for winning teams, that coach will win consistently and possibly dominate the league year after year even though this particular coach might not necessarily have any more coaching ability than the other coaches in the league.

If the situation is one in which youngsters have many opportunities outside of school to swim and play golf or tennis, coaches of these sports will have an advantage over coaches in a situation that doesn't provide these opportunities. If it is a community where children grow up with a football in their hands, which does occur in some communities, coaches can win, and win consistently. Sometimes, coaches in great circumstances make the mistake of overestimating themselves by assuming that success in winning is due to their own ability, and they fail to see and appreciate the importance of the situation and what it is doing for their success in coaching. A great basketball player, for example, can make a great coach. Adolf Rupp, the famed basketball coach at the University of Kentucky, once said about an All-American basketball player, "God taught that boy how to shoot, and I took the credit."

The eager coach who wants to pave the way to the big time of college coaching with championship seasons must, therefore, constantly be on the lookout for these great coaching situations. And these are not always in the most pleasant overall circumstances. This is probably the slowest and most difficult route to college coaching, however. When the dust of the competition finally settles, the great situation will normally produce the great coach, in the eyes of the fans and sports writers, at least. Coaches who accept jobs in impossible situations with the idea of rising to new heights because of their vast knowledge of the sport are overestimating themselves, and underestimating the importance of the situation. A bad situation or losing season is not always the fault of the preceding coach.

A high school coach must be aware, too, of the role a high school principal plays in creating an outstanding coaching situation, or in squelching one. A school principal who believes in excellence in all phases of the school program will do everything possible to help coaches realize this objective in the athletic program. On the other hand, if a principal is anti-athletic, coaching in that kind of atmosphere would be a constant series of frustrations and unpleasantness. A potentially great coach can consistently produce only average teams in these circumstances.

Many principals are former coaches. It would seem that these administrators would be willing to boost athletics in any way possible, but this is not always the case. Sometimes these people are the most difficult to work for, particularly if they had some success in coaching, even though it might have been with a single individual who became a state champion. In their minds this qualifies them as coaching experts in any sport, and they can become a nuisance to a coaching staff. If they were not too successful in coaching, they might be hesitant in providing the kind of situation that would breed success for others. There are also principals who are biased in favor of a particular team because they used to coach it. This can be good for the new coach, but terribly irritating for all the other coaches in the athletic program.

There are many ambitious high school coaches who are intelligent, extremely knowledgeable, and fine teachers, who never get the opportunity to coach on the college level. First of all, they don't know the right people, and second, they never coached in the kind of situation where they could become consistent winners. And, of course, there are some who have no desire to coach on the college level.

If a college coaching position is never offered, or if a high school coach decides to bypass this opportunity, one of the next points of decision could be whether or not to get out of the teaching field. Other opportunities often come to high school coaches in various kinds of sales positions, fields related to education or administrative positions in business. Frequently, these are most attractive simply because the financial rewards are potentially much greater than those of a public school teacher. The periods of time in a teaching career when these opportunities seem most appealing are somewhere in the first few years when a new teacher is discouraged, disillusioned or makes the discovery that teaching is no longer attractive. The other period occurs after six years or so when the thrill of coaching has worn thin, when teaching is no longer any fun or when an individual decides continuing in education is impossible for various reasons, including financial ones. This decision often has to be made several times at different points along a teaching career, and there probably aren't many teachers who haven't considered this possibility at one time or another.

One of the decisions many high school coaches have made when they get out of coaching is to become a guidance counselor. This is a natural progression, since this is a role a coach fulfills, unofficially, throughout a coaching career anyway. Many coaches begin preparing for this possibility by including guidance courses in whatever graduate courses they take en route to a master's degree.

Another point of decision occurs when a coach decides to give up coaching and must decide whether or not to remain on the faculty as a teacher, either in a classroom or gymnasium. Many people are schoolteachers primarily because that is the only way they can also coach, and when their coaching days are over, the prospect of spending 5, 10, or 20 more years in school as a teacher is not too appealing to them. This points up the necessity of coaches looking ahead early in their careers to determine what the possibilities are, and then attempting to determine primary and secondary goals.

The next possibility could be school administration. A coach can actively seek a position like this, in which case the decision is easy to make when the opportunity presents itself. But sometimes a position like this is offered when a coach hasn't asked for it, and at a time when it is still fun being a coach. At this point, the decision becomes more difficult, primarily because the coach doesn't know how much he'll miss coaching or else, how much she would enjoy being an assistant principal. There is no question that school administration is the one place where the best salary can be made in public school work, but it is also a very difficult position, and finances should rarely be the determining factor in the decision.

Another point of decision to be faced is the possibility of becoming an athletic director or chairman of physical education, which might or might not include athletics. Normally, this decision is not as difficult to make as others, but when a stipulation goes along with the position that the applicant must give up coaching in order to accept this position, this sometimes complicates things. This is especially so when a coach is relatively young and thoroughly enjoys coaching. The chief advantage in administrating the program is the opportunity to develop a sound, well-rounded program for boys and girls. To many people this provides much more satisfaction and pleasure than confining their efforts to one sport for just a short part of a school year.

It is possible that some individuals will decide to coach all of their working years, and be fortunate enough to accomplish this goal. It is also possible that all of these opportunities will present themselves at least once before retirement, some more than once, and some not ever. The main point is that coaches should be aware of all these possibilities, try to anticipate 5, 10, or 15 years ahead, determine priorities, and begin to prepare for them. In this manner, opportunities will not be lost because of a lack of planning or preparation.

SPECIAL RELATIONSHIPS

Administration

The relationship a coach has with the administration of the school is unique within a high school faculty, because the athletic teams and their accomplishments are so visible to the community. Most school superintendents would agree that the three most potentially explosive issues they are confronted with are: (1) professional negotiations, (2) building new buildings, and (3) athletic teams.

Because of the tremendous interest generated in high school sports, school officials are more apt to be approached by adults in the town over matters concerning sports teams and coaches more consistently than about any other single aspect of the school program.

Without a doubt, the first person coaches need to cultivate as a friend and supporter is the high school principal. The principal is the person responsible for every program that occurs in the building, and is, therefore, in a position to help programs succeed or to suppress them. Consequently, it becomes extremely important for coaches to convince a principal of the values of interscholastic sport, the values of participation, and the values of success in sport. The point is to let the principal know why this can be good for the school, and to also let that principal know that the coaches will help out in any way possible, and that the administrator can count on the coaches' support, both in and out of school. It is also advisable for coaches to make an effort to make sure the administration understands what is taking place in the athletic program. In this manner, a principal or superintendent can better answer questions or criticisms, based on the knowledge of the athletic program provided by the coaches. An administrator should never have to plead ignorance concerning the athletic program in a school.

One possibility is for the athletic department to submit annual reports through the athletic director; another is for individual coaches to submit short statements containing their philosophies of coaching and what they hope to accomplish in their particular sport. Still another possibility is for each coach to take it upon him- or herself to submit a short report to the principal and superintendent at the conclusion of each season. This report could be a short resumé of the program and its growth up to the present; it could include a section on athletes who have graduated and have received scholarships, or have accomplished other noteworthy goals; it could include a section on the upcoming season; and finally, whatever recommendations the coach feels are necessary to improve the program, that the administrator has the power to grant. This report takes a little time to put together, but it well worth the effort in helping to establish and maintain a good working relationship with the administrators, simply because they like to keep abreast of what is occurring in the schools, and they will appreciate this gesture. It can be embarrassing to a busy administrator when a parent levels criticism at a coach and the administrator knows so little about what is really going on that he or she cannot provide a good answer to this parent. The lines of communication between coaches and administrators should always be open and used constantly, primarily from the direction of the coach to the principal and superintendent. If there is an athletic director this should be one of his or her principle responsibilities.

Normally, obligations and responsibilities in athletic coaching are stated as guidelines for the coach, but the administration also has certain responsibilities to a coach.

Countless articles, pamphlets and books have been written concerning high school athletic coaches and their responsibility to (1) the community, (2) the school, (3) the school administration, (4) the student body, (5) game officials, (6) the boys or girls on the team, and (7) the hometown fans and their attitudes concerning sportsmanship — all of which imply that the burden is on the coach to shoulder all these responsibilities and that this is primarily a "oneway street."

Many questions might be raised concerning this implication, however, and the most crucial one is, "Should the school administration have any specific obligations toward coaches, and, if so, are these different from the obligations they feel toward classroom teachers?" Many believe that the administration does, in fact, have a responsibility toward the athletic coach, and that the nature of this responsibility is unique.

Consider: because of the very nature of the job, the coach lives in an atmosphere entirely different from that of any other teacher in the school. This is not necessarily good or desirable, but it is a fact. Coaches are subjected to certain kinds of pressures that most classroom teachers don't know exist and in all probability will never experience in their entire professional careers. For example, there is pressure to win from the "townies," the board, the parents, from the individual coach; pressure to beat a particular rival; pressure as to who will make the team; pressure as to not only who will play in the game, but also how much they will play; and in some instances, pressure from the high school administration in various forms and degrees.

Coaches live in a materialistic world in which success (winning) is the goal, but they work in a setting where academic and character development of students is supposed to be the primary objective of education. This situation produces a real dilemma: fulfilling their role as teachers and at the same time doing what they must in order to survive as coaches — winning games and satisfying the public.[2]

On the other hand, classroom teachers exist in the relatively secure environment of their own little domains, where they can practically isolate themselves and the class from the world merely by closing the classroom door, and rarely, if ever, have to put the class and their teaching ability on display in front of thousands of spectators once a week and be judged by numbers on a scoreboard as to their competence as a teacher.

The classroom teacher might fail 20 or more students in a certain subject, or discover that the majority of a class has failed a weekly test, without fear of criticism or of losing a job. At the same time, one athlete can make a single mistake that loses a game, and as a result the coach is subjected to a deluge of stinging criticism which, if allowed to go unchecked, can finally take its toll.

Generally, coaches are intense in their dedication to their job, and are sometimes criticized by other members of the faculty, and accused of trying to build a "monster"; but underlying this intense effort on the part of the coach is the knowledge that the coaching position, in far too many instances, depends on the performance of a group of boys or girls playing a game and that the coach will finally be evaluated by the message the scoreboard conveys. The coach knows, too, that if the high numbers are on the wrong side of the scoreboard too many times, the jury, sometimes known as the spectators, will find that coach guilty of poor teaching and the verdict will cost the job. To American business people, many of whom sit on boards of education, success is equated with profit. To make money is to be successful; to lose money is to be unsuccessful. Because most business people do not understand education, its ideals and principles, purposes and methods, because they do not comprehend the slow process of personality development in students, they can only understand and judge athletics by applying busi-

---

[2]Paul Governali, "The Physical Educator as Coach," *Quest*, VII (December, 1966), p. 30.

ness criteria to determine what success is. If the "business makes money, the board of directors retains the manager"; if the "company" loses, the board fires "the manager" and gets another.[3] What effect would a similar existence have on the methods, effort, and attitudes of the classroom teacher?

In view of these factors, it seems clear that athletic coaches are in a unique, and too often precarious, position in the school, and because of this position, the school administration has a moral obligation to these people that has not always been recognized or fulfilled. Very simply stated it is this: administrators should be absolutely honest with themselves, the community and the coaches as to what is expected of these individuals who carry the title "coach."

Sounds simple enough, doesn't it? But coaches are painfully aware that what is said to them in the privacy of the school administrator's office regarding winning and losing frequently is quite different from that which is left unsaid to the public by that same administrator. And how many times have coaches heard the painful, well-worn phrase that "we don't hire coaches, we hire teachers!" Coaches know, however, that in too many cases this is nothing more than lip service given freely while the team is winning, but when the wins are outnumbered by the losses and the criticism mounts, coaches suddenly find themselves out on a limb all alone and their job in jeopardy.

To get more directly to the point, one of the most important solutions to this problem lies in the communication between the school and community as to the reasons coaches are hired. Obviously there are many different reasons why schools hire the coaches they do, but some of the very real reasons are:

1. To reorganize the athletic program toward a reemphasis of the "major" sports.
2. To win.
3. To gain state ranking with the team.
4. To bring new recognition to the school and community through winning and state ranking.
5. To work for all-star and all-state recognition for some of the boys or girls on the team.
6. To satisfy the Booster Club.
7. To win championships.
8. To appease unhappy "barbershop quarterbacks."

While these reasons raise serious questions as to their educational value in any secondary school, they are in fact guidelines that are used in filling some coaching positions, but ones that few, if any, boards of education would ever admit!

Normally, the following criteria are the ones presented to the public:

---

[3]*Ibid.*, p. 33.

1. To teach youngsters in and out of the classroom, and let the wins and championships take care of themselves.
2. To keep athletics in proper perspective.
3. To conduct the best athletic program possible for the student body.
4. To be a teacher first and a coach second.

Whatever criteria are used in the hiring of a coach, the administration has a moral obligation to everyone concerned, and to the coach in particular, to be honest and state publicly what these criteria are, and toward what purposes this person is to work. In fairness to the coach, the time of hiring is not a time for hypocrisy, highsounding philosophical ideals that are meaningless, or a diplomatic silence from the front office (which allows everyone to draw his own conclusions), but for honesty, a trait that often demands a great deal of courage, and a trait that has not always been in evidence in administrators in the face of the kinds of criticism that arise over school athletic programs. In other words, if a coach has been hired to win, that coach should be told so and should be given every tool needed to accomplish this. If the administration is not concerned about championships and won't allow the coach to organize the kind of program that produces championships regularly, they should say so and then have the guts to back the coach when the critics scream, "Why aren't we number one?"

In most public secondary schools, coaches are required to teach a full load of regular classes in addition to their coaching duties — classes in math, history, science, and language, as well as physical education. Much to the dismay of the school administrator, the effort put forth in these classes by the coach is frequently a mere fraction of that put into the sport being coached, and consequently, the quality of instruction given in the classroom is not always satisfactory.

Certainly, there are a number of reasons for this attitude, but more often than not, the chief reason can best be summed up by a statement frequently made by coaches: "Look, I can fail a dozen students in my classes and nobody says a word, and I could continue to teach here forever, but if the team I coach fails to win, I've had it."

If a person is a classroom teacher and coach as well and feels that winning games is necessary to keep the job as coach, there is little question as to which part of the teaching will get the greatest emphasis and which part will be shortchanged. It is a simple matter of survival. Therefore, if a coach has been hired soley to win games, perhaps classroom assignments are not realistic.

On the other hand, if winning were not the primary objective the administration is concerned about, and if the community were aware of this and accepted it, it is the opinion of this writer that many coaches in this situation would operate under a different philosophy in their teaching, both in and out of the classroom. If the coach felt secure in the knowledge that the administration was sincere in its stated belief as to the value of athletics in the educational framework of that particular school, that the administration would make every effort to convey this belief to the community, and that they would support the coach as long as the coach worked toward these beliefs, regardless of the scoreboard, the coach could truly become a valuable asset to any faculty as an educator in this kind of professional climate.

The American Alliance for Health, Physical Education, and Recreation has stated that persons in athletic administration and coaching need particular competencies in public relations and courage to withstand pressures from noneducational emphasis.* This principle is just as appropriate, if not more so, for the administrators of a school in regard to the athletic program therein.

Faculty

In the eyes of the rest of the faculty, a coach is simply another faculty member and does not have any special status. However, coaches don't always give the impression that this is so, which in turn can create antagonism with other members of the faculty. There are many things that can cause ill feelings between a coaching staff and other teachers. One of the most common points of irritation is the extra salary many school districts pay coaches, which is normally quite a lot more than that of faculty members involved in other kinds of extracurricular activities. Regardless of the reasons and the justification for the difference, there are always some teachers who resent this and many a debate or argument has taken place over this matter. In the eyes of classroom teachers this automatically places coaches in a special category, and there are those who are particularly sensitive to this idea.

The vast amount of publicity sometimes given coaches can also cause ill-feelings among teachers. A classroom teacher can be very resentful over the fact that he or she is doing an outstanding job of teaching, and yet the only publicity appearing in the local newspapers deals with athletics. The classroom teacher sometimes gets bitter over the matter and assumes that very few people, if any, really care about what goes on in the classroom, but many people get overly excited about the condition of a star athlete's sore ankle. And even though a coach is not responsible for this publicity, some teachers will be resentful.

One of the techniques used by coaches to establish a good working relationship with other faculty members in a school is to check with various teachers periodically to see how the athletes are doing in their classes. Some coaches use a prepared form which they send around to each teacher inquiring about athletes' conduct in class, quality of work, and promptness in handing in assignments, for example. A coach should never interfere with a classroom teacher's method of grading, however, This can create tremendous problems.

---

*American Alliance for Health, Physical Education, and Recreation. Report of a National Conference, *Professional Preparation in Health Education, Physical Education, Recreation Education* (Washington, D.C., American Alliance for Health, Physical Education and Recreation, 1962), p. 6.

Checking on athletes' school work lets teachers know that a coach is anxious to help them with a student athlete, if necessary. It also alerts teachers to the fact that coaches are interested in a youngster's classroom performance as well as that youngster's athletic performance. A checklist such as this also provides a coach with a convenient tool to use in counseling a student, when it appears that there is a need for this. A coach can be quite an influence on an athlete's conduct in another teacher's classroom without interfering with that teacher's role. The following piece is a "tongue in cheek" example of the way some faculty members view athletic coaches' concerns about their athletes' progress in the class room.

Dear Coach Muscleman:

Remembering our discussions of your football men who were having troubles in English, I have decided to ask you, in turn, for help.

We feel that Paul Spindles, one of our most promising scholars, has a chance for a Rhodes Scholarship, which would be a great thing for him and for our college. Paul has the academic record for this award, but we find that the aspirant is also required to have other excellences, and ideally should have a good record in athletics. Paul is weak. He tries hard, but he has troubles in athletics. But he does try hard.

We propose that you give some special consideration to Paul as a varsity player, putting him if possible in the backfield of the football team. In this way, we can show a better college record to the committee deciding on the Rhodes Scholarships. We realize that Paul will be a problem on the field, but—as you have often said—cooperation between our department and yours is highly desirable, and we do expect Paul to try hard, of course. During intervals of study we shall coach him as much as we can. His work in the English Club and on the debate team will force him to miss many practices, but we intend to see that he carries an old football around to bounce (or whatever one does with a football) during intervals in his work. We expect Paul to show entire good will in his work for you, and though he will not be able to begin football practice till late in the season he will finish the season with good attendance.

Sincerely yours,

Benjamin Plotinus
Chairman, English Department[4]

The popularity a coach often has among the student body can disturb some faculty members who are concerned about this kind of thing. They sometimes view this as a personal threat and resent the coach as a result. This also involves petty jealousy and envy, both of which are not unknown within the teaching profession.

The enthusiasm coaches bring to their work is sometimes disturbing to members of the faculty who teach as though they are semi-retired and who have long since lost their enthusiasm for teaching. In their eyes, an enthusiastic coach is rocking the boat. This can be particularly upsetting to those people who are coasting, because they feel threatened by comparison with teachers who enjoy their jobs and work hard at

---

[4]Contributed to *College English*, April 1955, by William Stafford.

Photo by Dick Brown, Centre Daily Times.

them. Some teachers work themselves into a comfortable rut and are bothered by anything or anybody that might cause them to feel uncomfortable in their status quo.

Coaches who choose to ignore faculty meetings or other faculty functions are making a mistake. Their conspicuous absence helps create the impression that coaches think they are special people in the school and don't have to bother with minor activities as the rest of the teachers do, because they don't care about anything or anybody that doesn't have something to do with athletics. Coaches should always be represented on these occasions to eliminate this criticism.

Sometimes coaches will be given the use of a new automobile by some local car dealer who happens to be a great fan and who, by the way, doesn't mind the free publicity. To these coaches, this is a tremendous sign of status or prestige, since they now have their own "command car." In their eyes, this also adds to their stature when they wheel into the parking lot at a coaching clinic with the appropriate decals on the car announcing the fact that here comes the head coach of a certain sport at Blank High School.

This can help create a gap not only between a coach and other faculty members but also between coaches in the same school, some of whom coach the less privileged sports, and therefore don't enjoy this kind of fringe-benefit. This matter deserves careful consideration, and it might be contrary to school policy.

Basically these are the areas that can cause antagonism between coaches and other faculty members, and it may be that coaches can stumble into these situations oblivious to all the ramifications of the action as it affects their relationships within the school faculty. This is not meant to imply that all or any of the above are necessarily wrong and should be avoided, but it does imply that coaches must be aware that many teachers, rightly or wrongly, are suspicious and critical of coaches and their motives. Consequently, all coaches would be wise to work hard to educate a school faculty to the positive aspects of the athletic program, and to conduct themselves in such a way as to show a genuine desire to become an integral part of the faculty, with concern about all facets of school life. Coaches should avoid putting themselves in a special category and isolating themselves in their own little world within the school, if they ever expect any understanding and cooperation from the rest of the faculty when problems with athletes arise. A belligerent faculty will be unresponsive in this situation, and as a result, some boy or girl might be deprived of an athletic experience through some disciplinary measure of a disgruntled teacher. Getting a student caught in the middle of a misunderstanding like this is inexcusable, but coaches can help bring it on themselves.

Other coaches

All coaches have their own hopes and dreams involving the sport they coach. And it may be that these don't necessarily coincide with the attitudes of all the other coaches in the same school. When coaches are aware of these differences and respect them, it is not difficult to have a feeling of harmony among all the coaches in the athletic department. But when a highly ambitious or self-centered coach turns an athletic department upside down in order to better his or her own program, regardless of the rest of the teams, conflict will result. When this occurs, students become aware of it eventually and literally begin to choose sides, which in turn can cause all kinds of trouble, with unforeseen ramifications. A strong athletic director can do much to prevent this from happening, but if this individual is weak or unaware, or if there is no director, the problem can quickly get out of hand.

One of the practices coaches should avoid is exerting influence on an athlete to give up another sport for the one being taught by the coach — to give up football or field hockey, for example, to go out for cross country, because it will help the youngster become better in track the following winter and spring. This is not fair to a youngster, and it also tends to create tremendous ill feeling with the other coach involved.

There should also be a definite agreement among coaches as to when practice for a new season should begin, in order to avoid any overlapping with a season already in progress. In many instances, but not all, this is taken care of for some sports by state regulations Rarely does this include all sports.

The problem becomes acute when coaches get anxious and begin preseason practice before another season ends. If the season in progress has not been particularly successful, some of the athletes, particularly the substitutes who rarely get a chance to compete, will start thinking about the pre-season practices that have just begun for another sport. The current season is beginning to drag for them, and they are anxious for it to end. They also get concerned because they feel they are falling behind in the upcoming season because their friends are already practicing. This can affect their attitude in practice, and as a consequence, can affect the team as a whole. It can also hurt the coach of the season in progress. Obviously, this is not a desirable situation but one which exists all too often simply because coaches get selfish and forget about what their actions are doing to youngsters and to fellow coaches.

Frequently, there is a lot of overlap in practice time among athletes who participate in several different sports each year. Some coaches are willing to allow the players to begin pre-season practice for an upcoming season while finishing the current season. Since practice times do not always coincide, this is a possibility. Normally this is not good, and many coaches would not permit this to occur, but it is a possibility and it is something to consider.

Another situation that can cause tension is one in which a young, eager coach decides that his or her so-called minor sport is being ignored by students and fans. In a desire to right this inequity, the coach sometimes carries this feeling to the team, whereupon they too feel they are being neglected and, before too long, the attitude of the coach and squad is one of "our small, neglected, unwanted team against the world." In an attempt to change the image of this team, a coach is sometimes tempted to do things outside the policies and regulations of the athletic department in order to get other support for the program by going directly to parents or the community with requests and problems. This usually creates wider divisions in the department. This can only lead to more problems eventually, and possibly cause hard feelings that will affect the program for several seasons. The soundest and safest procedure to follow in these circumstances is through established channels within the school. If the situation is truly an unfair one and cannot be changed the proper way, the coach has four choices: (1) accept it and live with it, (2) stay and continue to try to make changes the proper way, (3) take it to court if it is in violation of laws like Title IX, or (4) leave.

One of the situations that causes the most grief involves the use of the gymnasium during the winter months, when facilities are limited and need to be shared by girls' and boys' basketball, wrestling, gymnastics, and volleyball teams plus intramurals. School principals and coaches have been tangling with this issue for years, with the girls usually getting the short end of the decision. This problem has gotten more acute, as girls' interscholastic teams have become more numerous.

Many solutions have been tried, such as not giving the gymnasium to the girls, using the fall for girls' basketball before the boys' season begins, using the gymnasium for practice in the morning prior to the beginning of the school day, letting the girls practice right after school and bringing the boys back at night, giving the girls the gymnasium one day a week right after school or letting the girls practice briefly after school every day followed immediately by the boys. There are many others being used by various schools and some are highly satisfactory, but the fact remains that in the vast majority of instances, when someone has to curtail a program, it is the girls who get shut out of the gymnasium.

Ideally, this is wrong, and legally, this is wrong. Male coaches counter with the fact that if their teams lose it could cost them their job, and this is not so where women are concerned — in most parts of the country anyway. The obvious solution is to build more facilities, but this is not always possible. Therefore, there is only one fair solution to this dilemma. The gymnasium should be shared equally between the girls' interscholastic teams and the boys' teams. The primary argument against this from male coaches is that they need the practice time. However, there is not one shred of scientific evidence showing that a high school team of any kind needs two hours of practice every day of the week to be successful. There is no evidence to suggest that two hours every day is better than an hour and a half every day, or even one hour every day. Coaches tend to be creatures of habit, and great copiers or imitators of other coaches, systems, and ideas. Most coaches believe in the two-hour daily practice because everyone else does, which, in reality, is no reason at all.

Conversely, some credence is given to the notion that teams reach a peak somewhere during a season, when they level off or reach a plateau of the benefits or improvements team members will receive through continued practice. There is some evidence showing that performance might decrease, especially during long seasons that are demanding both physically and mentally. The author coached football with a man who abandoned two-a-day practice sessions during the two weeks prior to the opening of school in favor of one two-hour session each day. His opponents were practicing twice every day and sometimes three times a day. When the season was over his team had won every game. In the final analysis, the amount of practice time was incidental. His team won, basically because he had more good athletes than anyone else, which is still the number one priority for winning teams, rather than time spent in practice.

Perhaps it is time for coaches to reevaluate their ideas about practice time. We might discover that one indoor facility is enough to take care of a boys' team and a girls' team as well.

Press

Sportswriters can do a great service for high school athletics by publicizing positive stories about games and individuals. Articles of this sort, emphasizing the behavior of teams and individuals that best exemplify the values claimed by athletics, can win more solid support for a high school athletic program than any other single method.

Coaches have a distinct obligation to the press, and that is to be honest. A coach is using the press when he or she issues false injury lists or other statements that are not true solely to "psych" an opponent; this is unethical and is not fair to the sportswriter who is also trying very hard to do an honorable job. False or misleading information given a reporter by a coach but printed under the writer's name can make that writer look very foolish.

School officials should also make an effort to provide a parking place at athletic contests for the press and provide reporters with working space in the gymnasium, press box, or wherever the event is being held. When sportswriters take the time to give coverage to a high school team, the school can reciprocate by making their job easier. When reporters do not cover a contest, the coach should make it a point to get the information to the press. This is no guarantee that it will appear in the paper, but if a coach wants publicity for a team, this might have to be done time and time again, until it does appear. This is also a good public relations gesture that will often pay dividends when a friendly press is needed.

It should be remembered that the sportswriter's interest is in writing stories; the coach's principle purpose is education. The newspaper reporter is concerned primarily with selling newspapers, and in most cases, has little knowledge of the educational aspects involved in athletics. It may be, too, that the people reporting the results of various games have little or no background in athletics. In cases like this, a coach or athletic director should make an effort to help these people become more knowledgeable about athletics by taking the time to talk sports with them, and by inviting them to practice. They should also be encouraged to write about the positive aspects of athletics rather than taking a sensational negative approach merely to increase the newspaper's circulation.

The press does have a definite commitment to high school athletics. A local reporter does the athletic program a great disservice when he or she becomes an authority and concentrates on playing the role of a critic. A sportswriter should work closely with the athletic department in publicizing the accomplishments of the teams and individuals, rather than assume the role of crusader and expose all the incompetents involved in the local high school program, including students who participate. The reporter should also be careful not to print derogatory comments about an opponent because these articles always have a way of appearing on that team's locker room bulletin board prior to their next game. More than once this has offended the pride of a group of athletes, or insulted their ability, only to help them become aroused to the point where they play a superior game and beat the local team.

The coach should make it a point to work with the newspaper people to help them understand the kind of publicity high school teams need, as well as the kind that can hurt not only the program but also the boys and girls who participate in it.

The newspaper reporter who seeks out a disgruntled athlete, and

Photo courtesy of The Pennsylvania State University Still Photography Services.

publishes this youngster's criticisms of the team, coach, and school is doing a great disservice to high school athletics, and the results might affect a team adversely for some time. Normally, this kind of writing serves no constructive purpose whatever, and should be discouraged.

In the final analysis, a coach should take the initiative to create a reciprocating, cooperative working relationship with the press, emphasizing the kind of publicity which is helpful to high school athletics, based on fact.

Athletes

Without any question, this is the most important relationship a coach must establish. Regardless of every other attribute a coach brings to the profession, that coach will fail without the proper relationship with the athletes. This will be discussed further later in the book, but basically it means putting the welfare of the athletes before everything else, including the coach's personal goals. Athletes are to be taught and not used. A genuine concern for them and what happens to them in sport and out of sport will be reflected by the way they perform under the leadership of this kind of coach.

An ambitious coach, in his or her eagerness to get to the top, sometimes spends more time on furthering a career than in establishing great rapport with the athletes, which is in the reverse order from a true educator.

Parents

A coach should make a maximum effort to involve parents in the program, by helping them to understand what he or she is trying to accomplish and why. A coach needs the cooperation and support of parents since they are the people with the greatest involvement in the sport, namely through their son or daughter. Their attitude toward sport, and their willingness to adjust the family schedule to fit the season, can affect the attitude of their offspring and their degree of commitment to the sport. It is the coach's responsibility to create the kind of understanding necessary for parents to become supporters of the program and the coach.

Techniques for doing this will be discussed in greater detail in a later chapter. One of the factors that upset families and create problems, that can be avoided very easily, is not letting parents know in advance what the hours for practice will be during the week, on Saturdays, and on holidays, as well as changes in practice times. A coach can easily forget that there are other things going on in the world besides practice sessions, and a simple change in practice plans over a holiday can affect dozens of people other than members of a team. For example, suppose a family has made plans to go out of town to visit grandparents over Thanksgiving and the day before the vacation is to begin the basketball coach, wrestling coach or swimming coach announces that there will be two days of practice during vacation and that everyone is expected to be there. This immediately creates turmoil within the family as well as a great deal of irritation toward the coach because of this apparent lack of consideration. Situations like this should never occur, if a good working relationship is to be established between a coach and parents.

Generally speaking, the concern of most parents is to have their youngster perform well and participate in all the meets or games. Very few parents ever become unhappy with a coach when their youngster is in the starting line-up. Normally, it is the parents of the substitutes who can get frustrated and critical.

The emotional involvement of parents when their youngsters compete can be total. This is particularly true in individual sports where youngsters win or lose on their own. The parents of high school wrestlers are the perfect example. It is not hard to pick out a boy's parents when a match begins. Generally docile mothers become screaming, fist-waving fanatics, and fathers have suffered heart attacks on occasion.

Parents simply want to see their children excel, and they suffer many of the same anxieties a coach does, and even more. When coaches understand this, it is easier for them to cope with irate parents. Whether or not a team is winning seldom makes much difference to the parents of a substitute. All they know is that their own pride and joy is not in the game.

It is the nature of parents to see their offspring with acute tunnel vision and bias. They also frequently have a total inability to view them with any degree of objectivity in relation to their athletic ability. This is normal; but a coach must understand this in dealing with unhappy parents.

It might be perfectly obvious to everybody in the football stadium that a boy does not enjoy physical contact because he tends to shy away. But his father, in most cases, will not see this because he doesn't want to, and he may be critical of the coach for benching his son.

Herein lies the greatest source of conflict between parents and coaches. It can be summed up in six little words, "Why doesn't my child play more?" This can also be described as the "every concept." That is to say: Every parent would like every youngster to play every minute of every contest, and for the team to win every game.

In some cases this concern is selfish in that there is a tremendous amount of ego involvement on the part of a parent. This is especially true when a parent never experienced much success as an athlete and is trying to accomplish something through a son or daughter. It occurs, too, when parents who were successful athletes relive past days of glory through their youngster's participation, and it becomes a source of embarrassment if a son or daughter sits on the bench.

Parents can become particularly hostile toward a coach when they feel that their child is being treated unfairly (sitting on the bench). This brings to the surface all of the human protective instincts, and a mother or father can become quite critical and vocal as a result, particularly if convinced the youngster has not been given a fair chance.

Some parents accumulate individual statistics on their child's performance during a season. There is nothing basically wrong with this, unless it affects an athlete's attitude to the point where he or she begins playing the game in such a way as to pad individual statistics, which can then become more important to the player than the success of the team. A youngster can become a selfish athlete because the concern now is individual accomplishments rather than the team's.

On the other hand, parents can be strong supporters of a coach and the coach's program. It all depends on the coach, the coach's personality and willingness to constantly sell the program to the parents. It is mandatory that they understand what is going on and why. Many of a coach's best friends in a community will be parents of athletes, not only while the youngster is in high school, but as long as the coach lives in that community, if the coach works hard to impress upon parents that their children are cared about. No one cares more about what happens to athletes than their families, and the coach needs to remember this.

The following points out some of the concern parents feel while their child is participating in athletics, and how they perceive the role of the coach. This letter was written by the author and published in the

Pittsburgh Press several years ago. I am certain many mothers and fathers feel pretty much the same way about a daughter's participation in sport.

Dear Coach,

We hardly know each other, and yet very shortly we will have quite a lot in common, namely, my son Mike. Now that your season is about to begin, we are "loaning" you one of the greatest possessions the Good Lord has seen fit to give us — our son, and make no mistake about it, coach, during these next few months he is yours!

To his mother and me he is still a little boy in many respects, but of course we wouldn't dare let him know we felt that way since he thinks he's quite grown up at age 15. To most coaches, he and his buddies are looked upon as young men because they have the backbone to come out for the team and to stick with it. Little boys couldn't do this, only "men" can take it, according to the coaches. But I guess most parents are hesitant to want to see their sons in this light because these youngsters seem to grow up so quickly anyway.

You know, Mike has been a hero worshipper ever since he was little more than a baby and I'm happy to say that at one small point in his life he even included me, but now, you are number one! In his eyes, you are the man. He believes in you. He believes in what you do. He believes in what you stand for and what you say. He doesn't miss a thing where you are concerned, and most importantly he believes in what you are! This, my friend, makes you a very special person fulfilling a very special role, with very special responsibilities, which far outweigh the limited message any scoreboard might tell.

Some of us have only one son to guide and enjoy, but you, coach, will literally have hundreds of "sons" to guide and enjoy over the years. In this respect, especially, you are a very lucky man indeed. Now, I'm not naive enough to believe that our son and his teammates won't keep you awake nights, make mistakes, frustrate you, lose some, win some, and cause you other kinds of problems, but in the final analysis it might be that this is because they are boys, not men. This might come as a suprise to you, but in some ways these things hurt the boys more than it hurts you since they are so anxious to please you. It might not show, but deep down they are disappointed when these things happen because they feel that they have let you down.

Ever since I can remember, this boy of ours has dreamed of the day when he would have his chance to "make the team." At the moment this is his one burning desire. He wants to be an athlete and be part of the team, and at this time and in this place he is ready to do what you tell him in order to accomplish this goal. As you might expect, like every boy, he dreams of glory and of becoming a superstar who always manages to come through when the team is on the brink of disaster! I guess this isn't too bad, for the moment, at least, since the hard facts of life bring us face to face with reality all too soon anyway.

Please do not misunderstand me, coach. I am not suggesting that he be treated any differently than anyone else because I feel that basically our boy is just like all the boys on your team. I don't know if he will ever be good enough to "make the first team," or whether he has any real athletic ability or not, but to us this is not our primary concern. I believe that I speak for most parents when I say that we are more concerned about what happens to our youngster through this experience and because you are his teacher. We hope that in spite of your busy schedule you will be able to see these boys as something other than X's and O's on a play sheet, or "tools" to be used in furthering your ambitions for that really "big job."

We hope, too, that our boy will not only learn the fundamentals of the game from you but also a respect for authority, the necessity of following rules and the penalty for violating them. He needs to learn that discipline is important to an individual and to a group in order to prevent chaos. He needs to develop an appreciation for hard work and the fact that this is still a good guideline for success in any endeavor. We think he should learn that loyalty is not a bad word and that being loyal to his team, his coach, his school, his family, his church and his country is good and necessary. Through athletics he should develop an understanding of the importance of taking care of his body and not abusing it by using tobacco, alcohol, or drugs. His experiences with you in athletics should also teach him to accept his fellow man for what he is and what he can do rather than the color of his skin or his nationality. No one enjoys losing, but youngsters need to get a taste of it in order for them to learn that the important thing is the necessity of "getting off the floor" and trying again. These are the little things that begin to make young men and good citizens out of little boys and I'm convinced that they can be taught through athletics without sacrificing any mechanical aspects of the game.

I realize that every community has its corps of "super-critics" who only have eyes for the scoreboard. But I am suggesting to you, coach, that if you teach "boys" instead of just a "sport," the boys and the parents will rarely, if ever, be numbered among the leather-lunged experts in row X and your personal scoreboard will record so many young men out of so many boys.

Good luck to you and the team.

Sincerely,
A Father[5]

Assistant coaches, their wives and husbands

The most important consideration in this relationship is the ability and willingness of the head coach to make these people feel that they are an integral part of the total program. Naturally, the larger the staff, the more complicated this can become, because of the various personalities involved. But the larger the staff, the greater the need to create a feeling of unity among these people.

Every coach on the staff has ambitions, hopes, dreams, and goals, as do their spouses. It is important that the contributions they make to the program are recognized publicly by the head coach. The perceptive head coach is aware of this, and never misses an opportunity to show appreciation to the assistant coaches about what they are contributing to the overall success of the team. It is a wise coach who works hard to establish the feeling of "us" among the staff, including their wives and husbands, since this helps create a genuine feeling of unity, loyalty and pleasant working relationships. This will eventually be reflected in the performance of the team.

There is little doubt that an unhappy husband or wife can affect a coach's attitude and job performance. Male coaches sometimes become so involved in a sport that the wives feel left out and neglected—hence the term "coaching widow." This problem, along with husbands' attitudes toward coaching wives, is discussed more completely in Chapter 4. It can be a real shock to a young bride or groom who has not been made to understand what the life of a coach entails. Every prospective coach should make it a point to explain this very carefully to his or her intended in order to prevent misunderstanding, resentment, or worse

---

[5]Reprinted by special permission from the *Pittsburgh Press*.

from arising after they become a part of a coaching staff.

The author received this letter from a former student and physical education major whose husband had just finished his first season as an assistant football coach.

> . . . I felt I had to write and say a few words about the coaching course I took last summer at State. I sometimes thought you were going a bit too far when you would describe the intricate ways in which you involved the coaching wives in the workings of the teams. Well, unfortunately, the coaches here are not aware of these finer points, and now, after less than one year of marriage, I have become what is commonly known as a coaching widow. I wasn't too crazy about that great game of football while I was an undergraduate, but I'm sure I'll hate it for the rest of my life after this.

This is a very sad situation in what should or could be an extremely exciting life for two fine people.

The roles of assistant coaches must be clearly defined so that they know precisely what is expected of them and what their responsibilities are. If the assistant coaches' basic philosophy of coaching is fairly similar to that of the head coach, and they have an opportunity to make important contributions to the team, this provides a basis for an excellent working relationship.

Band director

This relationship concerns just a few coaches within any athletic department, and these usually are the football coach and basketball coach. No doubt other coaches in various parts of the country work with the band director also, but generally, this is a concern of the football or basketball coach more than anyone else.

The first realization a new coach must come to is that the pre-game band show and the halftime performance mean as much to the band director and band members as the game means to the coach and players. There are people (parents) who attend high school games only because one of their youngsters is in the band. The people involved in marching bands work extremely hard so they can perform well, and the athletic department should cooperate to see that they get the chance.

For example, if the band needs eight minutes to take the field prior to game time, the coach should be willing to organize the pregame warm-up so that the team is off field at that time. At halftime, nothing infuriates a band director more than when a team comes out on the field and runs through the band and one of their formations. This is inexcusable, and can be avoided very easily, unless the coach sees the band as intruders in private domain. Even if a band is late in getting off the field, this action is inexcusable.

If the proper professional relationship exists, the band director would probably be more willing to reciprocate by having a pep band at bonfires, basketball games, or pep meetings or by having the band form a "funnel" through which a team enters the playing field. Another aspect involving cooperation is the student who would like to be in the band and also participate in athletics. There are situations, unfortunately, in which a contest develops between the coach and band director, neither of whom will compromise, and a student is forced to make a choice. When this happens, a student is cheated out of a valuable experience. In the proper atmosphere, a fall season athlete could still participate in concert band or a wintertime athlete could participate in marching band. If a student is involved in several sports, that student still should have the opportunity to be a member of the band, since they too have seasons.

It should be a source of pride when an athlete performs in the band, or when a musician participates in athletics. This cooperative spirit is also appreciated by parents, since a student isn't forced to make a choice and possibly give up music only to waste years of lessons plus the cost of the instrument itself.

There are situations in which athletic departments give the music department a part of the gate receipts as their part of the contribution in entertaining the spectators. If the athletic department is solvent enough to do so, this becomes a wonderful public relations gesture.

A great deal of friction can develop between a football coach and band director, unless they are willing to work together and compromise in order to establish and maintain a harmonious professional relationship. Both these individuals should be careful not to become so narrow-minded and self-centered that their only concern is their own program, to which they expect everyone else to adjust.

Guidance office

Coaches often work more closely with guidance personnel than most other faculty members. Guidance counselors know that coaches are sometimes aware of things about a youngster that no one else is, and this knowledge might be crucial in helping a youngster through some difficulty. However, the nature of privileged communication must be respected. Therefore, the coach or counselor must exercise good judgment when discussing a particular youngster in their desire to help him or her through some difficulty.

Coaches and guidance counselors frequently work together also when a youngster is being recruited by college coaches. Together they should provide sound enough advice concerning academics and athletics to enable a youngster to make an intelligent decision regarding the choice of a college.

Custodians

A good relationship with the custodians in a school is more important to a coach than to any other faculty member of the school. This is necessary simply because a coach asks more of the custodians than other teachers do. It is important that custodians be considered as important workers in the school and personal friends, rather than servants of the teaching staff. When custodians become friends of the coaches, there is no limit to the cooperation and assistance they will give, over and above the normal requirements of their job. There are countless ways custodians can help make a coach's job easier through their efforts in keeping the fields lined all season, keeping the locker room and coaches' offices clean, getting the ball diamond in condition for the game, keeping the grass mowed, and helping to repair equipment. These are just a few examples of the help custodians can give, and unless they do these willingly, because they want to, a coach can run into great difficulty if he or she has alienated them through thoughtlessness, or in some other way.

People in the community

There is an old adage stating that if these three questions were asked of any man the answer to all three would be yes:

1. Can you drive a car?
2. Can you build a fire?
3. Can you coach a team?

Not only would nearly everyone answer yes to the last question, but they would probably give the same answer if asked if they could do a better job than the present head coach. People are not hesitant to question coaches strategies or anything else they do with the team, often telling them personally. Some coaches resent what they interpret to be criticism by people who usually have little or no understanding of what is really going on, or who have an "axe to grind." These situations can often create antagonism, and they demand great patience and diplomacy on the part of the coach. The coach who responds to questions from fans with a declaration that "I'm the coach and I'll run my program however I see fit without any help from you" is probably correct in this belief but not too wise in the ways of public relations.

A coaching acquaintance of the author had what seemed to be a good technique for handling most grandstand coaches when they offered free advice. He would hear them out and then say, "You know, that might have possibilities." The fan would go away pleased and this coach continued to go about his business of coaching the team the best he knew how. He wasn't so sensitive or insecure as to see a situation like this as a threat to his undisputed role as king of the hill. Consequently, these things didn't bother him, and he thus avoided any real confrontations, which serve no purpose but to create hard feelings anyway.

Athletic equipment salesmen

The business of selling athletic equipment is highly competitive and in communities where there are several dealers, the competition for

school business is extremely high. When athletic equipment is purchased through bids, the relationship between the coach and sales agent
is not all that important, but in situations where the coach decides who
will get an order, the relationship with the sales agent takes on an
entirely different tone.

Generally speaking, there is little difference in the quality of comparable name brand equipment, and unless a coach has a preference for a
specific brand, an order should be placed according to where the coach
can get the best price, quality, and service for the school's dollar. If there
is no significant difference in price, the order will usually be placed with
the sales agent the coach likes best, and who gives the best service.

Salespeople are aware of this, and consequently they work to
cultivate friendships with the individual who spends the money. In
order to do this, sales agents will offer to take coaches out to dinner, give
them free gifts of athletic equipment, or give them huge discounts on
equipment they buy for personal use. They sometimes offer such things
as free golf clubs for a large order, or a pair of bowling shoes for a smaller
order, and so on through the gamut of needs the coach might have.

Accepting or rejecting offers of this nature is a decision every coach
must make in view of the fact that these could be considered as bribes,
and therefore, unethical. In spite of this, there are coaches who not only
come to expect this from salesmen, but actively solicit whatever they can
as a condition for placing an order. Not only is this highly unprofessional, but it also can be a source of serious trouble. If the school administration discovers that this is going on with one of their coaches, in spite of
the fact that better prices for similar equipment are being ignored, the
coach has cultivated a highly untenable situation, and if the abuse is
great enough it could cost the coach's job.

Occasionally, equipment companies will have dinner parties, and
invite many coaches as their guests, not only for dinner, but also to see
the latest display of equipment. Normally, this is a broad advertising
gimmick or public relations gesture which they hope will increase their
business, and doesn't carry any commitment for the coaches who attend.
These can be very pleasant occasions, and are not in the same category as
personal individual gifts.

The soundest practice is for the coach to stick to the basic principles
of purchasing equipment, such as cost, quality, service, and standardiza-
tion of style and need, and maintain an above-board relationship with
every salesman who can supply the quality necessary for the good of the
youngsters playing the game.

Cheerleaders

The purpose cheerleaders serve has changed somewhat in the past
few years. It seems that part of their function now is to perform, as
evidenced by the intricate hand and foot maneuvers and the precision
with which they do everything. They can still be of great assistance to a
team through their willingness to organize pep meetings and bonfire
rallies, and by posting signs throughout the school calling attention to,

and creating interest in, an upcoming game.

Cheerleaders often have a "closed shop" type of organization whereby they elect the cheerleaders themselves, draw up their own rules, and operate pretty much the way they like. Sometimes the advisor becomes a mere figurehead. In cases like this, a coach must use a lot of tact to get this group to do something special for a team or the cheerleaders could interpret this approach as outside interference. There are cheerleaders in schools throughout the country who cheer only at football and basketball games, or at wrestling matches, and virtually ignore every other sport in the school. It may be that they cheer only at games involving the boys', and never the girls', games. Coaches of these other sports often meet with resistance when they approach the cheerleaders about appearing at a swimming meet, for example. Unfortunately, becoming a cheerleader in many instances has become a social "plum," and their main interest is performing in front of large groups of people. Certainly this is not always true, but a coach should be aware of this factor in his dealings with cheerleaders. Some coaches will write letters of congratulation to newly elected cheerleaders. The group appreciates the gesture and it is very good public relations.

Another factor to be carefully considered by a young single male coach is his relationship with female cheerleaders. To begin with, a new coach might be only three years older than a senior, which hardly places him in the category of father figure in the eyes of an 18-year-old senior girl. The fact that he is a coach, young and single, means that everything he says, the way he says it, the way he looks at the girls, and the seemingly innocent kidding he does with them can all be interpreted a lot differently by these girls than if a 55-year-old married coach acted the same way. In short, a young single coach should be careful not to encourage these girls, or any other female student for that matter, because many of them probably have a schoolgirl crush on him already. While a situation like this can be an ego builder for a young coach, it can also be disastrous.

An occurrence like this happens more frequently to a male coach, but once in a while a young female physical educator becomes involved with the school athletic hero. Like the situation described above, this puts a teacher in competition with the students, involving possible dating of a high school student. Generally speaking, this should be avoided because of all the ramifications involved, not excluding the possibility that the teacher could lose her job.

TYPICAL WORKING DAY

One of the initial realizations a new coach experiences is how long and exhausting a working day is during the season, especially that of a head coach. Basically every day is the same, yet there is enough variety to prevent monotony from ever entering a coach's life. The demands on a coach's time depend a great deal on the sport being coached, the number of students involved, whether or not game films are used, incidence of injury to the athletes, and finally the coach's desire or willingness to work at the sport at times other than practice time. Assuming that a coach teaches a normal schedule, a work day could look something like this:

7:45–8:00	Hall duty or homeroom
8:00–11:00	Classes
11:00–11:30	Cafeteria duty
11:30–Noon	Lunch
Noon–3:00	Classes
3:00–3:45	Preparation period
4:00–6:00	Practice
6:00–7:00	Dress, shower, incidentals, go home
7:00–8:00	Dinner
8:00–9:00	Help children with homework; phone calls from parents about injured athletes and sportswriters, lesson plans, etc.
9:00–11:00	Review game films or scouting reports

Also to be worked into this schedule are evening meetings with assistant coaches, athletic board, booster club, league meetings, equipment salesmen who drop by the school to see if the coach needs any supplies for the team, and sportswriters who make it a point to call the coach at home to get their story for the week rather than attempt to get the coach out of class at school. Added to this are occasional visits from athletes who have some reason to talk with the coach at some place other than school, and it comes out to another full day in the life of the high school coach.

EMOTIONAL TENSION

This factor is the one that probably "wears out" more coaches than any other single thing. Unless a coach simply doesn't care about a team and what it does, this emotional strain is a very real thing to a coach. A coach becomes so involved, and gives so much of him- or herself to the team, that in most cases it just isn't possible to sit or stand along the sidelines without being totally involved in what occurs on the field of play. A doctor once said that treating a coach during a season was like a mechanic trying to repair a Boeing 747 jet in full flight.

Another factor which causes this feeling is the fact that there is always an element of suspense when coaching high school students. This suspense is not related wholly to the outcome of the game, but also to how the team will perform once the contest begins. Sometimes when a team seems absolutely ready physically and mentally, they literally collapse and play as though they had never been taught anything. At other times, a coach worries because they don't seem ready and when the game begins they catch fire and play a great game. The reason for the concern is simple enough. The way a team plays is a direct reflection on the coach and if the team looks bad, the coach looks bad. And if they look bad too many times the coach's job might be in jeopardy. A vicious cycle, but true in far too many instances.

The concern over winning and losing certainly adds to the emotional stress every coach experiences. This occurs in direct proportion to the ambition of the coach, the popularity of the sport involved, and the interest of the community toward that sport. In this regard, the stress may be entirely the result of selfishness, but it can take its toll nonetheless.

CRITICS

The Battle of Life

In the battle of life it is not the critic who counts; not the man who points out how the strong man stumbled, or where the doer of a deed could have done better. The credit belongs to the man who is actually in the arena; whose face is marred by dust and sweat and blood; who strives valiantly; who errs and comes short again and again because there is no effort without error and shortcoming; who does actually strive to do the deeds; who knows the great enthusiams, the great devotion, spends himself in a worthy cause; who at the best knows in the end the triumph of high achievement; and who at the worse, if he fails, at least fails while daring greatly, so that his place shall never be with those cold and timid souls who have tasted neither victory nor defeat.

Theodore Roosevelt

One of the difficult tasks or requirements for any coach is to learn how to live with critics, grandstand quarterbacks, or downtown coaches. Regardless of the size of a community or type of community, critics will exist, and it is not always a sorehead who is unhappy when a team loses. Coaches get criticized when they win by parents who think their youngster should have gotten into the game sooner, by parents whose son or daughter didn't get in at all, and by parents whose offspring was taken out of the game so others could play. There will be critics who think the score was too high, and some who think the points should have been piled on even more. There will be critics who call up the coach after a football game, for example, and complain because the team came out onto the field while the opponent's alma mater was being played and they didn't stop to take their helmets off (how the team was supposed to recognize another school's song might never be explained), and finally there are those who simply complain about the way the team plays.

The point is that people will always find something to pick apart, and the coach who keeps an ear cocked to hear what is being said or who tries to satisfy these "experts" is in trouble. An administrator once told the author that if whatever he did satisfied 75 per cent of the people he was doing a fantastic job.

The following story illustrates the folly of attempting to satisfy critics.

There was an old man, a boy, and a donkey. They were going to town and it was decided that the boy should ride. As they went along they passed some people who exclaimed that it was a shame for the boy to ride and the old man to walk. The man and boy decided that maybe the critics were right so they changed positions. Later they passed some more people who then exclaimed that it was a real shame for that man to make such a small boy walk. The two decided that maybe they both should walk. Soon they passed some more people who exclaimed that it was stupidity to walk when they had a donkey to ride. The man and the boy decided maybe the critics were right so they decided that they both should ride. They soon passed other people who exclaimed that it was a shame to put such a load on a poor little animal. The old man and the boy decided that maybe the critics were right so they decided to carry the donkey. As they crossed a bridge they lost their grip on the animal and he fell into the river and drowned. The moral of the story is that if you try to please everyone you will finally lose your ass.

The following article, written by the author and published some time ago, points out the inevitable presence of critics.

MEET HAL HUGEMOUTH — SUPER FAN

There is an old saying stating there are only two sure things in life — death and taxes. Like everything else in these times of change, we need to update this tired old cliché to include two other sure things — namely, the inevitable emergence of the pesty seventeen year locust bugs and the annual emergence of Harold Hugemouth, Super Fan and grandstand coach of this and every year!

In order to enjoy watching a schoolboy game, it is necessary for an individual to be able to identify "Super Fan" as quickly as possible, so as to be able to sit as far away from him as space permits. Even though Harold Hugemouth comes in various shapes and sizes, he is really very easy to recognize because of the one single distinguishing characteristic that pinpoints him immediately. You simply follow the loudest sound you hear until you see a mouth, surrounded by obnoxious abrasiveness. No question about it, you've spotted him.

He lives in Every Community, U.S.A. and his one purpose in life seems to be to criticize schoolboy athletic teams in general and high school coaches in particular. This individual normally goes into semi-retirement during the summer months in order to allow his lungs to recuperate from a long and tiring campaign of critical evaluation! Those long schedules make it tough on the old boy since he involves himself in every play and in every situation of every game he attends, but alas, his recuperative powers are marvelous! And, as a new school year approaches with the exciting possibilities of new "targets" to feed upon, Harold Hugemouth begins to stir with eager anticipation as visions of fumbles, blocked punts, missed foul shots and turn-overs dance through his head; it will be a glorious year, and rest assured, our number one fan will be ready!

The prerequisite for obtaining a "license" to practice as a full-fledged Super Fan is simple. He simply purchases one (commonly called a ticket) for $1.50 at the athletic ticket window and presto — an instant authority is born with full rights and privileges of castigating sixteen year old boys, your sons, and their coach! For $1.50 this has to be the greatest bargain in the world for Super Fan. This cost, by the way, happens to be quite a lot less than the "price" your son and his buddies have to pay to make the team or that his coach pays for the privilege of being a teacher of athletics.

Make no mistake about it, no athlete or coach is immune from Harold Hugemouth and there is absolutely no way that he can ever be satisfied with the game, the players or the coaching. No boy in the game is as tough, skillful, aggressive, fast, or as clever as H. H. was in his day; no team is as spirited, rugged, well coached or imbued with as much of the old "fighting spirit" as were the ones in his day; and it is plain to see, or rather hear, that Super Fan has forgotten more about coaching than that "dolt" on the sidelines will ever know.

When it comes to the coach, this is where Harold the Mouth really comes alive! All his frustrations, pet peeves, pettiness, and viciousness roll forth in an unending stream of vocal abuse toward that incompetent character on the sideline sometimes known as "coach." It makes no difference that the coach's wife and children are within hearing distance (who isn't!), and even though they try to ignore the criticism, it hurts. But according, to Super Fan, he paid his $1.50 and a coach is fair game — after all, isn't he responsible for everything that happens to the team during the game? The criticisms run the whole gamut from the uniforms to pre-game warm-ups, the game itself and of course, the final score. No matter what occurs during a game, it should have been better and would have been if the coach were really competent. But that guy — you can't tell him anything! The real "Proof of the Puddin' " though, is told by the scoreboard. And, if "our" team is on the short end of the score, that simply proves what Super Fan has been saying right along — this coach is a bum and he's got to go.

The saddest part of Harold Hugemouth's performance, though, is the part he saves for the boys. When a sixteen year old boy makes a mistake, and he will, this becomes an unforgivable sin that takes on catastrophic proportions in Super Fan's little mind and he never fails to rise to the occasion. He loudly challenges the boy's skill, courage, intelligence, desire, ancestry, and the coach's stupidity for allowing such an inept individual to stay on the team — let alone play in a game — all the same time and without pausing for a breath. It's an incredible performance and one that has obviously been toned to a fine pitch through years of practice and dedication to a labor of love! It makes no difference to H. H. that these are young boys simply playing a game the best they can because they like it. Nonsense, this schoolboy game will probably change the course of the world and as a result, Super Fan demands perfection. After all, he never made any mistakes, why should a sixteen year old boy.

Harold Hugemouth, Super Fan, Super Critic . . . who needs him?[6]

In spite of the nature of the profession, which requires much more of a coach than merely teaching youngsters to play a game, and in spite of the fact that there can be unpleasant aspects in coaching, it is still a fascinating way to earn a living.

DISCUSSION QUESTIONS

1. What are some typical problems that develop between coaches and administrators?

2. Many coaches feel it is important to develop a good rapport with various people within the school and community. Who are some of these people and how should a coach develop that rapport?

3. How should a prospective coach prepare for a job interview?

4. Discuss several things a coach could do to gain the support of parents and fans.

---

[6]Reprinted by special permission of the *Harrisburg Patriot*.

5. Even if successful, do you feel coaches can stay in one community too long?

6. Why do you want to become a coach?

7. Why is the phrase "all glory is fleeting" pertinent to the coaching profession?

8. What are some of the problems that can occur between coaches and other faculty? With other coaches?

9. Should athletes be permitted to begin practice in another sport before the current season ends?

10. Discuss the "every concept."

11. Should parents be permitted to attend practice sessions? Why?

12. Why should coaches be paid extra salaries when other teachers work on their courses after school hours also?

13. Explain the meaning of "great situations make great people." Give examples.

Photo by Ken Kasper.

2

THE ROLES OF A HEAD COACH

There is a natural tendency for young men and women preparing to become coaches to assume that the bulk of their time during a particular sport season will be spent in an athletic facility actually coaching boys and girls. As a result, prospective coaches often concentrate most of their thought on learning the mechanics of the game. After all, that's what coaching really is, isn't it?

As a matter of fact this is not what coaching is. If it were merely a matter of teaching youngsters the fundamentals of a particular sport, coaching would be relatively simple. However, coaching is a unique occupation and, as such, makes many demands on coaches. Consequently, there are many roles head coaches are called upon to fulfill. The degree of involvement in the various roles varies with coaches depending on the sport, the number of athletes involved, and the basic philosophy of the head coaches themselves.

The implications then are that undergraduates planning on becoming coaches must be aware that coaching demands many more competencies than just being able to teach youngsters how to score points in an athletic contest. This is not to minimize the importance and the necessity of having an intricate knowledge of the fundamentals of any sport. But this knowledge, coupled with an understanding of all the other aspects of the position, might help new coaches be more effective and more successful sooner than if these things had to be learned through trial and error "on the job."

Some of these roles are fulfilled constantly, with little or no awareness on the part of coaches. Others need to be dealt with periodically. Sometimes, depending on circumstances, possibly unpleasant, fulfilling a single role might necessitate an inordinate amount of time, which in turn might have some effect on the actual coaching of the youngsters.

The point is that every person who becomes a head coach will be

53

required by this position, to fulfill many different roles in carrying out this responsibility. The remainder of this chapter is intended to clarify these roles.

> Those who want to leave an impression for one year
> should plant corn.
> Those who want to leave an impression for ten years
> should plant a tree.
> Those who want to leave an impression for 100 years
> should educate a human being.
>
> *Ancient Chinese Proverb*

Teacher.   First and foremost, a coach must be a good teacher, in every sense of the word. Just as there are teachers of math, art, language, metal shop, and music, there are teachers of athletics. However, everyone does not see coaches in this light. Prospective coaches frequently hear comments during an interview to the effect that this school hires teachers first and coaches second. There are a lot of implications in this statement, and you should consider this carefully in order to develop a response that would help school administrators understand how you, in fact, do see your role as an effective teacher in that school system.

One of the important aspects in accepting the role as a teacher of athletics is to possess knowledge of what you will be expected to teach. Youngsters are alert and perceptive, and a coach with limited knowledge of a sport will not fool boys or girls very long. It is a mistake to try to fool youngsters by pretending to be knowledgeable about a subject when this is not the case. Once students see through this, any confidence they might have had in a coach will be destroyed.

The best source of preparation for a coach is actual participation in the particular sport that coach intends to teach. There are situations in the public schools where administrators will assign people, out of desperation, to coach an athletic team when they have had little or no background whatsoever in that sport. This not only puts the coach in an extremely difficult spot, but it is also unfair to the members of a team. Consequently, head coaches and athletic directors should make every effort possible to prevent this kind of thing from happening.

The next steps in developing knowledge of a sport are actual coaching experience and, finally, attendance at clinics. There is some doubt as to the value of much of the undergraduate classroom work in preparing men and women to actually coach a team.

Basically, there are three general ways in which teachers affect a student's learning.

Image.   There is an old adage which illustrates this point very well: "What you are speaks so loudly that I cannot hear what you are saying." In athletics, especially, it may well be that the most important lessons, and the ones most readily absorbed by students, are taught by the image the coach presents. Sooner or later, every teacher creates an image in the eyes of the students. Normally, the image students have of teachers occurs on the initial meeting. This may be re-adjusted then over a period of time, simply by circumstances and the teacher's reaction to them. Frequently, beginning coaches are not aware of this. Consequently, their image develops without intent, and sometimes it is a real shock when coaches discover how the athletes see them, how the student body sees them, as well as how the parents and other adults in the community regard them. Coaches are definitely at the center of attention, and very little of what they do or the way in which they do it goes unnoticed. This includes behavior in school, during practice, during a game and in everyday life in the community. Like it or not, this is part of the life of a coach.

Coaches create an image through their own physical makeup, personal appearance, language, behavior, and conduct. Teaching in this manner is more important to a coach than to any other member of the faculty simply because of the difference between many of the objectives of an athletic program and those of the English or math department, for example. Since coaches are concerned about teaching attitudes and behavior, among other things, these lessons can best be demonstrated by personal example.

The following poem illustrates this point further and should become an integral part of every coach's philosophy:

> I'd rather see a lesson
> Than to hear one any day,
> I'd rather you'd walk with me
> Than to merely show the way.
>
> The eye's a better teacher
> And more willing than the ear,
> And counsel is confusing
> But examples always clear.
>
> The best of all the teachers
> Are the ones who live the creed.
> To see good put in action
> Is what everybody needs.
>
> I soon can learn to do it
> If you let me see it done.
> I can see your hand in action
> But your tongue too fast may run.
>
> And the counsel you are giving
> Many be very fine and true,
> But I'd rather get my lesson
> By observing what you do!
>
> *Author unknown*

Verbal communication means precisely what the term implies, and occurs when a teacher talks to people, lectures, explains, and demonstrates. A common mistake among inexperienced teachers is to assume that this method of teaching is not only the best way but the only way to teach. In other words, they believe that telling is teaching, or that teaching is telling. Not only is this technique the most widely used but it is probably the most abused in that teachers frequently talk too much and become uncomfortable if something isn't being said at all times while they are in front of a group. We cannot underplay the importance and necessity of verbal communication in coaching, but it can begin to lose its effectiveness when used unnecessarily, especially during a practice session.

Unfortunately, verbal communication does suffer tremendous abuse in our society. It seems that many people have a difficult time getting to the point when they speak. Many have a hard time putting their thoughts into words so that everyone clearly understands what they are trying to say. There is also a tendency for some people to saturate their speech with words that are difficult to understand in order to impress listeners.

The necessity of clear verbal communication is illustrated in this short piece:

I know you believe you understand what you think I said, but I am not sure you realize that what you heard is not what I meant.

Author unknown

Photo courtesy of The Pennsylvania State University Athletic Publicity Department.

Nonverbal communication is an area in which a great deal of research has been and is still being conducted. It has become increasingly clear that, even though no verbal communication is taking place between a teacher and students, another kind of communication is occurring. Facial expressions or gestures on the part of a teacher showing anger, frustration, acceptance, empathy, disapproval, or pleasure can and do have an effect on members of a team or students in a classroom, and youngsters learn very quickly to interpret and react to this type of communication. This can be further illustrated by a situation in which parents become disturbed because their son or daughter is misbehaving in front of guests in a home. Not a word needs to be spoken, but with the proper facial expression of the part of Mother or Dad, the child gets the message and quiets down. This is nonverbal communication.

Pupils assume that nonverbal cues are more revealing of a teacher's actual feelings and thoughts than words. Consequently, when a contradiction arises between a teacher's verbal and nonverbal behavior, the students assume the nonverbal to be more valid. What a teacher says makes little difference if students perceive a different message from the teacher's facial expression, tone of voice, or gestures. The implications for a teacher are clear. "Body language" is a factor in communication.

> Many things are spoken which are not heard.
> Many things are heard which are not said.

Disciplinarian.   Without some measure of discipline there can be no teaching or learning. Unfortunately, most people associate punishment with the word discipline. This is not the sole meaning of the term in this text. Included in its application here are the ability and necessity of convincing youngsters of the importance of being precise in attention to detail, dependability, punctuality, personal conduct in practice, during the game and in school, and, of course, the necessity of following rules. In the history of sport, no team has ever been consistently successful without a high degree of team discipline. It is interesting to note that the ten "winningest" college football coaches in the last 27 years are among the strictest disciplinarians in coaching.

No person has ever been hurt by growing up with discipline used wisely and fairly, but many youngsters have suffered because of a lack of discipline altogether. To discipline youngsters is to love them. Today, this role of a coach is more difficult than ever, since the "in" attitude is for everyone to be able to "do his own thing." But make no mistake about it, much of what a coach does with a team ties in with discipline and the need to run an orderly program. The head coach must be "king of the hill," but tempered with understanding and good judgment.

The way in which an individual establishes discipline depends on many things, but primarily it depends on the personality of the coach and the situation in which the coach works. This also ties in closely with the image each coach creates in the eyes of the members of a team. In most communities, the parents expect teachers to enforce certain measures of discipline, since most adults recognize its benefit for their children. There are situations where parents will come to a coach and ask for help in instilling some discipline in a son or daughter, because they haven't been able to do the job and they need help. Even though youngsters themselves won't admit it, they want and need an authority figure, and if a coach doesn't provide this for an athlete, it may be that the youngsters will feel cheated in this situation and lose respect for the person in charge.

Salesperson. This attribute is particularly important to a coach, since the attitude of modern-day high school students toward athletics has changed. There are too many things competing for a youngster's attention, too many youngsters who own automobiles and motorcycles, too many youngsters with a pocket full of money with too many places to go, for a coach to assume that student athletes will come in droves to try out for the team. A coach has to sell the program to the students in such a way that they want to become a part of the team. They must be a sales agent to the school administration in order to get the kind of material support necessary to conduct a sound program. A coach must sell to the parents in order to help them understand all the purposes of the program and to get their support. And finally the coach must be a sales agent to the whole community in order to create a better under-standing of the role of athletics in a high school.

This aspect of coaching is important, also, when a coach fills a job that has just been vacated. Initially, everything the new coach does and says will be compared to the ways of the preceding coach. Consequent-ly, it is important that coaches "sell" their ideas and goals to those concerned as quickly as possible, in order to obtain the cooperation needed before too much valuable time elapses.

This role can be a difficult one to fulfill for coaches of teams that don't have great crowd appeal and the attention of the community. This is due to the fact that a lot of people just don't care about the "other" sports. This means that some coaches have to work harder at this role than some of their colleagues.

Public relations. Since coaches are in the public eye more than most faculty members, they have a great opportunity to fulfill this role. If coaches are interested in all phases of the school community, they can provide good public relations not only for the athletic program but for other aspects of the school as well. An open house for parents of members of a team, or a "meet the team" night for everyone in the community, is excellent public relations for the school and athletic department. The ability to perform this function of public relations is also tested periodically when adults in the community become vocal in their criticism of a coach, the team, or individuals on the team.

Good public relations develop, too, when coaches take time to participate in community functions which might or might not be school-related.

Guidance counselor.   It is not at all uncommon for youngsters to come to a coach with a problem or concern, seeking advice or guidance. Often athletes will be faced with a problem they feel they cannot discuss with their parents or the guidance counselor in the school and, because of the special rapport that develops between coaches and athletes, they turn to the coach. This can occur during a school day or at most any other time of day, and it is not unusual for athletes to call a coach or come to the coach's home late at night when they feel they need help.

One of the principles of guidance to be remembered by the coach is that when youngsters come for guidance, the soundest technique to follow is to let the student do most of the talking. The coach should try to help the student see both sides of the problem and to recognize all the possible solutions or courses of action. The student then decides what needs to be done. In guidance, the teacher gives help and advice, but should not tell the youngster what to do. Another consideration is that of privileged communication. A coach might be told something in strictest confidence because this boy or girl has faith and trust in the coach and doesn't know who else to turn to. If a coach feels the problem is serious enough that the parents should know but feels this confidence cannot be violated, the trick is to convince youngsters why, and how, they should confide in their family themselves.

Sometimes a student doesn't really need any advice, but simply someone who will listen. In spite of the busy schedule coaches live each day, no youngster should be turned away in this situation. In all of an athlete's career, this particular moment, in the long range, could be one of the most important to a troubled boy or girl, and a coach should never underestimate the importance of this role. Students never interrupt a teacher's work. They are our reason for existing.

Diplomat.   Coaches frequently play this role in their relations with parents and others in the community. One of the inevitable aspects coaches have always faced is the questioning of tactics, use of personnel, and performance of the team by "grandstand coaches." Sometimes this is done in a highly antagonistic way. For example, if a coach walks into a local shop and, before the door is closed, someone asks in a loud challenging voice why so-and-so played in the last game, because the youngster is a coward, a coach's first reaction is probably a violent one; but on second thought that coach might consider that there may be a better way to combat ignorance than to use a "sledgehammer" approach. This is not always so, and it is not always easy, but it is possible to answer such critics positively and still maintain a certain degree of dignity.

Sometimes it is much more difficult to be diplomatic where parents are concerned. This is particularly difficulty when a youngster very rarely gets into a game because this individual really doesn't have the "heart" for it, and the parents are very unhappy with the coach. The coach knows that the primary reason this youngster stays out for the team is because Dad or Mom wants it.

The first impulse might be to simply face these parents and tell them their son or daughter isn't playing because he or she doesn't really like the sport, and it may be, too, that in certain situations this would be the best course of action. But there is another consideration, and that is, if a coach feels it is necessary to be painfully blunt in order to stifle personal criticism, this might literally destroy a boy or girl in their parents' eyes. If the latter is the case, a coach needs to look for other diplomatic ways, less painful to all concerned, to answer parents of this type. It may be that, rather than destroy a youngster in the parents' eyes, the coach might elect to remain silent and take the criticism personally. The most important concern in this problem is the student and what happens to this student in the process. A coach's actions should be dictated by this concern.

Organizer.   The importance of sound organization should never be underestimated, regardless of the sport involved. there are three phases of organization. The first is for the head coach to begin by organizing a personal philosophy of coaching and to determine the way the program should be conducted. If the head coach is going to provide the proper leadership to a coaching staff and a team, it is imperative that this coach's thoughts be organized well enough to provide the necessary direction.

The next two phases deal with organizing the coaching staff and the team, both of which will be discussed in greater detail in subsequent chapters.

Example.   One of the greatest responsibilities of a coach is to set the kind of example that fits the expectations young people have learned to associate with a coach. This role should be fulfilled by design rather than chance. This is the primary difference between the image athletes have of a coach and the kind of example a coach wants to be for the athletes.

In learning to be civilized human beings, the process of identification and modeling is of tremendous importance, with parents the foremost, but by no means the only models. School age brings teachers as secondary sources of modeling and, particularly for the boy, the athletic coach. . . . For the boy, the athletic coach is an exceptionally powerful influence and model. Athletic skills, physical strength, and prowess are highly equated in our culture with the attributes of masculinity sought by the adolescent male and easily symbolized in the figure of the coach.[1]

Young people are sometimes critical of adults who, in their eyes at least, are hypocritical. An example would be a coach who stresses the importance of following rules, and then goes to great lengths to show the team how to take advantage of certain rules or officials. This lesson can be taught, too, by coaches who study the rules carefully to see how far they can bend them, to their own advantage of course, and then justify this by claiming that this is good strategy. Whether this is in the

---

[1]Sherwyn M. Woods, "The Violent World of the Athlete," *Quest*, XVI (June, 1971), pp. 56–57.

Photo courtesy of The Pennsylvania State University Still Photography Services.

spirit of the game or not makes no difference to this kind of person.

Then there are the coaches who smoke in front of athletes while telling the athletes that they shouldn't smoke because it is harmful to their health. Or the coaches who tell youngsters that they drink, but the athletes shouldn't because the coach is an adult and that this makes a difference. The old traditional attitude of an adult (coach) telling youngsters "to do what I say, not what I do" is hypocrisy at its worst, and this kind of example has to have an adverse effect on the respect and admiration athletes and many parents develop for a coach.

Through example, a coach has an excellent opportunity to teach such traits as honesty, integrity, and courage of convictions. By the same token, coaches can also teach dishonesty and many other undesirable traits by personal example.

According to Dr. Sherwyn M. Woods, psychiatrist at the University of Southern California:

> ... what he says is of minimal importance compared to what he in fact does ... the coach is one of the most potent objects for identification for the young male. He symbolizes the strength, competitive competence, independence, and masculinity that the child and adolescent are so desperately strug-

gling to attain. In the best of all possible worlds, where rationality prevailed, he would certainly be evaluated and paid not by whether his teams won or lost, but in terms of what kind of men he helped to build. . . . The way in which he handles his anger and potential for violence, his capacity for assertive force versus aggression and violence, the way in which he handles both winning and losing — all will be duly noted.[2]

It is possible that sport itself does not teach youngsters anything, but rather that they learn things through sport from the adult who provides the leadership.

The image just described by Dr. Woods obviously pertains to male coaches, and therein lies one of the problems of the role of a female coach. While the goals and objectives of women coaches are or should be basically the same as those of the men, the term *coach* immediately creates an image of masculinity in the eyes of many people. As a result, some women coaches prefer that their athletes not call them "coach." Women coaches have had to fight this image and attempt to create one for female coaches that would show that they have the same concerns for girls in sport as the men have for boys. Women have had to struggle, too, to counteract the "masculine" image of a coach by proving that women can be successful coaches and still retain the qualities our society equates with "femininity." The example, or role model, they set can and should be the kind that girls can identify with and that symbolizes all that young girls have come to expect of women teachers. This will be influenced by the coach's dress, language, conduct on the sidelines, and overall appearance.

The society in which we live has determined that certain personality traits are "masculine" while others are "feminine" and until such time as this attitude changes, women coaches will probably continue to be faced with a stigma of masculinity. This does not mean that they shouldn't teach girls to play to win, or make girls practice hard, or fulfill all the roles a male coach does; rather it means that women in our society are concerned about the example they set and the image they create in order to convince people that coaching is a respectable and natural role for women just as it is for men. Therefore, coaching should not have any effect on the feminine image of a woman.

One of the difficulties associated with this concern is the fact that there is no clear-cut definition of the word "femininity." Instead, it appears to be a word whose definition varies from one culture to another. Traits like aggressiveness, competitiveness, and dominance are words linked to the characteristics of a male coach. Consequently, women coaches who exhibit the same qualities are looked upon as unfeminine by some people. There are some who suspect that aggressiveness is a trait of the female of the species, more so than the male. What is needed is a less restrictive definition of femininity.

Detective.   While this is not one of the pleasant roles associated with coaching, it sometimes becomes a necessary role. In some situa-

---

[2]*Ibid.*, p. 59.

tions there might be stealing in the locker room of an athlete's personal property or athletic equipment. Frequently, this is done by someone other than the athletes, and is particularly troublesome if the athletic locker room is also shared by intramural teams and physical education classes. The responsibility for putting an end to this stealing often falls on the head coach since that is the person in charge.

One of the most unpleasant aspects of this role is that which occurs when it is reported that an athlete or group of athletes has violated a training rule, by being present at a drinking party, for example. Because of the nature of this problem, the principal of the school wants it cleared up immediately. More often than not this is a difficult thing for a coach to do and a logical course of action will depend on the coach, that coach's rapport with the team, the overall situation and circumstances. There is little doubt as to the importance of good judgment on the part of a coach in this situation or one similar to it.

Psychologist.   One of the coach's great concerns is to try to understand the personality of a team as well as the personalities of the team members, in order to be able to motivate them to perform well.

The days of the highly emotional, gimmick-laden locker-room pep talks as a steady diet are over. Youngsters today are perceptive enough to see through some gimmicks, and appealing to their emotions too many times is risky. A team can reach an emotional peak just so many times in a season before they fall flat, and this approach becomes meaningless. This does not mean that there is no room for occasional inspirational talks throughout a season, but to rely on this for getting a team up to play each game is a mistake. Jerry Kramer in his book *Instant Replay* produces additional insight into the psychology used by the late coach Vince Lombardi on two separate occasions. In the first situation the tension in the locker room was really high prior to game time. Coach Lombardi came in, recognized the situation and told a little corny story that was so bad it helped break the tension. On another occasion Coach Lombardi delivered a passionate pre-game talk quoting passages from the Bible which fired up every man in the room. Jerry Kramer goes on to say that "coach played up like a virtuoso." He had a knack for knowing how to say to right thing at the right time.

Beginning coaches will learn the proper approach through the trial and error of experience. The important thing is the necessity of establishing good rapport with the athletes and to try to determine as quickly as possible just what makes a team "tick" in order to choose the best possible approach. One caution for coaches is to be careful about doing something that is foreign to their nature. Generally, this will prove to be ineffectual and create an adverse effect on a team.

This concern for motivation is also critical where individual athletes are concerned. Again the key word is motivation, and the quicker a coach can determine how to reach each boy or girl, the sooner this youngster can begin to reach whatever potential he or she possesses. A common mistake of most beginning coaches, of team sports especially, is to assume that everyone on a team can be motivated the same way.

This is not true. Each individual is different and a "shotgun" approach in motivating a group of athletes is not the best way of achieving the desired results — peak performance and winning.

Drs. Bruce Ogilvie and Thomas Tutko, of San Jose State College, both of whom are psychologists, have done a great deal of work attempting to identify personality traits of athletes, in order to determine how each individual can best be motivated. They have identified certain personality traits that create high degrees of anxiety among athletes, traits that indicate which athletes can and should take a good scolding and those who cannot, and traits that indicate which athletes need to be left alone or praised.[3]

It may be that they are simply reinforcing what coaches have been aware of for a long time, but haven't taken the time to practice. At any rate, Professors Ogilvie and Tutko claim to have enough evidence to be convinced that motivation of individuals according to their personality is the crucial element determining the success or failure of many athletes. This element, in fact, has a great deal of bearing on whether or not athletes will finish a season or quit the team.

Judge and jury.   Regardless of the number of coaches on a staff, in the final analysis this role belongs to the head coach. There are many situations in which the head coach must be both judge and jury simply because of being head coach and having the final responsibility for everything that takes place concerning the team and staff. When questions are asked, the head coach is the one who must come up with the answers.

This role not only concerns the staff and the team, but also concerns decisions involving individual team members. In every situation, all the assistant coaches can do is advise and offer opinions. This becomes more evident in potentially troublesome or controversial situations such as disciplining an athlete, dismissing a boy or girl from the team, in certain policy statements, in deciding whether or not a boy or girl will be allowed to come out for a team because of previous difficulties in or out of school, and in cases in which a decision must be made in the absence of any existing school policy. When the "chips are down," the head coach must cast the deciding vote. This is the head coach's role and it cannot be delegated. Good judgment, usually based on experience, is the key.

This role can become an unpleasant one on occasion, but it cannot be ignored. This situation demands that a head coach have the courage of convictions, and the backbone to live by them in the face of criticism. This also points out the importance of a head coach's formulating a personal philosophy of coaching and athletics upon which to base decisions of this sort.

Leader.   There are three kinds of leaders:

1. *row boat* — this leader goes only where pushed;

2. *sail boat* — this leader goes in the direction the wind blows;

---

[3]"Some clinical aspects of sport psychology." Quest (Jan., 1970), Vol. XIII, pp. 12–17.

3. *motor boat* — this leader determines a direction and plows ahead to reach a goal.

A famous coach once described leadership this way:

Leadership is not so much leading as having the people led accept you. You know how you do that? You've got to win the hearts of the people that you lead. The personality of the individual has to do it.[4]

Another definition of dynamic leadership is:

When in doubt — ponder.
When in trouble — delegate.
When you don't know — mumble.

Which of these definitions would best describe you and your leadership ability? How do you think your colleagues would rate you? There are three primary areas in which a coach must establish leadership: (1) to the team, (2) to the staff, and (3) within the school faculty. There are many obvious ways to exhibit leadership in the first two areas—image, example, dedication, personality, knowledge, courage of convictions, integrity, dignity, and loyalty. Most coaches are well aware of these and the importance of fulfilling the leadership role, but often coaches forget or ignore the importance of establishing this role within the faculty of the school.

One of the criticisms frequently leveled at coaches is that they often live in their own world, with little regard for anything else or anyone else, or with little concern for the school as a whole. In some situations, no doubt, this is a legitimate criticism, while in others it may be unjustified. However, when coaches get so involved in a sport that they make little or no effort to show interest in other facets of the school community, the assumption is that they just don't care.

Coaches should not allow themselves to be identified with this kind of image. It is important that the rest of the faculty realize that coaches do care about something other than sports. Members of the faculty are more apt to cooperate with the athletic department when necessary; teachers are more willing to help athletes when they are having difficulty and it establishes a much more pleasant working relationship among various departments in the school. This also eliminates the idea that coaches set themselves apart from the common folk (teachers) because they occupy a privileged position in the school.

Coaches can utilize their leadership ability through attendance at teachers' meetings, membership on teachers' committees, such as those involved in negotiations on salary and professional rights and responsibilities, and by serving as heads of some of these committees as time permits. Some of these might be short-term obligations and can be completed in the off-season.

[4]*National Observer*, Oct. 20, 1970, p. 12.

Accepting these kinds of responsibilities adds to a coach's stature among faculty members, contributes to the good of the school and helps prevent criticism of athletics on the part of faculty members who might otherwise resent a coach's isolation from the rest of the school life. Attendance at the school band concerts and plays is something else coaches should consider as a genuine gesture of interest in other phases of the school. Added to this is the impression this makes on athletes if they are also participating in one of these events. This sometimes helps youngsters to see coaches in a light other than that of the locker room or playing field.

Mother figure—father figure. This role is played to varying degrees, according to the age of the athletes and the school situation. As might be expected, boys and girls who come from a home that has only one parent, from an orphanage, or from a home where parents do not care have the greatest need for a relationship such as this. They need this special relationship and frequently look to a coach to fill it. They need someone to talk to, they need someone other than a parent to listen to them, and they sometimes simply need some adult advice from someone other than a member of their own family.

A coach soon discovers that this need also exists among students from affluent communities and homes, and is not specific to children in the inner city or rural areas. Young people need a relationship such as this in addition to the home environment, or because it doesn't exist at home. In our modern-day society, with the breaking down of the structure of families, it may be that a teacher who really cares could be the most influential person in a youngster's life.

A problem that can arise in this regard specific to girls and female coaches is that of a feeling of jealousy or resentment on the part of some mothers when their daughters begin to confide in or seek advice from a female coach, especially if the coach appears to be encouraging an extra close relationship with the athletes by being a pal or big sister type. Consequently, female coaches need to be careful in handling this situation so that mothers don't feel they are competing with a coach for their daughter's attention.

Dictator. There are a lot of connotations associated with this word, most of them uncomplimentary. But in this context it will be described as that of a benevolent dictator, and this makes a great difference. In this light, it means an individual who cares about the program, the team, and the people involved, but who nevertheless finds that there are times when a decision must be made without any time for discussion. A benevolent dictator makes these decisions according to what is best for everyone concerned, and since the head coach is the individual in charge, this is the way it must be. In certain circumstances the head coach's word must be final.

When coaches on a staff disagree or cannot come to any agreement about some item concerning the team, the head coach must out of necessity exercise this right and make the decision that everyone will be expected to abide by. In other words, if there are four assistant coaches on a staff, the head coach always carries five votes when necessary. This is not to say that the democratic procedure has no place in coaching, but coaches and athletes must also learn that in the excitement of competition there are circumstances which demand that the players react instantly and without question to decisions and instructions of the head coach. This is no time to call time-out and have an election. A good leader will tolerate uncertainty only up to a point.

Politician.   Regardless of the provocation, a coach should make every effort to avoid antagonizing people, particularly the parents of boys or girls who are members of a team. A good "politician" learns how to do this very quickly. Perhaps this role goes hand in hand with diplomacy. When a straightforward, honest answer to a parent or other adult concerning a youngster might be particularly embarrassing to everyone concerned, or when it might have an adverse effect on the relationship between a youngster and that youngster's parents, the coach will be found playing this role.

This role is important, too, in dealing with critics in the community. Ideally, they don't exist, and if they did, we could ignore them and simply coach the team. But in reality, they cannot be ignored, nor should they be. If left unchecked, these critics sometimes grow like a cancer and create serious problems for a coach. The coach who is also a "politician" can do a great deal toward preventing this kind of situation from getting out of hand or being forced into a confrontation.

Good "politicians" also know that the time to make friends and firmly establish themselves is when the team is winning and at the top. When the tide turns, and cycles do happen in high school programs, the coach and the program will need every friend they can find, and if this didn't occur when the team was riding the winning crest, it surely won't happen when they are losing. Winston Churchill supposedly said that the most important qualification for a politician was the ability to predict what will happen tomorrow, next week, next month, or next year — and to explain afterward why it did not happen. Could he have also been talking to coaches who end up on the wrong side of the season's won–lost record?

Actor.   An illustration of this point occurred in a scene in the movie *Patton*. The general had just finished "chewing out" his staff because a job needed to be done and he was not satisfied with the progress being made. After the group left, Patton's aide turned to him and said, "You really didn't mean all that, did you, General?" to which Patton simply replied, "No, but they don't know that." The point is, he was acting a role in order to get a job done. In this respect, coaches find it necessary, too, to act out certain parts when the situation demands it.

Sometimes the situation necessitates an acting role unusual to a coach's personality, such as scolding an individual or team, or remaining very calm while feeling like exploding. It might be for the good of an individual, staff, or entire team. The pitfall to be avoided is that of being "phony." This would destroy what the coach was trying to do, since youngsters are not to be fooled for very long by insincerity. But, if the coach believes in what he or she is doing and recognizes that the situation calls for the role to be played, a coach will find this to be an effective tool in accomplishing whatever the particular goal is at that moment.

The perceptive teacher seldom fails to recognize when these situations arise. However, these cannot always be anticipated, but with experience and common sense a teacher will be able to make a quick judgment as to the proper response to select.

The ultimate in fulfilling this role is the coach who, while being driven out of town by an irate community, looks like the leader of a parade.

Fund raiser.   Rarely do coaches ever feel that they have enough funds allocated to them to purchase the kind of equipment they would really like to have, and in the amount they think necessary. As a result, these coaches often dream up fund-raising projects in order to supplement their approved budgets. Candy, cookie, and hoagie sales are just a

Photo courtesy of The Pennsylvania State University Still Photography Services.

few examples. These campaigns might take place in school, out in the community or in both places at the same time.

Some school districts have strict policies prohibiting this kind of thing, because it can create public relations problems in a community already financially burdened with supporting the schools. Consequently, coaches should check with the school administration before launching a fund raising campaign, to avoid finding out after the fact that they are in violation of school policy.

Director.   The degree to which this role is experienced depends on the number of coaches on your staff. In any event, the head coach should be the director of the entire program and normally the team reflects not only what the head coach believes in but the coach's personality as well — specifically aggressiveness, enthusiasm, fair play, and class.

Field general.   This role evolves from the director of the whole program — junior high, freshman, and junior varsity team — to the specifics of coaching the team. The important element here is the coach's ability to make quick and accurate judgments and decisions in the excitement of competition — the ability to keep cool while everyone else falls apart. A sound knowledge of game strategy is also crucial if a coach is to be successful in this role.

Equipment manager.   Unless the head coach is fortunate enough to be in a school that pays some other individual for this assignment, the ultimate responsibility for purchasing, issuing, policing, collecting, and inventory of equipment falls on the head coach. For coaches of some sports, like golf, this might amount to very little, while to a football coach this aspect of the job can assume monumental proportions.

Organization and delegating responsibility are the keys to fulfilling this role.

Trainer.   Every coach should have some background in first aid and the treatment of athletic injuries. The most obvious reason of course is that most high school coaches also serve as team trainer, simply because the school district will not or cannot employ a certified athletic trainer.

Add to this the fact that coaches cannot expect to have a medical doctor at every practice, or at every scheduled contest for that matter, and it becomes readily apparent which person will be in charge of the care of injuries, taping, and so on.

Another very important factor to consider is legal liability. This alone would dictate that all coaches protect not only the athletes' welfare, but their own, by obtaining a solid background in the proper legal procedures involved in the whole area of athletic training (see Chapter 10).

Citizen of the community.   There are basically three kinds of coaches. There are those who live in the community, there are those who live off the community, and finally, there are those who live for the community.

The coach who merely lives in the community is one who does the job at school and cares not one whit about what goes on in the community, and therefore makes no contribution toward making the community a better place in which to live.

The coach who lives off the community is the individual whose interest is primarily selfish. This coach is only concerned with using the community for personal gain, that is, moving on to a better job, getting special deals from the merchants in town, and being concerned only with what the community can do for him or her.

The coach who lives for the community has a genuine desire to be a part of his community and to contribute whatever needs to be done in order to help in any way possible. This often means serving the P.T.A. in some capacity, working as a member of a service club, participating in the work of a civic group, helping to organize the neighborhood Fourth of July parade, or volunteering time to the cancer crusade.

The point is, regardless of personal goals and ambitions, coaches are missing some of the pleasure of being a coach and occupying that special role in a community if they don't take the opportunity to become a part of that community. No matter how short a stay may be before a better position comes along, coaches could feel a tremendous inner satisfaction if they felt that a community was just a little better place in which to live, for a moment anyway, just because they were there. This is not to be confused with conceit, but rather is a good feeling that comes with the knowledge that you have made a contribution to something or somebody just because you wanted to.

Citizen of the school.   Coaches often isolate themselves in their sport for various reasons. This tends to bring on criticism by other faculty members since they make the assumption that the coach doesn't care for any part of the school or anything in the school that doesn't pertain to that coach's team. In the eyes of the faculty this type of coach is not fulfilling all the obligations of a teacher, and they resent it. The responsibilities of being a teacher do not begin and end with teaching classes or coaching a team. The beginning teacher quickly discovers that there are many other duties and obligations involved in teaching, and everyone is expected to share in these as much as possible, including coaches.

The excuse many coaches use is that they don't have time. The argument gets no sympathy from fellow faculty members, because in most cases coaches are paid extra for coaching. So, while other teachers spend time after school at committee meetings, without pay, the coach is spending time after school with pay, and this becomes a very touchy point.

In light of this, coaches should make a genuine effort to participate on faculty committees when possible, and to take part in social functions of the faculty on occasion. This creates the opportunity for the teachers to get to know the coach and eliminates any suspicion they might have that all coaches see themselves as privileged characters who have little regard for others on the faculty.

Sometime when you're feeling important
Sometime when your ego's in bloom
Sometime when you take it for granted
You're the best qualified in the room.
Sometime when you feel that your going
Would leave an unfillable hole
Just follow these simple instructions
And see how it humbles your soul.
Take a bucket and fill it with water
Put your hand in it up to the wrist,
Pull it out and the hole that's remaining
Is the measure of how you'll be missed.
You may splash all you please when you enter
You may stir up the water galore
But stop and you'll find in a minute
That it looks just the same as before.
The moral of this quaint example
Is do just the best that you can
Be proud of yourself, but remember
There is no indispensable man.

Author unknown

COACHING IN THE INNER CITY

The roles of a coach in an inner-city school are basically the same as those discussed already, but the situation itself is quite different. It is extremely difficult to comprehend school life in the inner city, without actually living in this environment and experiencing it first hand. Vicarious experiences can help the prospective inner-city coach prepare for this venture. The prospective coach who can spend a number of days observing in an inner-city school will begin to sense some of the uniqueness of this situation. This student should read extensively, particularly books and articles dealing with the inner-city family, the values of inner-city students, and the economic expectations of minority groups. Discussing inner-city coaching with people experienced in this area will be highly beneficial. Most importantly, the prospective inner-city coach must attentuate any preconceived ideas of what coaching in an inner-city school is like. By doing these things, a coach can approach this difficult assignment realistically.

The inner-city school environment is unique in several ways. The coach faces the problem of working with young athletes who often have no father in the family unit and a mother who is too preoccupied with providing for her family to have time to encourage any one of the children either academically or athletically. In many cases, the lack of parental involvement is the result of the parents' unawareness of the coach's philosophy or of what the athletic program offers their children. As long as their children seem happy and content, the parents will usually leave it up to them, knowing that if their children are unhappy, they can quit. Parental involvement in the high school athletic program, consequently, is practically nonexistent.

Photo courtesy of Bob Nastase.

This lack of parental involvement has other ramifications, for it forces the inner-city athlete to develop a values system which originates in the street. Since inner-city youngsters are usually uninformed about life beyond this environment, they learn through trial and error, and some view stealing as a means of getting even with a society that they blame for their poor economic condition. Another school of thought is that this stealing is for survival. If an inner-city youngster needs something, and doesn't have the money to get it, stealing seems a valid alternative. For most youngsters, ego satisfaction arises from fitting into their peer group, and they will do just about anything to be accepted. In the inner city, this can include stealing.

Inner-city youngsters often view all adult authority with apprehension, and they seem to thrive on confusion and conflict, holding a value system based on an enormous sense of distrust and suspicion. Since the inner-city athlete does not accept adult authority as a matter of course, the coach must earn this authority. This can be done by being consistent, demanding, and uncompromising, once the behavior expected of the athletes has been made clear to them by the coach. This is of the utmost importance.

The inner-city coach will face a generally negative attitude toward education from the athletes. Since these youngsters are not pressured either from home or by environment to learn at school, they believe that educational pursuits are rarely beneficial, feeling that social and economic factors are always working against them. Inner-city youths see all society beyond their environment as the province of the white man;

no matter how hard they work, they do not believe they will ever receive the same benefits from education as their suburban counterparts.

Statistics compiled by *Life Magazine* a few years ago seem to lend credence to this belief, showing that a black with twelve years of education earns $500 per year less than a white with eight years of education; that the black, college educated person earns $750 per year less than a white, high school educated person. If inner-city youths do well educationally, peer pressure operates against them, and their attitude remains unchanged. The inner-city school meets with little success in reversing the negative attitudes the athlete brings from home, or in counteracting the negative influence of failure-oriented peers.

The inner-city coach has a large number of physically endowed and athletically interested prospects from which to form athletic teams. Since the inner-city youth usually lacks the financial resources to travel, and to take part in swimming, golf, skiing, tennis, and other sports requiring elaborate equipment, settings, and fees, they are forced to occupy their leisure time with activities requiring little space, equipment, and money. Often having an excess of leisure time, inner-city youngsters find themselves devoting many hours a day to play. This play builds them physically and competitively and gives valuable experience. Unfortunately, inner-city athletes are often motivated by a long-standing myth that through athletics, they can gain fame, fortune, and a way out of that stifling environment. Statistics, however, show that only a very small percentage of aspiring athletes ever reach this goal.

The economic situation of the inner-city school often poses additional problems with which the coach must contend. Inner-city schools have limited resources which manifest themselves in numerous ways. Buildings are often antiquated and run-down, with inadequate athletic facilities, limited seating capacities, and poor lighting. Equipment is often limited and in poor condition. Monies are rarely available for employing the ideal number of coaches. Occasionally the inner-city coach must contend with the possibility of the athletic program being discontinued, a possibility which has endangered the Philadelphia public school system, where budgetary cuts threaten the existence of the entire athletic program.

This inner-city school environment dictates a number of roles that the coach should play. Whether they like it or not, inner-city coaches will find themselves functioning as guidance counselors in a very short period of time. The inner-city athlete, however, has an aversion to guidance counselors, for they feel the counselors have no personal interest in them and make no demands of them. The athletes feel that counselors do not want to discuss problems that are important to the youngsters, and furthermore, the youngsters accommodate them so that they can get by on the least amount of work. Coaches, therefore, should not let athletes know that they are assuming the role of counselor. A common interest in a sport serves to draw coach and athlete together to work, to learn, and to experience success and failure in a way rarely achieved in a classroom or a guidance office. This common interest serves as an excellent base for the coach to begin breaking down an athlete's distrust and hostility. This common interest also provides coaches the opportunity to extend themselves to show interest in the athletes as individuals, rather than just as members of the team.

As rapport between a coach and athletes develops, the coach can then begin to influence the players' values systems. Coaches can help players to recognize their responsibility for their behavior in light of the total environment, and to see themselves realistically. The coach emphasizes the players' strong points and questions them to make them aware of what they are doing. When the players recognize their responsibilities, regardless of the situation, both learning and self-discipline begin.

Coaches should never use the players' past as a means of humiliating them; rather, the past is only used as a learning tool from which the athletes might profit. Everyone wants to be treated with respect. In this feeling, inner-city youth are no different from any other youngsters, regardless of circumstances. Coaches should also be aware of the fact that the inner-city youths react violently to criticism from the peer group. Team members should not be permitted to criticize each other, because it can lead to major dissension on the team. Coaches have to emphasize the fact that they alone are to correct errors. They must also refrain from embarrassing an athlete in front of others. Constructive criticism, and a re-run of the skill so that player can be successful, leads to harmony on a team.

The coach also helps the athletes to establish individual goals that are realistic and achievable and that will help each individual, both in and out of school. If a plan fails, the coach then helps the player establish a new plan. The players should be aware that failure is a state of mind, that failure can be a building block, not a stumbling block. The coach helps the players experience success through a gradual progression of events. The ultimate goal is to have the youngsters become success-oriented and able to use these principles in all aspects of life.

In addition, the coach should serve as a guidance information system. The coach should help the players establish career goals, by directing them to the people who can give them the information they need in order to understand any career and its requirements. Whenever possible, the coaches should use their community influence to help the players secure part-time or summer employment. Through such efforts, the coach gives tangible evidence to both the player and the player's family that the concern for the athlete is genuine. This kind of concern is what helps develop trust in the athlete.

Some coaches believe that another important role that the male inner-city coach might fulfill is that of father figure. Since many inner-city athletes do not have their fathers living at home, male coaches will often find themselves functioning as a surrogate father. Other coaches are of the opinion that this relationship should be more of a "big brother" type, since many inner-city youngsters feel hatred toward a father who left his family. Many do not know their fathers, and often respond negatively to any mention of their father. If a coach can establish the "big brother" idea, it becomes a friendship without the feeling of oppressive authority a father figure might give. Whatever he decides, the male coach must offer these athletes an outstanding model to emulate: the coach should be success-oriented, be willing to work as hard as he expects the players to work, and give evidence of growth in both the sport and in his personal life.

Both male and female coaches will find numerous opportunities to approach the players on a personal level; consequently, the coach must treat the players as mature people, by talking over problems honestly, offering appropriate advice, and respecting the players' positions. The coach should develop a genuine "my office is open to you anytime, if you want to talk or if you need help" approach. The coach, however, must be aware of the pride of the athletes and must be prepared to seek out the athletes if aware that they are having problems but fail to ask for help with them. If the coach has been successful in building trust with the players through the assorted roles of counselor and surrogate father, that coach may even find inviting the team home for a picnic, or a meal followed by a "rap session," an extremely rewarding experience. In any event, the coach cannot limit his or her involvement with the players to the school and practice day; the coach must be available for help and counseling both after school and evenings, if necessary.

Perhaps one of the most important roles coaches fulfill in an inner-city school is that of disciplinarian. The role of disciplinarian, however, should not be construed to mean "playing the heavy" or keeping the player in line in other teachers' classes; coaches should avoid being an extension of the administration. However, if coaches in the inner city expect to be successful, they must make demands on the athletes. They should clearly outline exactly what they expect from the team, and insist that each player adhere to these expectations.

Coaches must impose an almost military regimentation on the athletes or they will view a coach as weak and take advantage of the situation. The inner-city athlete tends to equate strength in a coach with the demands the coach places on them. Consequently, inner-city coaches must not compromise on these demands. Coaches should also make it clear to the players that they are interested in winning, that they know far more about the game than the youngsters do, and only productive players will be on the team. At the same time, the coach should make it clear to the players that they are needed to meet these goals, just as they need to the coach to meet theirs. The coach uses this role as disciplinarian to help players evaluate themselves, set goals, develop procedures and skills necessary to meet these goals. The coach also helps the athletes to re-evaluate and re-establish goals in the face of defeat, and to carry these learned skills into other areas of life. In effect, discipline involves all of those skills and techniques a person must use to meet a goal, and few people in any school are in a better position for helping young people do this than coaches.

The inner-city athlete poses two special problems for a coach: the first is coachability. Normally, coaches in the inner city will encounter two traits in the athletes—a lack of trust and defensiveness—which must be overcome if any coaching is to be successful. The socio-economic position of the coach automatically causes the athlete to view the coach with suspicion, a suspicion which is easily translated into a lack of trust. The player initially doubts the coach's intentions, and it is only after the coach establishes sincerity and honesty, and breaks down barriers, that trust emerges. Because of this lack of trust, the athlete is always defensive, almost to the point of being aggressive. "Street methods" are adequate for most purposes and are, therefore, resistive to any suggested changes. Inner-city students like to insist on doing things their own way.

Contrary to what many people believe, it really does not matter to the inner-city athlete whether a coach is black or white. The inner-city athlete distrusts any symbol of authority and must be convinced that the coach is sincere. The problem usually centers on the inability of the coach to adjust to the athletes who are used to speaking their minds, and who must be convinced that the coach's way is better than their own. The "because I say so" philosophy will never work in the inner city.

In addition to the problem of coachability exhibited by the inner-city athlete, the coach must also contend with the problems engendered by the stereotype of the "dumb nigger." Too many people, including some coaches, view the inner-city black as being unreachable. This stereotype labels black athletes as disruptive, violent, vulgar, generally deficient, and negative. A popular view is that these people are best left alone, since nothing that is done will really change them. The perceptive coach realizes that though individuals may exhibit one or more of these traits, the inner-city athlete is reachable and teachable, provided the coach uses sound methods of approach. Coaches must realize too, that they are as much their brother's keeper as the next person, and to neglect this role in the present is only to insure a greater problem in the inner cities in the future.

In spite of the numerous problems explored above, a coach will find many advantages and rewards in working with the inner-city athlete. A good coaching situation exists due to the lack of outside interference: the coach coaches players and not parents. In addition, the inner-city athlete is aggressive and exhibits a competitive style of play obtained from the playground and streets by playing with older and more experienced players. The athlete's skills and physical strength are finely toned from frequent competition. These traits free the coach from teaching the basic, fundamental skills and allow concentration on more advanced techniques. The coach receives great personal satisfaction from directing negative thinkers into positive

Photo by Patrick Little.

thinking, cooperative individuals. These changes help each player develop his or her own personal leadership. The coach who helps the athletes develop more wholesome life styles reaps an immeasurable reward.

Despite the problems that exist, many school administrators are convinced that athletic programs are a positive influence in the inner-city schools. One of the most vocal supporters of this idea has been a former Superintendent of Schools in Cleveland, Ohio. He believes:

The last place to cut a budget is in the areas of health, physical education, recreation and athletics. We have to be active in athletics . . . and we have to double the programs of America. We have to use our programs to break the isolation of the ghetto. We have to use our programs to keep the children in school, to teach them discipline, and how to live with each other. We have to use the wholesomeness of the athletic field and the athletic plant to do these things.[5]

[5]Paul Briggs, *Athletic Educators Handbook* (1976), p. 52.

Through a number of articles and speeches he has also made the following points:

1. Athletics do things for youngsters that cannot be equaled anywhere else in school. He said he has seen youngsters headed for trouble —academic, personal, legal — until they get involved in athletics and begin to find themselves. Because he has seen so many success stories come out of athletics, he has become one of the strongest advocates in the country for effective athletic programs.

2. Athletics provide discipline, orientation, and focus. These things are lacking in the inner-city where strong athletic programs can help young boys and girls develop self discipline, make decisions, and take pride in their accomplishments.

3. Athletic programs help inner-city youngsters break through their isolation. Many never get more than a few blocks from their own ghettos, but participation in sports gives them opportunities to visit other areas.

4. Participation on athletic teams is a great tool for keeping youngsters in school. The dropout rate of those involved in sports in five Cleveland schools is significantly lower than for those who do not participate on any athletic team.

5. Success in sport can provide future educational opportunities for the inner-city athlete.[6]

DISCUSSION QUESTIONS

1. How can a coach be him- or herself and still fulfill the roles discussed in this chapter?

2. "What you are speaks so loudly that I cannot hear what you are saying." Discuss this phrase and the image you plan to present as a high school coach.

3. What is the difference between image and example?

4. What does the term "coach" signify to you?

5. Give some examples of ways in which a coach can be a citizen of a community.

6. Should coaches live in the community they teach in? Why or why not?

7. What kind of image do you think high school athletes have of male coaches; of female coaches?

8. How would you describe non-verbal communication? Give some examples.

9. What does it mean when a team or athlete is described as "disciplined?"

10. Interpret this statement: "To discipline youngsters is to love them."

11. How can the inner-city coach motivate athletes to do well in the classroom?

---

[6]Briggs, p. 55.

12. What environmental factors force the inner-city coach to play certain roles?

13. How can the inner-city coach break down the inner-city athlete's distrust and hostility?

14. Discuss the importance of the role of inner-city coach as a disciplinarian.

15. How can the inner-city coach make athletes believe that the coach's way is better than what the athletes have learned playing in the streets?

Photo courtesy of The Pennsylvania State University Still Photography Services.

3

THE ASSISTANT COACH

THERE IS A VAST DIFFERENCE BETWEEN MAKING A SUG-GESTION AND MAKING A DECISION.

There are several points that should be made at the outset of this chapter.

1. Not all head coaches have assistant coaches.
2. Some coaches of some high school teams will never have assistant coaches.
3. With the exception of football, most head coaches who do have assistants will probably have between one and three people on their staff.
4. All assistant coaches are not necessarily qualified for the position.
5. Head coaches do not always have a voice in hiring assistant coaches.
6. Many head coaches do not know how to effectively utilize assistant coaches.
7. Many assistant coaches do not understand their role in the overall program.
8. One of the primary tasks of a head coach is to make clear to assistant coaches their basic responsibilities and duties in order to prevent any misunderstandings later on in the season.

The information that follows is for the consideration of coaches who do have assistants, or who expect to, and for those young men and women entering the profession as assistant coaches.

Being an assistant coach, or associate coach as some refer to this position, can be a very rewarding and satisfying experience in which a young coach can begin to feel the excitement and fun of coaching while growing professionally. On the other hand, this experience can be a very frustrating, stifling, and unhappy one. The determining factor

81

usually is the head coach and that coach's personal philosophy of coaching, which includes the role of assistant coaches and how it is perceived. Consequently, it becomes extremely important that a head coach and prospective assistant clarify their beliefs to each other about coaching during the interview or some other time prior to making the final decision on this particular position.

Sometimes beginning coaches, in their eagerness to get a coaching position, forget to investigate this aspect of the job. If their points of view are drastically divergent, it would probably be a mistake for these individuals to coach together since it would breed frustration and discontent in the assistant. At the same time, the head coach would also be unhappy with an assistant who disagreed philosophically with the basic foundation of the program. Neither the love of a sport nor the love of coaching will compensate for this.

If this situation exists, a prospective assistant should be careful not to overlook it and accept the job anyway because of being impressed by the reputation of the school or the coach. By the same token, a head coach in this case should be careful about hiring an assistant simply because of the prospect's reputation as a player. Friction will be inevitable unless, of course, the head coach believes that the assistant's beliefs can be altered enough so that they are fairly compatible in the coaching situation. The implication to the new coach is that while it is wise to enter the profession with certain ideas, ideals and principles, it is also important to keep an open mind and to be receptive to new ideas and thoughts. Dogmatic, uncompromising individuals tend to destroy unity within a coaching staff.

This is not to say that assistant coaches should never disagree with the head coach. They not only will disagree, but they should and they must, if the program is to grow and improve. But these disagreements should concern themselves primarily with the mechanical aspects of the game. Philosophically, they should believe basically in the same things in order to maintain a degree of harmony and unity, both of which are important to the effectiveness of a coaching staff.

A simple example of differing philosophies would be a case in which one coach believes in teaching by being an "iron hand" — screaming at the youngsters all the time, cursing at them, booting them and doing whatever is felt necessary to win, including bending the rules — working with a coach who believes just the opposite. In this situation, someone is going to be unhappy.

When interviewing for a job, a person should keep in mind that all interviews should be reciprocal exercises. That is to say, the person being interviewed should also have an opportunity to ask questions of the prospective employer. There is no single best set of questions for every prospective assistant coach in every situation. Obviously all individuals have their own concerns about a job along with a list of priorities for these concerns. Note: There is a comprehensive list of questions in Chapter 1.

However, there are some basic concerns specific to coaching prospective assistant coaches should consider asking if they are truly interested in being an effective coach in a particular situation. They are:

1. How did this opening occur?
2. If I filled this position, would it create any hard feelings because someone already on the staff wanted this position?
3. What is the head coach's philosophy?
4. What does the head coach feel about winning and losing?
5. Precisely, what are the requirements for this position?
6. What would I be expected to do in this position?
7. What would my basic responsibilities be?
8. Do assistant coaches have an opportunity to contribute to the program?
9. How many people come out for the team?
10. What kind of attitude do these students have toward this sport?
11. Does the administration support the athletic program?
12. Does the community support the athletic program?
13. Is there pressure from the administration or community to win?
14. Do we have a chance to be competitive in the league?
15. Do assistant coaches have opportunities to attend coaching clinics?

Another consideration for the head coach in choosing an assistant is not to make a choice based on the applicant's athletic accomplishments, awards, and honors. Performing well does not insure success in coaching. No doubt having an All-American on a coaching staff would impress members of a team and add prestige to the group, but the ultimate concern still has to be how well this individual can teach. One school of thought is that the outstanding performer sometimes has more difficulty in teaching average boys and girls than an "occasional" player does, because a "star" cannot appreciate the problems of being average. The bench warmer, or someone who had to struggle to accomplish anything in athletics, might tend to have more empathy and patience for young boys or girls. This, of course, is a gross generalization, but is something to think about, especially if the coaching position is in junior high school, where a high level of performance is not to be expected.

Assuming that most would agree that head coaches should be careful in their selection of assistants, when they get the opportunity; and that young coaches should be discriminating when accepting a position as an assistant, philosophical differences between a coach and the assistants can still occur after they begin to work together. The attitude of many school administrators is such that a head coach is never given an opportunity to interview prospective assistants; they are simply assigned. In cases like this it means that the coaches never meet until after the vacancy has been filled. The false assumption made by administrators is that all coaches think alike and since they have a particular sport in common they will get along famously. In these situations a coach or athletic director has to attempt to "educate" the administration as to the necessity of involving head coaches in interviews with prospective assistant coaches, in fairness to all parties concerned. In the final analysis this is for the good of the students. If there is friction on the staff it will affect the team and this isn't fair to these youngsters. The administrators need to understand that a coach is not attempting to tread on their domain by taking part in an interview, but rather that this will be important to the boys or girls who are members of the sport involved.

On the positive side, being an assistant can be quite rewarding when an assistant and the head coach agree, generally at least, on what they both consider to be a sound philosophy of coaching a high school athletic team. It is absolutely crucial, then, for the head coach to clarify the exact responsibilities for each assistant. There can be no doubt or confusion over the role an assistant coach is to fill if the staff is to be efficient and do a good job of teaching. If the head coach is one who believes in delegating responsibilites, an assistant coach should be able to make a signifciant contribution to the team and be recognized for it. This usually provides great satisfaction and motivation for the assistant as well as creating a good feeling throughout the staff. This also creates an atmosphere of unity since, instead of a situation in which the head coach does everything and assistants simply put in time, everyone is deeply involved in preparing the team.

Photo courtesy of The Pennsylvania State University Still Photography Services.

There are two basic schools of thought concerning the advantages or disadvantages of a first-year coach's acceptance of a position as an assistant coach versus a head coaching job. There are those who believe that a coach's first job should definitely be as an assistant. In their view the new coach is in effect serving an internship while making a contribution, but is in reality learning how to become a coach. Since the pressures associated with being head coach are not involved, the assistant is free to learn through actual coaching experience and by observation. Another consideration is that before a person can be an effective leader, that person must first learn how to be led. Thus, by experiencing the role of an assistant, an individual will gain greater insight as to how to establish the most effective kind of working relationship between a head coach and a staff when and if the assistant becomes a head coach. An advantage, too, is that an assistant can and should benefit from the experience of the head coach. There is little question in the minds of experienced teachers that the first year of teaching is primarily one in which the teacher frequently learns more than the students and it isn't until about the second or third year of teaching that a teacher really begins to become effective. This is a generalization, to be sure, and naturally there are exceptions, but there is enough pragmatic evidence among teachers to provide some basis for this observation.

On the other hand, there are some who believe beginning coaches should make every attempt to become a head coach in their first position. In this manner they can try out their own ideas and learn by trial and error. It means also that a naive, idealistic young man or woman can begin coaching without being influenced by a head coach who might have become cynical, lazy, or unethical after prolonged involvement with high school athletics.

The question of which position is best is something each individual must determine individually prior to accepting that first coaching job.

Even though an assistant coach bears less responsibility than a head coach, the nature of this position requires that certain roles be fulfilled over and beyond that of coaching. In order to be an effective coach, the assistant must also possess certain characteristics and qualities. These characteristics and qualities of an assistant coach merit consideration.

Loyalty. Of all the qualities of an assistant coach this one ranks highest of all, for without it any other quality would be of little value. Loyalty, in this regard, refers to others on the coaching staff, the head coach, the team and the school. There is an old saying about loyalty:

Loyalty

If you work for someone, in heaven's name work for him; speak well of him and stand by the institution he represents . . . remember — an ounce of loyalty is worth a pound of cleverness . . . if — you must growl, condemn, and eternally find fault, why — resign your position and when you are on the outside, damn to your heart's content . . . but as long as you are a part of the institution do not condemn it — if you do, the first high wind that comes along will blow you away, and probably you will never know why.

Elbert Hubbard

It is a very rare individual, indeed, who will always agree with everything a head coach does and says about coaching a particular team. Actually, this is a healthy situation as long as there is general agreement on a philosophy of coaching, and any disagreements end once a staff meeting is over. The worst mistake an assistant coach can make is to "undercut" the head coach and to criticize the head coach somewhere other than at a staff meeting. This is a potentially explosive situation and can do much toward tearing a staff or team apart. The organization of a staff should be such that coaches can disagree strongly at a staff meeting, but when they walk out the door they walk out united toward whatever was finally agreed on by consensus or by edict. This becomes a way of life as the number of coaches on a staff increases and their background and experience vary. But this is the way the best decisions, hopefully, are finally arrived at—by the give and take of dissent and agreement. The important thing is that if an assistant hasn't been able to sell an idea the assistant must then be willing to accept the decision of the group and work as hard as possible to make it succeed.

Teacher and technician. As was stated earlier, every coach must be a teacher, but the teaching job of an assistant might only involve some six to a dozen or so athletes, depending on the size of the staff. Consequently, it is imperative that the assistant coach possess a thorough knowledge of the techniques of the game since this is pretty much the scope of this coach's teaching. The teaching done by an assistant coach is a great deal more specific than that required of the head coach. To beginning coaches this is one advantage of starting out as an assistant since this position makes it possible to concentrate on just a few aspects of teaching the game rather than overall responsibility for presenting the "big picture" to a large group.

Enthusiasm. Genuine, spontaneous enthusiasm is contagious. It is an important criterion in teaching athletic skills, especially in preseason practices when chances of boredom setting in are great. An exciting, enthusiastic teacher can take some of the dreariness out of a practice session and get great response from youngsters as they react to this kind of example. Enthusiasm for coaching is particularly important because when a coach begins to lose enthusiasm for the job the "parade" will quickly pass that coach by.

Knowledge of the sport. Beginning coaches bring this characteristic to a staff in varying degrees and the greater the knowledge, the more valuable a coach becomes and the greater is the contribution to the whole program. Playing experience must be supplemented by a thorough study of the sport, methods of teaching, and areas related to teaching. This particular process should never end for coaches who

Photo by Laurie Usher.

desire to improve and grow in the profession. A coach must stay abreast of the latest ideas and techniques in order to keep pace with his competitors.

Unfortunately, not all assistant coaches have had playing experience in a specific sport, or in any sport for that matter. On the other hand, some might have participated in athletics, but are not otherwise qualified on the basis of a lack of professional preparation in coaching. In spite of these shortcomings, school administrators continue to assign these people as coaches, for various reasons.

Using a strict definition of the word, these people are not assistant coaches, but helpers. In cases like this, a head coach has no choice but to teach these individuals what to teach the athletes and how to teach them. These individuals can become effective coaches in time. However, many coaches find this becomes an annual exercise as these "assistants" leave the program after one season, only to be replaced by similarly unqualified people.

Initiative. This requisite is not a difficult one to fulfill when an individual is genuinely enthusiastic about being a coach. When this is the case, an assistant is constantly looking for things to do to improve the program or to improve a particular phase or aspect of a program. This individual is also concerned with doing whatever is necessary to become a better coach. All of this is done without instructions from the head coach and it is done because an assistant is dedicated to doing everything possible to contribute to the success of the team. This also relieves some of the burden the head coach carries all season long.

Coaches of this type generally do make great contributions in many different ways because they make things happen. The coach who fills a place on a staff with the expectation of doing only what the head coach says to is really not fulfilling all the requirements of the position and should do some "soul searching" to see how much he or she is really enjoying this work.

Dependability. This is an important quality in any teacher, but particularly so in a teacher of athletics. When a head coach asks an assistant to perform certain tasks or to assume certain responsibilities or to get specific things accomplished, there should be little doubt that this will be accomplished, and promptly. An assistant should perform these duties in such a way that the head coach does not have to spend valuable time double checking to see if the job is done. The head coach should be able to have complete confidence in the assistant coaches.

One of the lessons coaches attempt to teach members of a team is the importance and necessity of being dependable. Therefore, this makes it mandatory for coaches to exhibit this same quality in order to make the lesson more meaningful to the athletes.

Philosophy. Regardless of whether an individual is seeking a position as head coach or as assistant coach, it is imperative for prospective coaches to begin formulating a sound philosophy of coaching during their undergraduate days. These early beliefs will be influenced by a person's own high school coaches, playing experience, college coaches, college playing experience, and courses in professional preparation. Each individual should take advantage of every opportunity to constantly test ideas on others in order to help clarify thinking and adopt other sound ideas. The college classroom is the ideal setting for this exercise. It is highly unlikely that a philosophy of coaching that is formulated while in college will stay unchanged after an individual actually begins coaching. This is not necessarily good or bad, but inevitable. Every coach needs to constantly reevaluate personal beliefs about coaching, and such reevaluation should be based on the valuable lessons learned through experience.

Clarifying one's beliefs while still a student helps prepare for the job interviews that follow. On the basis of these beliefs a prospective coach should be able to answer questions more confidently and to ask intelligent questions specific to the particular job.

Desire to be a head coach. A head coach should encourage this desire on the part of assistants. This sounds strange because it means that a coach will lose members of the staff periodically. But the advantages far outweigh the disadvantages. When assistant coaches have no desire to be a head coach or lose this desire, the limits of their professional growth frequently diminish in direct proportion to this frame of mind. People in this situation often perform as though they were "semi-retired" in that they tend to do only what the head coach tells them and little else. These coaches tend to show little initiative and enthusiasm and are generally uninspired in their teaching, which severely limits their effectiveness and contributions to the team. The motivation of coaches like this is usually the extra money they get paid for coaching or the chance to identify with an athletic team — neither of which justifies their position on a coaching staff.

On the other hand, those who have a burning desire to someday be a head coach operate with an entirely different attitude. In reality, what they are doing, while a member of a staff, is preparing themselves to be head coaches. Consequently, they study, question, suggest, advise, argue, debate, try new and different techniques and ideas, and constantly evaluate what is taking place in the program. Throughout this process, and because of it, their contributions to the program are limitless. When all the coaches on the staff have this desire, there is an air of electricity surrounding the group and the members of the team receive the benefit of genuine, unbridled, enthusiastic teaching on the part of their coaches.

One caution to keep in mind is that, in this ambitious desire to become head coach, the assistant doesn't begin to take aim at the head coach with whom the assistant is working. This is not only unethical, but dangerous, because it can create all kinds of dissension within a coach staff, as well as on a team if youngsters begin to pick "sides." At the same time there are head coaches who discourage assistants from leaving by hinting at early retirement as head coach, in which case the assistant could move up. In this case, an assistant would be wise to carefully assess the situation, and set a time-table to see if the head job does, in fact, open at that school, and if it does not, to begin an active search for a head job elsewhere. It can be very frustrating to hang on for years, while the head coach dangles the bait of retirement in front of an assistant's eyes. In too many cases like this the head coach finally does retire and a new head coach is brought in over the long-time assistant, because the Board wants a younger person or someone who has had head coaching experience. This can be a great disappointment, and if so, will create a great deal of resentment.

Playing experience. Of all the lessons in professional preparation, playing experience is the greatest single factor in preparing to become a coach. Game time is not the critical issue, but being on the squad is. Experiencing, both physically and mentally, what you will teach provides a much sounder basis for coaching than any textbook ever written or any lecture ever delivered. There are people who become good high school coaches in a sport in which they did not participate, but this is an exception rather than the rule, and often there are other extenuating circumstances.

The question of playing experience is not as critical in small colleges as it is among physical education majors in a large university. Even though everyone is not big enough, fast enough, or good enough to make the team in a large university, it is still possible to be a part of the team as a manager, statistician, trainer, or a walk-on in order to learn more about that sport. Another possibility for a "non-team

Photo courtesy of The Pennsylvania State University Still Photography Services.

member" is to get permission from the various head coaches to attend some of their practice sessions. In this manner it is possible to learn a great deal of observing and by listening.

Attendance at clinics. This is one very good way in which coaches can continue to learn about the latest ideas in whatever sport they are coaching. Naturally, there is a limit to the number of clinics a coach can or should attend; therefore they should be chosen with specific purposes in mind, based on who the speakers are and what topics are to be discussed. Assistant coaches who are dedicated to the coaching profession should take advantage of this opportunity, while the "semi-retired" type of assistant should be required to attend.

It may be that attendance at a clinic will not cause a staff or coach to make any changes, but all clinics should cause coaches to do some self-evaluation, and this is good. This either creates a change in a coach's thinking or reinforces that coach's belief in what is already being done. In the case of young assistant coaches, this provides an opportunity to become aware of what other coaches are doing in similar programs. They can then compare other ideas to their own and apply them to the situation they are in. The greater one's understanding of the many different ways of successful coaching, the better teacher one should become.

A word of advice is to be careful not to be lured to clinics by the appearance of professional athletes on the program. Most of them are entertaining but have little to offer to a high school coach. The experiences of a professional athlete have little significance for anyone involved in a high school or junior high school athletic program, since professional sport is a "world" of its own, and what takes place there is hardly appropriate for teen-age athletes.

Many times a clinic composed of high school coaches only is the most meaningful to other high school coaches. They talk the same language, understand the problems and live in the same "world." Consequently, what they say is relevant to any other high school coach.

Attendance at clinics serves one other purpose, too. They provide great opportunities to meet coaches from different areas and to learn about coaching vacancies. There is no way of knowing when some chance meeting with another coach will pave the way to another job one day.

Rapport with athletes. This is crucial to any teacher, but particularly so to coaches. Without good rapport there are limits to the athlete's acceptance of a coach and what that coach tries to teach, regardless of how sound the techniques are. Again, this emphasizes the importance of a teacher's concern for the students rather than for "things," or the mechanics, of teaching. It also means that the students respect the coach, respect what kind of person the coach is and what the coach knows, and like having this individual as a coach.

The assistant coach has a great opportunity in this regard that a head coach does not have, solely because of the basic nature of each position. Someone has to be the boss, the ramrod, the driver, and the pusher, and in practically all cases this is the head coach. Obviously, the image these roles create for a head coach in the eyes of the team members helps prevent the close working relationship with every member of the team that an assistant can establish with the small groups the assistant teaches. An assistant is primarily concerned with teaching the assigned group, establishing good rapport with them, and getting them to want to do the best they can. If this is a normal-size coaching staff, the number of athletes the assistant coach is responsible for could be very small. Consequently, the athletes identify with the assistant more readily than with the head coach.

There is another way in which rapport develops between members of a team and an assistant coach. This occurs when the head coach finds it necessary to scold or discipline athletes and the student really gets discouraged, so much so that it affects that player's performance. In this situation an assistant must back the head coach, but should also make an effort to boost the morale of the individual and provide whatever kind of encouragement is necessary to get the student back in the proper frame of mind. Special efforts like this do much to enhance rapport between an assistant coach and athletes.

Liaison between players and head coach. Because of the special rapport that should be deliberately cultivated by assistant coaches, they also fulfill this function. The head coach needs to be constantly aware of the feelings of the players, their concerns, the morale of the team, any grumbling that might be going, any unhappiness on the team, any athletes who think they are not being treated fairly, and how the team is reacting to certain things the coach says or does.

Not many boys or girls will go to a head coach and volunteer this kind of information, nor be perfectly frank when asked. The perceptive coach usually is aware of these situations when they exist, but this is not always possible, especially with a large squad. At the same time, the coaching staff might decide that, because of certain circumstances, the head coach should do or say certain things to the team in order to create or cause specific reactions. A teacher cannot always tell what impact these actions are having on students, but should, if they are to be truly effective. The assistant coaches can find out easily whether or not a move has had the desired effect on the team.

It is possible, too, for assistant coaches to serve as a liaison between athletes and the head coach when they themselves see something the head coach is doing that is having a negative effect on an individual or a team. The atmosphere within the coaching staff should be such that an assistant can do this freely without causing any resentment between the head coach and the assistant.

Willingness to work. Even though the final responsibility for an athletic team rests with the head coach, a good assistant is more than willing to carry a fair share of the load prior to or during the season, and even after the season ends. Coaching is a lot of work, and assistants should never adopt an attitude of sitting still and doing nothing until the head coach has everything organized for the season. This is what the "semi-retired" assistant coaches do. Good assistants never do this, and if they had to, would probably feel very frustrated and useless because they weren't making more of a contribution.

Willingness to work means attendance at clinics, evening meetings after a long day at school, meeting with the head coach in the summer or Christmas vacation to make plans for the upcoming season, scouting, and the willingness to do what the head coach believes is necessary to have a good program for the students. If an individual cannot fulfill this role without resenting it, in fairness to the other coaches and the members of the team, this assistant should give up coaching, at least in this particular situation.

Contributing ideas. The head coach should encourage the sharing of ideas among coaches on the staff. If the assistant coaches have come from different colleges or universities, they have all been exposed to different ideas and techniques. Sharing them can make the program better and serve as inservice training for everyone concerned.

Brainstorming sessions provide a good setting for this. In brainstorming people simply begin to throw out ideas, no matter how wild they might seem, and allow everyone else to react to them. Frequently, these ideas trigger ideas or possibilities in someone else's mind, and changes in the program can follow because of this. Industry has been using this technique for years among company personnel. This is an exercise in reaping benefits from the abrasive effect of one sharp mind on another.

The opportunity to present an idea and have it become a part of the team is a tremendous morale builder among assistant coaches. If assistants are high-caliber people they should not only present their own ideas, but also have an obligation to add their thoughts to the ideas of others, to help make the team a better one.

DISCUSSION QUESTIONS

1. Before accepting an assistant coaching position, what kinds of questions should an individual ask to make sure the position is a desirable one?

2. What are the top three qualities an assistant coach should possess, in your opinion?

3. Why should loyalty rank so high as a quality of an assistant coach?

4. There is a vast difference between making a suggestion and making a decision. What implications does this have for an assistant coach?

5. Why should a head coach be involved in interviewing a prospective assistant coach? What kind of questions should a head coach ask a prospective assistant coach?

6. What are some ways an individual can prepare to become a better assistant coach?

7. How can an assistant coach act as a liaison between athletes and the head coach? Give some examples.

CHAPTER 4

Photo courtesy of Bob and Pam Carroll.

4

THE COACH'S FAMILY

Not too many years ago, any discussion of a coach's family usually dealt with the impact the job had on a man's wife and children. Since interscholastic sport for girls was not as widespread as it was for boys, or non-existent in many parts of the country, there were relatively few women high school coaches. As a result, few people paid much attention to the concerns of a coach's family from a female coach's point of view.

Because of the tremendous growth in interscholastic sport for girls that is occurring, and the corresponding increase in the number of women coaches, any discussion of a coach's family today must take into account whether it is the wife or the husband, or both, who is coaching.

It is not necessary to draw distinctions between male and female coaches in most phases of coaching, because basically there are no significant differences in the way teams are organized and coached.

However, when it comes to the coach's family, it is necessary to make a distinction — because while there are some similarities, there are also many significant differences, problems, and concerns, depending on whether it is the wife or husband who is coaching.

SIMILARITIES

It makes little difference whether married coaches want their spouses to become involved in their job or not, because there is simply no way to avoid this completely.

On the one hand, there are the "non-coaching" husbands and wives who want to be a part of the program, while on the other hand, there are those who want no part of it, and expect the coach to leave the job at the school.

Regardless of personal desires, coaches and their families soon discover that the job does "come home" in several ways. Depending on the sport and the interest of the community in that sport, the job affects the home through (1) telephone calls (some anonymous) from parents, fans, students, or the athletes, (2) athletes dropping by either for a friendly visit or because of a problem, (3) listening to critics or "grand-stand coaches" during an athletic event, (4) publicity about the coach and the team in the news media, (5) incidental contact with parents of the athletes in various places in the community, (6) adjusting to the late hours the coach comes home, (7) Saturday contests, (8) attending coaching meetings, possibly in the coach's own home, and (9) the coach's frame of mind during the season, especially if the team is not doing well.

Depending on the circumstances, some of these might not be of any real concern. But the most difficult aspect to control is the coach's frame of mind during the season. This factor becomes important in direct proportion to the individual coach's degree of commitment to coaching. That is to say, to some, coaching is not only a profession but an obsession, while to others, coaching is merely something to be tolerated because it does provide some extra pay.

It is not too difficult to understand why people become obsessed with coaching when we consider that it is: (1) a person's chosen career, (2) a person's means of livelihood, (3) a possible step to better jobs, (4) a matter sometimes of great ego involvement, and (5) a direct reflection of a coach's ability to teach.

It is rare to find individuals who have the ability to completely disassociate themselves mentally from coaching once they leave the locker room for the day. The excitement, problems, happiness, anguish, and plans usually go home with the coach either consciously or subconsciously. At any rate, the family will be well aware of these inner feelings and be affected by them.

The coach's children cannot escape involvement if they are school age. They will be the envy of many in their peer group because one of their parents is a coach and will often be told how lucky they are; others will not hesitate to tell them what a terrible coach their mother or father is and it is their parent's fault alone when the team loses. A coach's children learn some lessons of life early, but when they feel they are a part of what is going on in the planning for the season and individual games, they wouldn't trade places with any other boy or girl in town.

There is no way a coach's family can be completely insulated against critics; consequently, it is wise to include the family in the "inner circle" of the operation of the team. This will help the family face whatever they come up against in the stands, in the town, at school, or at home.

When this occurs, a coach's family will be less apt to resent the coach's preoccupation with the season or with the time spent in preparation for each game, because they feel they are a part of what is occurring and so they understand.

Coaches frequently make the mistake of assuming that everyone

Photo by Bruce Feimster, Asbury Park Press.

around them, including their family, shares their boundless enthusiasm for the sport they are coaching. This definitely is not always the case. Making this assumption can breed serious problems in a new marriage. A coach just entering the profession, who plans on getting married, should not assume that the future spouse will automatically become the perfect, understanding coach's partner just because of being married to a coach. Unless the future spouse has a tremendous interest in sports, or has grown up in a coaching family, he or she probably has no idea in the world what kind of life awaits. It is imperative that a prospective coach make every effort to explain what the coaching profession is all about, especially the demands it makes on a coach's time, thought, and energy. The "non-coaching" member of the family will need to be willing to adjust a household to fit the "merry-go-round" life every coaching family experiences. The coach's spouse must learn how to ignore criticism and to live with the various moods the coach passes through during the course of a season, ranging from the exhilaration of a great win to the depths of despair over an unexpected loss. If the husband is a head coach, the wife will often be expected to help and encourage the families of the assistant coaches to become involved in the excitement of the season. If she elects to take this role, she can be especially helpful to these families in their adjustment to a new community. The prospective husband of a head coach should be prepared to become similarly involved. In short, it takes a very special person to be a coach's husband or wife. Coaches fortunate enough to have this kind of spouse should count their blessings.

This aspect of coaching is one not often considered, but is an area that should not be taken lightly. An unhappy marriage partner, in this demanding profession, can have an adverse effect on the efficiency of a coach.

THE MARRIED FEMALE COACH

Traditionally, it has been the wives who have had to make many adjustments at home for husbands who were coaching athletic teams. However, since people have finally begun to pay attention to the meaning of anti-discrimination laws such as Title IX and their impact on athletic programs, many men now find themselves making adjustments at home because their wives are coaches.

Frequently, part of a husband's attitude toward a coaching wife and the time she spends with the team stems from his belief that basically he is the breadwinner of the family and must work. He does not believe the wife is expected to support the family forever, and as a result, her involvement in coaching and all its ramifications and effects on the marriage are simply not necessary. So, when problems occur, or when the wife is unhappy with some part of her coaching, her husband is likely to say, "Why don't you quit?" In his mind the aggravation just cannot be worth it; the economic impact would be almost invisible, and besides "it's only a game," and really not too important.

Obviously, this attitude can create a great deal of friction if the wife is committed to coaching and pursuing excellence in her profession. If a husband is a physical educator or a coach his attitude is likely to be far different from one who is neither, and who might never have participated in sport. The coaching husband can be a great help by officiating, helping at games, or by just understanding the concerns of the wife. Of course, having a husband who is also a coach can create some problems, too, if he is overly aggressive and begins to interfere in his wife's program.

If the husband is not in physical education, this can lead to a feeling of loneliness on the part of the coaching wife. Her husband might not care about the team since he has problems in his own job which might seem far more important to him than his wife's concern over a 16-year-old girl having problems shooting foul shots, for example:

Life for a married female coach is very demanding. Not only must she teach all day, coach after school, and take her team on lengthy trips, but she also has the joint responsibility of the house with her husband,

Photo courtesy of Judy Anderson.

and possibly the care of children. Someone has to cook, wash and iron clothes, clean the house, and shop for groceries. Even when these chores become joint efforts between husband and wife, many men are notoriously bad at household chores because they never learned how, they do not want to learn, or they believe this is women's work.

In order to investigate the question of how men see the role of their wives who coach, we conducted a survey of married women high school coaches in the state of Pennsylvania. We were anxious to see, through the use of a questionnaire, if the kinds of things married female coaches were saying would be supported by husbands.

Obviously we cannot say that the results of this survey absolutely represent the attitudes of men throughout the nation, but there is a strong suspicion that the following information would vary little among men, from coast to coast, at this point in time.

The questionnaire and results follow.

1. Some men feel it would be very exciting to be married to a woman who was a coach. How do you feel?

A. 41 per cent said yes, it was exciting
B. 27 per cent said it didn't make much difference
C. 32 per cent said no, it was not exciting

In addition they said:

1. I am glad she is working with young girls
2. It gives me a chance to meet new people
3. I'm happy she likes what she is doing, and if she's happy, I am happy
4. It is exciting if she is having a winning season
5. I respect her for her effort
6. Her coaching creates too many problems at home — late dinners, different schedules, transportation problems, dirty house, babysitters, too much time away from home

2. What do you see as the three biggest problems/concerns you have to deal with since your wife is a coach?
A. late dinners
B. her emotions, anxiety, frustration, depression, and anguish
C. too little time together during the season

Additional concerns were:

1. Neglect of family responsibilities, housework, and child care
2. She is worn out when she gets home
3. She gets home too late

3. Does your wife leave her coaching at school or does she bring it home with her?
A. 68 per cent said yes, she brings it home
B. 15 per cent said she did sometimes
C. 17 per cent said no

How would you prefer it?

A. 44 per cent said they preferred she bring it home
B. 34 per cent said it didn't matter because she brought it home anyway
C. 22 per cent said they preferred she did not bring it home with her

4. Do you believe it is important to be a fan of your wife's team?
A. 80 per cent said yes
B. 15 per cent said no
C. 5 per cent said they didn't think it mattered

Comments:

1. Yes, it supports her effort
2. No, but it makes living with her easier
3. We can share a common interest

5. What advice (men) would you give another young man who was

considering marrying a woman who is a high school coach or who plans to become a high school coach?

I would advise the young man to:

A. be aware of the amount of time she will be spending with her team
B. get involved in her sport and share her interest in it
C. be understanding, patient, and support her
D. realize that she will be tired and irritable when she gets home
E. spend time together whenever possible
F. establish an open and honest relationship before he gets married

Other responses that are of interest:

1. Learn how to cook
2. Be willing to share the sports page
3. Marry her . . . she has a job
4. Buy a crockpot

6. What advice (men) would you give a female coach who was about to marry a "non-coach"?

A. Make sure your husband-to-be understands the amount of time your job as a coach will require away from him—time factors such as clinics, practices, games, banquets, coaches' meetings, tournaments, and league meetings
B. Get him interested and involved in some way
C. Make up the time spent away from him
D. Be a woman first and a coach second
E. Never let coaching become more important than your marriage

7. If there are children, do you see any special effects her job has on her relationship with them?

In 44 per cent of the cases there were no children involved. Those who had children made the following comments:

Bad effects:

A. She only gets to see the children a few hours a day
B. It is especially bad when the children are young
C. She is too demanding of the children
D. She lacks patience with the children

Good effects:

A. Helps her get the children involved, so the whole family is involved. It makes for a closer family relationship
B. Gives the children more responsibility at home
C. Exposes children to athletics in the home

8. Does criticism of your wife from "grandstand coaches" or parents bother you? How do you handle this?

34 per cent said yes it did

66 per cent said it did not bother them

1. Most of the husbands said they ignored the critics
2. They said they would keep quiet unless the comments were rude, personal, or bothering her
3. They said they tell the critics to try coaching themselves
4. They realize that we are all grandstand coaches at one time or another

9. What is the best part of being a coach's husband?
   A. I am happy she enjoys what she is doing
   B. the extra pay
   C. sharing her success and failure
   D. free tickets to the games
   E. a winning season
   F. there is no best part in being married to a coach
   G. it makes my life more interesting
   H. it keeps me close to athletics
   I. getting to know the girls on the team
   J. loving the coach
   K. the night after a win
   L. the end of the season

10. Do you wish your wife would give up coaching?
    12 per cent of the husbands said yes
    63 per cent said no
    25 per cent said it makes no difference

Implications

In reading through the completed questionnaires, it became clear that the one consistent negative thread in all of them was concern with the demands on the wife's time. In fact, there seemed to be an underlying resentment on the part of many of the husbands over the amount of time the wives spent at school.

It is possible for a woman to be a wife, a mother, *and* a coach. Yes, there are problems, but with a lot of cooperation and understanding it can be done. What we are suggesting is that it is of great importance to have, prior to marriage, clear, frank communication between a young woman and man regarding the fact that she does intend to coach, that it is important to her and as a result there are some ramifications that need to be understood. If there is unwillingness on the part of the man to accept this, prior to marriage, there is some question about whether his attitude will get any better after the marriage.

Finally, it does not seem to be necessary for a woman who wants to be a coach to choose between that career and marriage.

THE MARRIED MALE COACH

Another point of view about the role of a high school coach's spouse and family involvement was expressed by the author's wife to a group of prospective coaches in a seminar at Penn State. This point of view is that of a coach's wife, and it provides a great deal of insight into the importance of the wife's role in the coaching situation — the feelings a wife experiences throughout a season and some concrete examples of responsibilities the head coach's wife must accept if she wants to be an asset to her husband in his career as a coach. Here, then, is a summation of her presentation to the seminar:

When this idea came up, I didn't know what I could say to you young people regarding the life of a coach's wife. Then I sat down and began thinking about some of the experiences we've had and the things we did as a football and baseball coaching family, and discovered that there really is a lot involved in being married to a coach, particularly if he is coaching a sport with several assistants and a good number of athletes involved. As new men joined our staff, they and their wives were guests in our home soon after they arrived in town. Often these young men were just newly married and reporting to their first coaching position. We would sit and talk about things in general and about what they could expect to be happening in their young lives within the next few years as they began to grow in the coaching profession. This always seemed to mean a lot to them, simply because they were not really aware of many of the ways coaching would influence their lives.

Perhaps you wonder why it is important that the woman in the family be aware of or understand what it means to be a coach's wife. Well, she must understand what kind of life she is getting into, and the young man

Photo courtesy of Dick Taylor.

must point this out to her very early before they decide to get married. She must realize what will be expected of her very early, or it will be a shock as time goes on. She must understand that coaching is going to demand a great deal of her husband's time and thoughts, and there will be lots of times when she is going to feel second in line of importance to her husband's team, and for a young bride this can come as a real disappointment. It is important that she understand this occurs because to her husband his coaching is not just a little boy's game. Instead, his team's performance is a reflection of his ability to teach and is displayed in front of thousands of people several times over a season, on the field, in the gymnasium, pool, or wherever the contest takes place. To him it is more than a game, it is his chosen profession and life's work.

Basically there are three kinds of coaching wives: (1) those who know something about the game and become involved because they want to, (2) those who don't know much about the game and don't want any part of it, and (3) those we can classify as ambitious wives. The last kind becomes a problem only when she feels her husband is not being given enough credit for his contributions and begins to suggest that he really should be head coach anyway. This is a potentially explosive situation and the head coach's wife must work hard to make this wife feel that she and her husband are important to the program.

There are three things the new coach's wife will find are inevitable—sometimes the team wins, sometimes it loses, and her husband will be criticized in either case. When the team wins, it is a great feeling and everyone is happy. When it loses, this can put a damper on the atmosphere around home for a short while or several days. The critics have a field day when the team loses, and when the team wins the critics are often parents of the substitutes, who don't understand why their son didn't get into the game sooner. The only consolation is that it is easier to take negative comments after a win.

One of the happiest thoughts I have is remembering all the wonderful parents we got to know and became friends with, as we shared their sons through athletics. It is a nice feeling to be known by so many parents and of course your paths always cross while shopping, in church, or at other community functions. A coach's wife shares a lot with parents, especially during the athletic event itself. You both hope the boys do well — and if they do, you cheer with them, and if one or all the boys don't do well, you share disappointment with them also.

A coach's wife must also expect to receive telephone calls about her husband. Some can be very bad, but many can be quite complimentary too. Why people call the coach's wife to complain instead of talking directly to the coach remains a mystery, but they do. A wife whose husband has been the long-time football coach at Ohio State used to completely disarm anonymous phone callers (according to the *Columbus Dispatch*) who would call to tell her that her husband was an incompetent coach. She'd say she quite agreed and she thought the coach made some bad decisions during the game in question, too. This usually ended the conversation abruptly!

Shopping at the local grocery store was always fun after a win because everyone was so happy and anxious to discuss the game. The atmosphere was not quite the same after a loss, but I made it a point to shop after every game simply to let people know our world didn't come to an end just because the team lost a game. It was always a thrill when the clerks in the store called me Mrs. Coach.

The fans who were the hardest to take were the ones who were so critical of the boys. When they criticized the coach, the coaches' wives turned a deaf ear to this because we had come to expect this as part of the game, but it would make us angry to hear a grown man verbally attack a young boy because he made a mistake in the game.

Getting to know the young athletes was a most rewarding part of being a coach's wife. I think athletes are extra special anyway and to have them go out of their way to speak or call across the street to say hello gave me a real feeling of pride inside, because these fine young men were recognizing me as coach's wife. Now if your husband establishes a close rapport with these boys, they will find all kinds of excuses to drop in at your home, and frequently it will be around the dinner hour, as all young athletes are always hungry, it seems. So it isn't unusual to have unexpected company for dinner, even though this young man may have just gotten up from the dinner table at home before he decided to stop in to visit the coach. When you have children of your own I can't think of any kind of young people I'd rather have in my house around my own children than well-disciplined athletes. This is particularly so if you have a young son who also happens to be a hero worshipper.

At the same time, some of these visits would come late at night, when a boy had come up against some kind of problem and almost automatically came to the house to talk to the coach. The rest of the family learned how to make themselves scarce in a hurry.

We also felt it was a privilege to take these young men to college athletic events as they began to think about college, and when we did, our whole family went along. It was not uncommon to take a group of boys to a Saturday afternoon football game and another group to a night game the same day. Often their mothers would send picnic lunches along, or a cake, and the trip became a big picnic.

It is a great pleasure to have some of these boys go away to college, only to return to your home for a visit during their college days or after graduation. Often they would bring their new girl friends along for us to meet and, if the boy was a physical education major, it was easy to imagine that he was showing his wife-to-be his former coach and family. One of our proudest moments came when our family was invited to commencement at Yale some years ago as one of our former athletes, who had been elected Secretary (president) of the senior class, gave a commencement address.

If your husband stays in coaching long enough, some of his former athletes will have graduated from college and will apply for a coaching job on his staff. This happened to us on several occasions, and was always a source of great pride as we watched these young men begin their careers and families. Many of these young men that come to your husband as shy young high school boys will become your lifelong friends, as do their parents. This is one of the major rewards in being a coaching family.

As you might expect, the next step was receiving wedding invitations in these growing-up years. This often put a dent in a coach's limited budget, but was a very pleasant part of our lives, too. It was a good feeling to think that these young men thought enough of your husband to invite him to one of the most important events of their young lives. It never failed, though, that before the reception was over, a group of the athletes and the coach would be in the corner reliving past glories while the bride wandered about the room, pretending not to notice.

One of the most important relationships the head coach's wife must cultivate is with the wives of the assistant coaches. The wives share so many feelings and emotions during the course of a season that this provides enough common ground upon which to develop the unique feeling of "in-ness" among coaching families. The larger the coaching staff, the more important this becomes. The two problem areas that may arise revolve around the wife who doesn't join the group and the overly ambitious wife. In the first instance, the head coach's wife should make an effort to include this individual in every situation where the group will be together socially or at a game, and try to impress on her how much more fun being a coach's wife is when you feel a part of the program. In this manner there is a sense of belonging, rather than a feeling of being neglected and left out.

The overly ambitious wife creates another problem that is much more serious. When a coach's wife is ambitious for her husband to the point where friction begins to develop within the group, this problem is one that is not easily resolved. This situation can destroy the unity among the coaching families, cause wives to "draw up sides" and possibly spread to the point where the coaches themselves are affected by it. There are really only two basic solutions, and the first and most obvious is for the coach to resign and look for another coaching position. But until that happens, a lot of damage can be done, so when and if the head coach's wife senses this problem is brewing, and if she feels it is impossible for her to handle, she should let her husband know of the problem.

At this point, if the head coach has established a good working rapport with his staff, he should sit down with the husband of this particular wife and calmly discuss the situation to see what the problem is. It may be that the assistant coach is not aware of the problem or it may be that there are other problems causing his wife's behavior. At any rate he needs to understand the ramifications of any significant division within the coaching family, including the effect it could have on his own career, and the head coach must urge him to handle the problem quickly. This is not easy to do, and requires a great deal of tact and diplomacy on the part of the head coach, but as was mentioned before, there is more to coaching than simply coaching.

One of the most important contributions the head coach's wife can make is to serve as a committee of one to help the wives of new coaches get acquainted in the community as quickly as possible — in other words to be a one-woman "Welcome Wagon Hostess." It is easy for people who have been settled in a town for several years to forget the trauma that is often associated with moving into a brand-new community. This is particularly true when a new young coach joins the staff right out of undergraduate school, and has just recently been married. If neither of these people is familiar with the community, their adjustment problems can be painful, and so the head coach's wife should take it upon herself to help ease the jolt of being "new" by helping these folks feel at home instantly.

There are so many ways she can help. One is to offer this young couple a place to stay while they look for a place of their own. She can also guide them around the community, showing them the various sections of town and possible living accommodations in relation to the location of the school and shopping areas. They need to arrange for a family doctor and dentist, and should see where the various churches are located. It is a good idea, too, to take the new wife on a shopping trip, so she can learn something about the stores, where the best bargains usually occur, and where the best place is to purchase meat and groceries. This also provides a fine opportunity to introduce her as the wife of one of our new coaches to as many merchants as you happen to know. This is one of the first steps in making a new family feel welcome, and a good way to let them know that you are glad they are joining your coaching family.

Sometimes a new assistant who is unmarried joins your staff. In this case, the head coach takes care of orienting him to the community, but you will find that this young man will be a frequent dinner guest in your home. Not only does the young man get some home-cooked food but he has a chance for a close look at a coach's family during the hustle-bustle of a busy season. If he takes a bride while still on your staff, you like to think part of this is because he liked what he saw while visiting with your family in your home.

Another method for creating the feeling of "in-ness" among wives is to arrange to go to all the games together. The wives can take turns driving to the games, but all meet at one house to save time.

We always sat together at both home and away games, and after every game we all met at someone's house for a post-game get-together. This I think was one of the best things we ever did, because it was one of the few opportunities the whole group had to be together and relax for a while during the season. If the team won, everyone wanted to be together to enjoy the win. If the team lost, we felt it was necessary to be together rather than brooding individually. I guess being together served as group therapy. Sometimes these sessions would last until three or four in the morning. Many cups of coffee were consumed as the husbands unwound and replayed the game over and over again. But these evenings were a wonderful part of coaching that helped create a real closeness within the whole group. The wives felt responsible for these get-togethers and looked forward to them. Sometimes the evenings were painful at the beginning because of a disappointing loss but more often, over the years, they were happy occasions.

When there weren't too many seniors on the team, we sometimes invited their parents to these functions at our homes. We did this in order to get to know the parents better, and also to give them a chance to know us better and to see how winning and losing affected us, too. Often, as the group began to thin out, some parents would linger to talk about their son and his future, now that he was a senior. These were very rewarding moments and many lasting friendships grew out of these times.

Then, too, there are the inevitable coaches' meetings. Rather than have each wife sit at home feeling neglected, we decided to meet also. The wives with small babies would bring them along and put them to sleep in their car beds — we'd put on the coffee, talk, knit, and get to know each other better. Those who didn't know how to knit learned, and sometimes when the coaches finished their meeting, they would come to the living room and have to wait for the wives to finish what they were doing.

We soon discovered that, after all these fun times together, we usually missed them and each other when the season ended, so we decided it was important to continue to do things together all year long. Coaches usually like to eat, so at least once a month we would all go out to dinner, have a picnic, or plan a progressive dinner, and we would take at least one camping weekend each summer. Obviously, we didn't want anyone to feel that they weren't an important part of a close-knit group, so we worked hard at it.

Another consideration is the wives of other coaches in the school— coaches of other sports. In order to prevent any misunderstanding about creating a feeling of "in-ness" within a coaching staff of one sport only, it is a good idea to invite coaches and their wives who are involved in other sports to some of the social functions your group has during the year. This helps create a good working relationship between all the coaches, and it can be an effective tool to help maintain harmony among the coaches of various sports. The athletic director and his wife often joined us in these get-togethers also. Occasionally, we would include the high school principal and his wife, or other faculty members who would enjoy the association with a group of coaches.

Naturally, the head coach is too busy to think about these kinds of things, so it becomes the sole responsibility of his wife to organize this facet of coaching. This serves a lot of useful purposes, and makes the coach's wife feel as though she is making a significant contribution to the overall program.

It is also important for a coach's wife to attend other functions in the school with her husband — school plays, concerts, P.T.A., and so on — to show that they are not narrow and selfish in their interests but care about the total school program. Owing to the nature of his position, your husband is highly visible to the community, and attendance at these functions does not go unnoticed.

The wife who resents these kinds of experiences and involvement is missing some wonderful and meaningful moments of sharing all the excitement of her husband's career. This also puts her husband in an uncomfortable situation in that he either attends all these functions by himself or doesn't go at all.

Since we were primarily a football coaching family, the weeks during a season generally followed the same pattern. The first six days of every week our schedule revolved around Father's schedule, but we made certain that Sunday was a special day for the family. We always spent the day doing something together totally unrelated to athletics. Everyone was fairly relaxed the first part of the week but as the days passed and game time approached, the tension in Father began to affect the whole family so that, by game night, dinner was a very sparse occasion because everyone was too excited to think much about eating. To make the children feel extra special, they always were let in on some special play that would take place during the game, and of course this made them feel quite knowledgeable when they went to the game and told their friends to watch for it and then pointed it out when it happened. This is all well and good, but it backfired on us one night. Our daughter explained an unusual play in great detail to an inquisitive fan during a game, only to discover that he was a scout for our next opponent.

One role a coach's wife rarely escapes is that of laundress. It isn't unusual for the coach to come home with one or two duffel bags full of dirty scrimmage vests or other paraphernalia to be washed in time to take back to school the next day.

She might also be called upon to chauffeur a group of athletes to a baseball game, tennis match, or other athletic contest when school buses aren't available. She may find herself hostess to 30 or more boys for a team picnic, because her husband thought it would be a good thing for the boys. Or on occasion, she will find herself going to the hospital with her husband late at night after a game to visit a player who has been injured. There is no question about it, a coach's wife is a lady for all seasons and a woman of many traits. It is truly an exciting way to live when you pitch in and join your husband.

When our daughter was very young she took a long look at our busy lives and very seriously announced that if she ended up marrying somebody poor instead of somebody rich she hoped it would be a coach. At the same time, our son wanted to know, "Why doesn't dad go to work every day like other kids' dads?"

In order to provide a broader look at how other coaches' wives viewed the impact of coaching on themselves and their family we surveyed a random sample of married men coaches throughout Pennsylvania, using the same basic questions we asked husbands of women coaches.

The coaching families were involved in team sports, individual sports, high visibility sports (football, basketball, wrestling), sports that did not receive a great deal of publicity, and sports in which there were no assistant coaches.

The questions and responses follow.

1. Some women feel it would be very exciting being married to a man who was a coach. How do you feel?
   A. 67 per cent said yes it was
   B. 13 per cent said no it was not
   C. 20 per cent said it didn't matter that their husband was a coach

In addition they said:
   1. It is hard to deal with the pressures of his job, anxiety, demands, loneliness, time he is away, and frustration
   2. Too many hours away from home
   3. I'm very proud to be the wife of a coach
   4. It is best when you get involved by getting to know the kids and going to the games
   5. It is exciting because you know that your husband has a part in the success of so many students
   6. It's even more exciting when you are winning
   7. I'm happy because I know that he's happy

Photo series by Bill Dettlaff, Oshkosh Advance-Titan; *courtesy of Bob and Shirley White.*

2. What do you see as the three biggest problems/concerns you have to deal with since your husband is a coach?
   A. his time away from home, the children, wife, and family
   B. his health, i.e.: tension, anxiety, worry, pressure of the job, exhaustion, ulcers, and possibility of heart attack
   C. irregular home schedule—meals, trips, and transportation problems

   Other comments were:
   1. my ability to cope with criticism of my husband and his team
   2. a losing season, or losing in general
   3. use of my spare time
   4. property damage from unkind fans during the season
   5. parents' telephone calls to our home
   6. the tremendous demands on the coach's time

3. Does your husband leave his coaching at school or does he bring it home with him?
   A. 72 per cent said yes he brought it home
   B. 5 per cent said sometimes he brought it home
   C. 23 per cent said he did not bring it home with him

How do you prefer it?
A. 73 per cent said I prefer him to bring it home
B. 12 per cent said I prefer him to leave it at school
C. 15 per cent said it really doesn't matter

Comments:
1. It gives me a chance to share his interest
2. I know what is going on with the team
3. I can help relieve his anxiety by listening
4. It helps me to get to know him better

4. Do you believe it is important to be a fan of your husband's team?
A. 79 per cent said yes
B. 21 per cent said no

Additional Comments:
1. Yes, it gives him support
2. Gets me involved in his interest and makes me feel part of the team
3. No, but it makes things a lot easier
4. Yes, it is important for survival
5. No, we have small children that take up most of my time

5. What advice (women) would you give another woman who was considering marrying a man who is a high school coach or who plans to become a high school coach?

I would advise the young woman to:
A. Learn the sport that your husband coaches
B. Be prepared for long hours away from him
C. Support your husband in his coaching
D. Find some interest of your own
E. During the season be ready to be number two
F. Be patient, loving, cheerful, understanding, and a good listener
G. Don't throw away scraps of paper—they might have a play on them
H. Learn to fix late warmed-up meals
I. Understand that coaching is important to him
J. Be ready for losses by his team
K. Be prepared to meet a lot of new people
L. Be flexible
M. Be his number one fan; at times you'll be his only fan
N. Marry a doctor

6. What advice (women) would you give a male coach who was about to marry a "non-coach"?
A. Include your wife in the sport; share with her your problems and concerns about the team. Take her to games and any social events surrounding the team
B. Let her know the amount of time you will be away from her, the kids, and the family
C. Let her know coaching means a lot to you

D. Encourage her to find hobbies of her own
E. Don't bring your problems home
F. Marry the girl, not the sport
G. Find someone who likes sports
H. Be considerate of your time together

7. If there are children, do you see any special effects his job has on his relationship with them?
   A. Yes, it does make a difference in that the children get to see him less during the season
   B. The mother has to take care of disciplining the children
   C. It's nice when the children can go to practice and spend more time with their father this way
   D. The children are proud that their father is a coach
   E. The entire family gets involved in the sport
   F. He is short-tempered and impatient during the season
   G. He misses a lot of his own children's activities
   H. Having a father as a coach helps the children get interested in sports and to become better athletes

8. Does criticism of your husband from "grandstand coaches" or parents bother you? How do you handle this?
   A. 55 per cent said yes the criticism bothered them
   B. 45 per cent said no it did not

   How do you handle this?
   A. ignore them
   B. sometimes I say something back to the critics
   C. get up and leave
   D. keep quiet
   E. stare at them
   F. I know they don't know anything anyway
   G. I try to consider the source

9. What is the best part of being a coach's wife?
   A. knowing that my husband is happy, satisfied, and doing what he wants to do
   B. knowing he is satisfied with the team's performance, that they are winning or having a winning season
   C. seeing the respect he gets from being the coach
   D. getting to know the boys on the team
   E. being proud of him for working with young men and teaching them positive attitudes as well as skills
   F. being part of the fun and excitement of the game
   G. when the season is over
   H. loving the man, my husband, the coach
   I. getting the extra pay
   J. discounts from the local sports store
   K. the pride involved
   L. sleeping with the coach
   M. being able to share a big part of his life with him; being able to support him and listen to him
   N. the tournaments, games, and the travel

O. watching some of the boys become successful in high school
and in later life

P. sharing the "ups and down" of coaching, together

10. Do you wish your husband would give up coaching?

A. 15 per cent of the wives said yes

B. 63 per cent said no

C. 22 per cent said it really didn't make any difference

Conclusion

In general the women who responded to this questionnaire wrote
long, thorough comments to our questions. Many not only answered the
questions but added other bits of information they felt were of value. It
was almost as though some of the wives found an outlet all of a sudden to
let go with some thoughts they had been harboring for some time.

At least one woman wrote specifically to this point when she said,
"I've been married to a coach for 25 years, and this is the first time anyone has really asked me about my attitude toward his job."

Some of the wives said that being involved in one sport season was
fun and exciting, but when their husband had to coach more than one
sport, they weren't too happy about that. The biggest complaint from
their point of view was the amount of time the husband spent away from
home, which is considerable.

One of the areas not included in this survey was coaches' salaries.
Many wives covered this in their responses anyway. For example, they
said:

1. Coaching is not worth the time my husband spends on it when you
look at the money he receives.
2. If all his time were spent in some other occupation he would be
making a lot more money.
3. My husband's coaching salary breaks down to 35 cents an hour—
while another lady said her husband's pay for coaching figured out to
be 25 cents an hour.

Few people who coach would dispute these figures. This might lend
some support to the notion that people don't stay in coaching for the
money, or conversely, if a person is interested in making money, coaching is the wrong occupation to follow.

Another observation is that it was apparent that most of the wives
were willing to adjust themselves and their families to the unique
demands inherent in the responsibilities their husbands faced as high
school coaches.

Our final reaction to what the wives wrote was that many of them
felt very proud and happy about the respect shown their husbands
throughout the various communities because of their role as a coach.

There is no doubt that a man's involvement in coaching does affect
his wife and family, for better or worse. This in itself is not necessarily a
revelation to any married coach, but the important thing is to be able to
put coaching, and particularly the time factor, into proper perspective.

Photo courtesy of Jack and Ann Infield.

That is to say that more than one coach has devoted years of time and energy to "the team" and other men's sons, only to give up coaching one day to discover that his own family has grown up on him and moved away.

Coaching is a demanding occupation — that is a fact. But it is also a fact that it is possible to be a family man or woman and coach, too. When a person quits coaching and the scores of all those athletic events have long been forgotten by practically everyone, the family ties still remain — and it may be that in the final analysis, this is what really counts. At any rate, it would seem that a coach's family deserves the same kind of interest, concern, and dedication he or she gives the team. At least this seems to be part of the message that comes through to us from this survey.

DISCUSSION QUESTIONS

1. Would you like to coach your son or daughter? Why?

2. What are some ways in which a coaching staff can involve their wives and husbands in their coaching?

3. How will you advise your spouse or children to handle critics in the stands?

4. Is it really necessary for coaches to spend so much time on the job? Explain your answer.

5. Should coaches involve their families in their jobs? Why?

6. How can a husband or wife in coaching create problems in a marriage?

7. What is your reaction to the husbands' survey? The wives' survey?

8. Of what value is this chapter to prospective coaches like you?

Photo by Laurie Usher.

5

QUALITIES OF A GOOD COACH

A head coach's personal philosophy will dictate everything that he or she does as a coach. This philosophy grows as a composite of all the coaches the individual has played for, what has been learned and observed as an assistant, and ideas gathered at coaching clinics. It is important that coaches use a great deal of discretion and evaluate, critically, all that they see and hear from other coaches in order to determine what is best for them in their particular situations. Techniques and methods that have proved successful to one coach might prove disastrous to another because of circumstances and personalities. Therefore, beginning coaches should exercise caution in attempting to pattern themselves after a famous "name coach" or in trying to imitate this person. To emulate a great coach is one thing—imitating this same coach might be a serious mistake.

For example, a highly successful coach was once described as an ingenious architect, efficient contractor, and relentless straw boss. He was also a tyrant, father-protector, Moses figure—and a winning coach.

Another big-time coach has been referred to as the cruelest coach in football, and in terms of victories, one of the most successful.

A long-time Big Ten coach has been known to take off his watch, throw it on the ground, and smash it by jumping on it or tear his ball cap to shreds when things go wrong at practice — and his teams win consistently.

On the other hand there are coaches who run low-key practices, who don't scream at their athletes, who don't act like maniacs during an athletic event, who are fairly calm people — and their teams win also.

The point is that there is no single right way or best way to coach, and beginning coaches should not look at another individual's won-lost record and then imitate those coaching ways because they believe that is the way to be successful. It is dangerous for high school coaches to pattern themselves after successful big-time coaches when the name coaches' techniques are foreign to their own personalities. Each coach's philosophy of teaching, their own personality, and circumstances will determine how they should conduct themselves.

Transparent realism.   Frequently, coaches attempt to project an image based on a preconceived notion of how they think youngsters view coaches. For example, some coaches might attempt to portray toughness, aggressiveness, manliness, or femininity, depending on the image they want to create for the athletes. Consequently, youngsters frequently never get to know their coaches, and leave school with a distorted view of what they were really like. Many coaches have fallen into this pattern. It really isn't necessary and, in fact, might hinder accomplishing some of the goals they set for the team. One of the qualities good coaches should develop is transparent realism. This means coaches should allow their human qualities to show and not pretend to be something they are not. These human qualities include such things as empathy for individual athletes, concern for individuals, anger, sorrow, tenderness if need be, as well as toughness and aggressiveness. To be truly effective as a teacher, in the broadest sense of the word, a coach must be seen in these various moods rather than merely as a "sledgehammer" personality whose only purpose in life is to win games. Some coaches look at the idea of allowing their human qualities to show as a real threat to the long established image of toughness in a coach. This is more a matter of insecurity on an individual's part than sound educational practice.

Reasoning.   Coaches should always have well-thought-out reasons for everything they do in their program. This not only concerns offense and defense or practice plans but also includes the way they conduct the entire program. Every decision, with all its ramifications, needs to be carefully considered before a coach acts. Coaches need to look at all phases of their program, as well as their personal philosophies, and simply ask themselves, "Why are we doing this?" or "Why do I believe this?" One of the important reasons for doing this is that it forces coaches to evaluate everything they believe and do in coaching. Time is always a factor in coaching a team and unless a coach has a reason for doing specific things a great deal of time is wasted and these things should be eliminated. This is a luxury very few teams can afford. If coaches cannot justify or explain everything they do in coaching, in their own minds at least, they shouldn't be doing them. A good mind is constantly revising when it comes to organizing athletic programs.

There is little question that coaches are subjected to all kinds of criticism from many sources. There are times when their methods, techniques, and beliefs are questioned by adults in the community, or by the school administrators themselves. In situations like this coaches will experience great difficulty if they have not carefully thought out precisely why they conduct the program or certain aspects of it the way they do. This doesn't mean that coaches have to explain everything

Photo by Dick Brown, Centre Daily Times.

they do to every critic, but the important thing is that they should be able to. A coach should not do things in athletics simply because someone else does. If a school superintendent asks a coach why he or she did things in a certain way, the coach should be able to answer the question clearly and intelligently if the reasons have been thought out beforehand.

Whether or not anyone outside of the coaching staff agrees with the coach's reasons is not of prime importance. What is important is that the coach has justification for what has taken place or is taking place.

Interest in individuals.   A coach also needs to possess an intense and continuing interest in the overall development of each individual on the team. It is too easy to forget what is happening to youngsters after a season is over, when they are not directly involved with a particular coach every day. When this occurs, it lends credence to the critics who insist that coaches care about youngsters only during the season, and then only because they are doing a job for the coach, but once the season ends the coach cannot be bothered with them anymore. Coaches who care about people could not and should not allow themselves to fall into this mold.

This genuine concern for athletes should carry over into all phases of a youngster's school career and should continue after high school days are over. This means that while they are in school, a coach is concerned about the students' academic achievements, conduct, problems, concerns, and successes. It means that a coach is willing to help, if need be, in guiding a youngster to make the decision concerning college or the choice of a profession. It means a coach is ready and willing to offer assistance in times of difficulty, as in serious illness or death of one of the athlete's parents. In times like this the coach's presence can serve as solace and strength for a young person when comfort is greatly needed.

There will be times when athletes earn the lead in a school play or participate in a band concert. Coaches should feel great pleasure in seeing athletes excel in something other than sports and be willing to share in this experience by attending these functions. This means a great deal to youngsters in that someone other than members of their family — someone who is important to them and is special in their eyes — has taken the time to watch them perform in something other than an athletic contest.

Occasionally a coach will be blessed with athletes who go on to college and are skillful enough to participate in college athletics. When possible, a coach should make an effort to attend at least one of these games during a season. It means a lot to athletes when their former high school coach comes to campus to watch their team compete and it also lets athletes know that the coach is still interested in their achievements even though they have graduated from high school.

The ultimate in satisfaction, for a coach who cares, occurs years after an athlete has left high school and has become successful in whatever field he or she has chosen to pursue. Long after the games have been played, this is really what counts. This is the time that a coach is permitted the luxury of thinking that the experiences this individual had as a member of a particular team might have helped this person to become what he or she is, as an adult and a citizen of the community. There is no known scientific research to substantiate this, but coaches receive enough feedback from former athletes to know in their hearts that some of the lessons they attempted to teach through the discipline of athletics have made enough of a difference in the lives of these students to make it all worthwhile.

Respect.   The next quality a coach should strive to achieve is that of being respected. Respect is something that a coach cannot demand, dictate, or purchase—it must be earned. Generally speaking, teachers earn the respect of their students by how they treat them. Beginning teachers often confuse respect with popularity, and there is a great difference. It is possible for a teacher to be liked as a person, but still not command respect. On the other hand, a teacher might not be very popular among students, but have the respect of all who know that teacher. New teachers, in their desire to have students like them, often go easy on discipline and try to establish a friendly "one of the gang" type of image. The biggest difficulty in this approach is that once a teacher crosses that invisible line between student and teacher, and becomes a buddy, maintaining any kind of discipline becomes extremely difficult and often breeds resistance or resentment from the students.

The teacher who is fair, maintains certain degrees of discipline, and lets the students know what is expected from them and what they can expect in return, who holds the line between student and teacher so that the students are always aware that the teacher is their teacher, rather than a buddy with back-slapping or first-name familiarity, will be on the way to earning respect from the students. Once this feeling develops, the teaching-learning process is enhanced greatly.

Coaches should conduct themselves in such a way that respect comes not only from members of a team but also from the student body, faculty, school administrators, and people in the community. When coaches are eager to fulfill all the responsibilities of the position and to be effective teachers and leaders, it is mandatory that they work hard to earn and keep the respect of all who know them. Because of the nature of the position, coaches are constantly in the public eye and when they are respected for what they are, what they do, and what they believe in, this makes the job much easier. This is especially so when and if the team has a bad year in the eyes of the community (the team loses more than it wins). The critics will have their say as usual, but this is less of a threat to the coach who is highly respected as a teacher of young boys or girls than it would be to another kind of coach. People tend to be more tolerant of those they know and respect, and particularly critical of those they don't.

Ability to motivate.   It has been said that motivation is the key to learning. When youngsters are ready to learn both physically and mentally, and want to learn, they will learn and not before. Therefore, the primary task for coaches in motivating athletes is to make them want to

Photo by Laurie Usher.

learn how to become better athletes, better competitors, a better team, and winners.

The best kind of motivation, without question, is self-motivation. Some youngsters who participate in high school athletics have a high degree of self-motivation, while some have little or none. The highly motivated individuals are referred to by coaches as real competitors. Normally these people are the easiest to coach because they "come ready to play."

For a high school coach to consistently find teams made up totally of highly self-motivated boys or girls is extremely rare. It is when there are few such members that a coach's ability to motivate, to make a group of young people want to work to excel, is tested.

If we agree that motivation is the key to learning, is there then a key to motivation in sport? The answer is yes and that key is challenge. If a youngster is a competitor, challenge can be extremely effective as a motivational tool. However, it is very important that challenges be realistic or they become meaningless. This requires coaches to know their athletes as individuals. It also demands sensitivity and a feel for the personality of a team and the individuals on the team.

The ability to motivate athletes is essential. Many coaches believe that when all factors are fairly equal, teams or individuals who win are those that are the most highly motivated and prepared mentally.

When coaches are able to instill a burning desire to succeed in a group of athletes, that team will be a difficult one to compete with; and, while they might get beaten, they never lose. In other words if they come up short on the scoreboard, it is because their opponent was better, and not because they themselves played a poor and uninspired game.

Everyone wants to win, but it is the individuals who don't want to lose who are the most successful. Many coaches believe this is the goal of motivation in sport.

Some will argue this point and insist that the goal of motivation is to instill a desire for excellence. Some also believe that playing to win can in fact hinder excellence because the only thing that matters is the score — and never mind how the points come just as long as we have more than the opponent at the end of the contest.

On the other hand, many coaches believe that winning is excellence and that you cannot have one without the other. Ultimately the answer to this argument comes down to each coach's own philosophy of sport, including the importance of winning.

There is the belief, too, that the basic purpose of motivation is to make youngsters competitive. Competitiveness in this context is defined as the desire to succeed in "the game," to show superiority over an opponent.

Whichever way coaches view the purpose of motivation, one fundamental fact overrides all else, and that is that youngsters bring different degrees of competitiveness to sports. Much of this depends upon their past environment, both familial and social.

If boys or girls grow up in highly competitive situations where this quality is rewarded, they are more likely to respond to motivation than youngsters who come from an environment where competitiveness was minimized. This appears to be more of a problem for girls than boys, simply because girls growing up in America traditionally have been taught to be "nice." This means they have not been raised to be aggressive, tough fighters and competitors.

The ability to motivate people to consistent levels of readiness is a fascinating process and a difficult one. The basic problem is that there is no one best way or right way that fits all people all the time. As a result, coaches constantly strive to discover effective ways to accomplish this task.

There are as many ways to motivate athletes as there are coaches. Most coaches would admit that they have tried them all at one time or another. To further complicate matters, the method that worked in motivating a group today might not work tomorrow, next week, or next year. People change, circumstances change, moods change, and the personalities of teams change.

In their desire to become motivators of athletes, some coaches become "gimmick" coaches. These are coaches who rely a great deal on things like inspirational slogans, music, signs in the locker room, and various awards throughout the entire season. Their belief is that these gimmicks will excite the athletes, fire them up, and help get them into the proper frame of mind for competition.

There is nothing wrong with this approach, but too much of anything can become counterproductive, and so it is with gimmicks. The real danger in this approach to motivation is that coaches can get so wrapped up in gimmicks that they neglect to teach youngsters how to play the game.

In other situations coaches rely on noise or complete silence, inspirational talks, humor, pleas, or threats to motivate a team. Attacking an individual's ego or pride can sometimes be a very effective technique in motivation. The coach's personality is the key, more so in this situation than in one in which gimmicks are relied on. The slightest amount of motivation will affect performance to some degree, but an attempt to increase motivation excessively may actually result in poorer performance. The problem is to determine how much and what kind of motivation it takes to get a team to its peak. The drawing at the top of the next page illustrates this point.

This aspect of coaching is probably one that causes the greatest anxiety for a coach, because it is so difficult to tell whether or not the team is mentally ready to play their best. This is particularly crucial among teen-aged athletes, but is a concern, too, among college and professional athletic teams. Therefore, the coach in a normal high school setting cannot always be sure what the team will do once they take the field or court, and this uncertainty can be particularly disturbing to a coach.

The timing involved in motivation is also crucial. The right thing

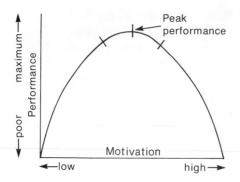

said at the wrong time can cause an adverse reaction. Too much motivation too soon can leave an athlete or team literally exhausted before the competition begins. Generally, the soundest technique is to begin preparing the athletes mentally, several days or more prior to the contest, and build to a peak at game time.

Playing on the emotions of an individual athlete or group of athletes is a delicate technique since there is such a fine line between too little motivation, too much, too soon, or too late. One of the cautions to be considered in attempting to get athletes "psyched up" for athletic contests is to try to avoid the "peaks and valleys" of emotional readiness.

No athlete can survive an entire season at the peak of emotional arousal. Somewhere along the line there will be a letdown; when that occurs, performance suffers. Many experienced coaches have learned this the hard way.

Frequently, when a team gets sky-high for that really big contest—win, lose, or draw—the athletes are drained emotionally and, as a consequence, might not perform well for one or more contests afterwards. It is also possible that if a team or individual gets keyed too high, performance will suffer as a result.

The trick is to keep the athletes consistently on the high side of the scale toward the peaks with infrequent attempts to reach the peak of emotional readiness. As some coaches have put it, you can only go to the well so often before it runs dry. Often when a team fails to perform well it is due to this motivational factor rather than to how well they were taught the mechanics of the game. The ability to consistently motivate people to do their best might be one of the most important qualities a coach can possess.

Coaches often get so involved in the organization and mechanical aspects of sport that they sometimes neglect the personality of the team and begin to take motivation for granted because they themselves are

Emotional arousal

peaks

valleys

Photo courtesy of Judy Anderson.

highly motivated. Coaches should make every effort to develop and perfect the ability to motivate throughout their coaching career.

Dedication.   Dedication is another quality of a good coach—dedication to doing the best job possible, year round, to becoming a better coach, and to making the sport the best it can possibly be for the youngsters who participate. The coach needs to have a burning desire to be the best and do whatever preparation is necessary to reach this goal. When coaches do not possess this kind of dedication they will probably never advance beyond the level of mediocrity as a coach. An assumption coaches frequently make, especially new coaches, is that a high degree of dedication also exists within all members of a team, otherwise they wouldn't be there. This is not true. Youngsters participate in athletics for many reasons and in a squad of 20 to 100 boys or girls it would be an extremely rare situation if all were as dedicated to the sport as the coach.

To the coach, this sport is both profession and livelihood, and winning and losing do matter. But to an average 14-year-old or 17-year-old boy or girl this is merely a game and their involvement or dedication varies according to their personal motivation, worries about school, girl friends or boy friends, how they look, problems at home, and other personal concerns. They have other things on their minds, and coaches need to realize this. If a student is out for basketball, for example, that student may like the sport and enjoy playing it, but might really like baseball or softball better, and if the basketball team doesn't win the state championship, this is not the end of the world to this player and others on the team. This doesn't necessarily mean they won't work hard and compete well; the point is that winning just doesn't happen to be the most important thing in the world to them, as it is for the eager, ambitious coach whose coaching future depends on boys and girls who are similarly dedicated.

This difference in degree of dedication between coaches and athletes can create frustration for the coaches. This in turn can affect their relationship with athletes, if they fail to recognize that all high school students bring varying degrees of dedication into their participation in sport.

Ability to discipline.   The need to be a firm disciplinarian is an integral part of teaching. Youngsters need guidelines and they need to know the limits of their conduct. There is nothing wrong with telling youngsters what they can or cannot do or in teaching them how to respond to an authority figure. In spite of desire for individuality and "doing your own thing" in today's society, there is and always will be a necessity for discipline to guarantee some form of order. Young people still need to learn to follow rules, as well as learning the consequences of breaking rules. Today, it might be rules of the game, but tomorrow it will be the rules for an adult in society. There is no concrete proof that the discipline a youngster experiences in athletics will necessarily carry over into any other walk of life — only the belief teachers have that it does, and occasional firsthand experience when they can see that it does.

The keys to maintaining discipline are firmness, fairness, and consistency. Whatever rules are made must be reasonable, have a purpose, and be understood by everyone concerned. Once rules are established it is absolutely necessary that coaches be consistent in the way they handle any situation involving discipline, regardless of who the offender might be. Exceptions to established rules can breed additional problems for the coach. However, there are circumstances when coaches must exercise the option to treat disciplinary cases individually. Therefore, it is essential that coaches not issue ultimatums along with the rules. If they do, they leave themselves no alternatives.

Identification of goals.   In order to be an effective teacher, it becomes necessary for a coach to identify goals for him- or herself and the program. Establishing specific objectives is a basic principle of teaching, and when these are made clear it provides direction for all facets of the activity, including the way the coach performs within this framework. Out of necessity, some of these goals will need to be accomplished immediately, while some are medium-range, and still others will be long-range goals.

It normally takes several years to accomplish all these goals, and it may be that some will never be reached. The important point here for the beginning coach is to recognize the need for patience with him- or herself, the athletes, the program, and the administrators of the school.

A coach needs to learn to cooperate with the inevitable. This planned timetable, along with the objectives, might have to be reevaluated and readjusted several times as time goes on. The coach might have overestimated his or her abilities; he or she might have misjudged the capabilities of the athletes, or a coach's goals might change as that coach becomes more experienced and begins to mature in the profession. This is normal, and coaches should not be so impatient that they become discouraged if things move slower than planned.

The effect on the program by the administration often requires a great deal of patience also. Administrators are sometimes slow to help bring about all the changes coaches desire in order to upgrade their program, but the coach must keep working to bring these about. If it appears that the administration is stifling and will continue to stifle the growth of a program, so that a coach feels frustrated in reaching specific goals, the coach should then consider moving to another coaching position.

The quality of salesmanship is tied in closely with this point. Unless a new coach is given carte blanche in organizing a specific program for a high school — an unusual situation — meeting some of his or her objectives will depend a great deal on salesmanship. Assuming that this sport is already in existence at a school, a newly appointed coach will find that there are already policies, goals, traditions, and ways of doing things, some of which the new coach will want to change. If the preceding coach was successful and well liked by athletes, this presents the kind of problem which really demands great salesmanship. This becomes even more of a challenge if the team is composed of many seniors and they happen to be unhappy over the circumstances which created the coaching change. Not only does this require that the coach be able to sell him- or herself and the accompanying ideas, but it requires much patience and understanding as well.

If a coach's predecessor had a different philosophy toward coaching and organizing a program, this will try the new coach's salesmanship also. For example, if the preceding coach had a lackadaisical approach, did not maintain good discipline, was not a demanding coach, or spent little money on good-looking uniforms, a new coach obviously has a great selling job to do if this coach doesn't believe in running the program the same way.

Ability to recognize talent.   Player evaluation, or the ability to recognize talent, is another quality every coach must develop, and the only sure way to do this is to watch an athlete compete. Skills alone do not indicate a player's true talent, nor will this player's physical make-up, speed, strength, or the fact that a father, brother, or sister was a great athlete. Physical skills are not so difficult to recognize and, in some individual sports like tennis, track and field, or swimming, the stop watch, height of the cross bar, or challenge match usually determines who will participate in the contest. The great difficulty in player evaluation is to try to determine as quickly as possible how each athlete will perform in the game or contest. A coach must identify as quickly as possible who the "winners" are. These are athletes who, regardless of skill, size, speed, or whatever, simply get the job done. And this cannot always be determined before a season begins or without seeing a youngster in game competition.

Drills will not serve this function in every case, although they frequently indicate certain qualities a coach will be looking for in an athlete. One of the drawbacks in relying solely on drills to evaluate personnel is that if the sport is a contact game, like football, a coach can take two boys and match them in a drill that demands a lot of aggressiveness. In spite of the fact that one of the boys might be timid, he will stand and fight rather than be embarrassed in front of his teammates. This can give the coach a false impression, because when that same boy practices with a whole team, he will not compete well, since all eyes are not on him and he literally loses himself in the crowd. All other things being equal, the best evaluation of a player's overall ability occurs through game participation.

There is no way to predetermine what is in the heart of athletes regarding their reaction to game-time competition — the game itself must reveal this. Consequently, a coach should organize practices as nearly like game situations as possible and use pre-season scrimmages to find out who the competitors are. Techniques and methods of evaluating personnel will be discussed in greater detail in Chapter 7.

Ability to utilize available talent.   Along with the ability to evaluate personnel, the ability to improvise with the talent on hand is also of great importance as a step in achieving a successful season. It is a rare situation when a high school team has no weaknesses or shortcomings in personnel. Whereas a college coach can recruit athletes to fit a particular system, the high school coach must make a system fit the talent on hand, and this changes year by year as the talent cycle evolves. Consequently, it is a manifest waste of time for high school coaches to keep saying, "If we had stronger athletes, faster athletes, more athletes," and so on. The point is that they don't; those now on the team are the only athletes available. Therefore, the coach must improvise with what is available, do a great job of teaching, devise strategy that will give these athletes the greatest chance of competing well, place various athletes in different positions if necessary, and, finally, camouflage whatever weaknesses still exist to prevent an opponent from detecting them. Do not let what you cannot do interfere with what you can do. The good coach will take what talent is there and do the best possible job with it, and not spend time in the futility of looking at a squad and saying, "If only we had this or that." It is also a study in futility to watch a coach try to fit athletes to a particular system when they are not capable, rather than adjusting the system to fit the talent.

Enthusiasm.   Enthusiasm on the part of a head coach is necessary because what the head coach does and the way in which things are done permeate the entire squad. This is especially important during pre-season practice sessions, when monotony and boredom become a threat. The enthusiasm of the head coach and its effect on the rest of the staff and athletes help make practice less of a chore and more fun. Enthusiasm is also important to a coach personally. It is this trait that helps create the desire and willingness to spend long hours working during a season, to attend coaching clinics, and to make a continuing effort to learn more about coaching, year after year. Without this quality, coaching is no longer any fun, and it is time to give up coaching.

Intense desire to win.   Every coach should possess, along with enthusiasm, an intense desire to win. The personality of a team normally reflects that of the coach, and having the desire to win is no exception. There is nothing wrong or sinister in teaching people to play to win, providing it can be accomplished within the rules and in the spirit of the game. One of the coach's major obligations is to attempt to instill the desire to excel in each member of a team, and in sport the measuring stick of excellence is the scoreboard, stop watch, or tape measure. This is not any different from other fields—mathematics, for example, in which the math teacher who works very hard to teach students how to excel in math uses a test grade to measure the individual's degree of success.

This doesn't mean that if a team or an individual fails to win every time, something is seriously wrong with the athlete, the coach or both. When success and winning are equated, every athletic contest then

Photo courtesy of Tom Billman.

becomes an all-or-nothing event. There are varying degrees of success or excellence, but the most important thing is that coaches, through their intense desire to win, instill this desire for excellence in each athlete. When athletes learn to do their utmost and give maximum effort both physically and mentally to win the prize, and do this within the rules, they have learned a valuable lesson that will eventually make them winners. A coach has an obligation as a teacher to instill the desire to excel in each student.

There is a danger present in this quality, however, and that is the temptation of the coach to win at any cost, by breaking rules, using and abusing athletes, abusing officials, or by using unethical tactics to gain an advantage over an opponent. Poor conduct on the part of coaches is often justified on the grounds that they hate to lose. This is pure rationalization. The desire to win does not excuse any of these acts, nor do they have any place in high school athletics. No one enjoys losing; therefore, using the desire to win as a reason for the poor behavior of a coach is not justifiable. This idea simply breeds a great deal of malpractice in high school athletic programs. In these situations the game ceases to be a game, becoming instead an ego-satisfying experience for the coach.

Willingness to work.   Another quality of a good coach is the willingness to work hard and to put in long hours when necessary. When the school day ends a big part of the coach's day is just beginning, and the end of practice does not necessarily mean the end of the working day. Because all the members of a coaching staff have teaching responsibilities, staff meetings will have to be held in the evenings; there might be films to review, practice plans to develop, phone calls to make, phone calls to answer, and injured athletes to care for or take home, to mention some of the possibilities.

There are many situations in which coaching a particular sport has become a year-round occupation, rather than seasonal. This usually occurs because the coach wants it to be that way, or feels it must be done in order to compete well against the teams on next year's schedule. There might be league and state rules which prohibit off-season coaching, but there are many related activities which can be done legally. For example, there are physical conditioning programs, clinics to attend, notebooks to be revised, films to review, and staff meetings to review the season just passed and to make plans for the one to follow. In the normal high school situation, all of this must be done on the coach's own time because the daily teaching schedule does not provide any time for this type of work.

Even though coaching does take a lot of work, coaches need to be careful not to create work for themselves just for the sake of working. There comes a time when this extra work reaches a point of diminishing return, and coaches should develop the ability to recognize how much is too much. A weary coach or weary staff will not be effective. In the final analysis, the key to a successful team is still good athletes, and all the meetings in the world will not change this fact. The most important consideration then, for each coach, is efficiency of time, rather than the amount of time spent in planning.

There is another aspect of this quality to be considered, and this is that athletes tend to be more willing to work hard themselves when they know the coaches do. This is a further illustration of teaching by example.

Knowledge of the sport.   Knowledge of the sport was discussed earlier as a quality of an assistant coach. This quality is just as critical, if not more so, for a head coach. An assistant coach can be very effective by possessing knowledge of a particular phase of a sport, whereas it is mandatory that a head coach have a thorough knowledge of all phases of the sport, to be able to organize and supervise the whole program properly and efficiently. The head coach is in effect the master teacher, and therefore must develop a great knowledge of all the intricacies of the sport.

Dislike of mediocrity.   Coaches must also have an intense dislike of mediocrity in anything that concerns the program in any way. They must develop in the athletes the attitude that whatever is done must be done the right way, the coach's way, and anything less than that will not be satisfactory. There is a right way or a wrong way to do the right thing, but there is no right way to do the wrong thing. There are a lot of different ways to accomplish a certain task in any sport, but the athletes must understand that, based on all factors concerned, such as personnel, ability, speed, and so on, there is one best way for this group to get the job done, and not only is it important that everyone do it this way, but they must also do it the right way. Mediocrity breeds mediocrity. Abraham Lincoln once made a statement to the effect that an individual cannot help being born average, but no one has to stay that way.

In athletics, the average high school youngsters will not drive themselves to rise very far above mediocrity unless they have a high degree of self-motivation. Consequently, the coach must insist that each individual strive to become the best that he or she can. This is a responsibility inherent in teaching.

> If you can't be a pine on the top of the hill,
> Be a scrub in the valley — but be
> The best little scrub by the side of the rill;
> Be a bush if you can't be a tree.
>
> If you can't be a bush, be a bit of the grass,
> Some highway happier make;
> If you can't be a muskie, then just be a bass—
> But the liveliest bass in the lake!
>
> We can't all be captains, we've got to be crew,
> There's something for all of us here,
> There's big work to do, and there's lesser to do,
> And the task we must do is the near.
>
> If you can't be a highway, then just be a trail,
> If you can't be the sun, be a star;
> It isn't by size that you win or you fail —
> Be the best of whatever you are!
>
> *Douglas Malloch*

One way to avoid mediocrity is to insist on precision in everything affecting the team. The first step in precision is punctuality. Tardiness on the part of the athletes or the coaches should not be tolerated. There are coaches who deliberately set odd times for meetings to begin or for a bus to leave for a game. For example, to make people more aware about precision of time, a coach can set a meeting for 8:13 rather than 8:00 or 8:15, and then start the meeting at the set time. Precision is also important in the way the athletes and coaches dress for practice, because they are members of a team and as a team they will succeed together or fail together. The coach should also insist on precision in practicing or teaching the techniques that will be used in a game.

The greatest benefit to be achieved through this quality is teaching people to be thorough and to pay attention to detail. Regardless of the sport, the movements involved, or the plays executed, all are made up of many small details. If details are ignored, the final product will reflect this by lack of continuing excellence. Youngsters are impatient to play the game and do not like to work on details or fundamentals, but coaches cannot afford to take short cuts. Attention to detail is the foundation upon which consistently strong teams are built.

Understanding boys and girls.   The next quality every coach should develop is an understanding of teen-aged boys and girls. In order to motivate them and teach them, it is necessary to understand and appreciate their concerns, problems, worries, anxieties, interests, physical capabilities, and mental characteristics. Since so many physiological and psychological changes occur in each individual during his or her teens, a coach should realize that most of these youngsters have many more concerns on their minds than sport alone. To most of these young people, a game is a game, and winning and losing do matter, but only for the moment. There are too many other things clamoring for their attention, whereas a teacher making a living coaching teams sees this same situation from an entirely different point of view. Unless a coach is aware of this vast difference in outlook, that coach might make the assumption that the players don't care that they lost a game, because they seem to get over the disappointment so quickly. Before too much time has passed they are already talking about other things. This can breed frustration and anger on the part of the coach, but not if the coach remembers that this is only a game to these youngsters.

One of the false assumptions that coaches also make, and which creates some misunderstanding, is that youngsters come out for a sport and stay on the team because they love it — just as the coach loves the sport. Nothing could be further from the truth. There are many reasons why young people go out for athletic teams, over and above love of the sport, such as:

1. SOCIAL PRESSURE.   This might come from a girl friend, boy friend, or group of friends. Peer pressure is one of the strongest influences on youngsters of this age. Not only might this influence their decision to try out for a team but it also sometimes dictates which team.

2. UNIFORM WEARER. There are youngsters who stay on a team just for the opportunity to be seen wearing a game uniform. They enjoy the pre-game warm-up because they get a chance to show off a bit, but when the game begins, they are satisfied. They have had their moment of glory, and they really don't care to play in the game. These are the people who sit on the end of the bench, and when the coach turns around to look for a substitute, they quickly look in the other direction hoping the coach won't notice them.

3. PRESSURE FROM MOTHER OR DAD. One of the saddest reasons youngsters have for being on a team is that their parents want them to be. In cases like this the youngster is usually unhappy and learns to hate every minute of practice. When coaches are unaware of this they can add to the misery by "getting on" this youngster because he or she isn't doing a good job in practice.

This is particularly true when the situation concerned involves a highly aggressive sport with body contact. A youngster in these circumstances suffers a great deal of inner torment because the situation is so disagreeable and unpleasant.

Youngsters who stay out for a sport because mother or father expects it are to be pitied for the unhappiness being forced on them. If the coach becomes aware of this and feels strongly that this youngster would be much better off if he or she weren't part of the team, the coach should consider talking to the parents to try to make them aware of what they are forcing their child into. On the surface, this might sound very easy, but in reality it can be quite difficult. There are parents who will refuse to listen, because they don't believe what the coach is saying, or they don't want to hear what the coach is saying. Either the parents were athletes, and they want their children to be athletes also, or they were not, and they are trying to live this experience through a son or daughter. In either case, it takes a great deal of tact and diplomacy in dealing with parents like this, and even then a coach may fail.

Another possibility to consider is to cut the student from the team. By doing this the coach has taken the youngster out of an untenable situation and still not destroyed the youngster's relationship with the parents because he or she didn't quit the team — the coach made the cut. If, in the judgment of the coach, this is the best course of action for the youngster's mental and physical well-being, that coach should be willing to do this in spite of the criticism forthcoming from the frustrated parents.

4. LOVE OF THE GAME. There are still people who go out for teams because they enjoy the sport and love to compete. These people are in the majority and in spite of all the criticism leveled at sport in our modern society there are still hundreds of thousands of youngsters across the country who play the game because they love it and everything that goes with it. The coach simply needs to recognize that not everyone on the team feels this way — there are exceptions.

5. EGO INVOLVEMENT. This is also a big factor in being a member of the school team. There is evidence to suggest that, without

this, youngsters will not play, or if they do, they won't really put out. The perceptive coach attempts to identify this need in each athlete, and then uses it to get each athlete to do the best job possible, in order to help the team succeed.

It may very well be, too, that ego involvement on the part of a coach is what keeps men and women in the coaching profession for as long as it does!

6. ATHLETIC SCHOLARSHIPS.   There are individuals who participate on teams because there is always the promise of a scholarship, and, with it, the opportunity to go to college. For some, this might appear to be the only way they will ever have to get a college education, and as a result, this provides tremendous motivation for them to excel.

Generally speaking, these are the reasons that high school students try out for athletic teams. In inner-city or ghetto schools there are additional reasons why students participate in sport. These reasons are unknown to youngsters from the more affluent areas, simply because of circumstance. They are as follows:

1. Athletics might be a way out of the ghetto. Excellence in athletics might provide a "ticket" to new and great opportunities for the underprivileged individual, through athletic scholarships. This is an opportunity to get an education and to learn a profession. In addition, the super-athlete might have the opportunity to become a professional athlete with the possibility of a lucrative contract.
2. Athletics provide an opportunity to satisfy the urge to excel.
3. Athletics can serve as a constructive outlet for the pressures, problems, and frustrations of life in the inner city.
4. Sport is a way to earn respect from fellow students. It provides an excellent opportunity to establish a good reputation in the school com-

Photo by Dick Brown, Centre Daily Times.

munity, and to be known. To be somebody is important. Through success in athletics, the individual's self-image is enhanced also. These factors are important to any youngster, but more so in ghetto schools, where daily circumstances do little to satisfy these needs and, in fact, stifle them. Participation in athletics provides this opportunity.

5. Many youngsters who grow up in the ghetto have little or nothing, in contrast to the more affluent suburban children, and athletics is something real and concrete that they can really get involved in. In many cases athletics is the only thing that keeps young inner-city students in school.

6. In situations where basketball shoes are issued to people who make the team, some students try out for the team to get a pair of shoes. These shoes become a matter of prestige, and indicate a certain level of accomplishment for that individual.

These reasons do not fit comfortably into all the idealistic principles and theories of play that physical educators have been mouthing for many years, but they are real and they do exist.

Know what factors make the difference between winning and losing.   Another quality of a good coach is the awareness of the factors that make a difference between winning and losing. The most important of these factors are discussed below.

1. SUPERIOR PERSONNEL.   The prime prerequisite for winning is great athletes. No team has ever consistently won without them, regardless of the ability or intelligence of the coach. Beginning coaches who have been blessed with outstanding athletes and start a coaching career winning sometimes fail to appreciate the contribution of the highly skilled youngsters, and assume that the winning occurs because the coach is extraordinary. In situations like this it is very easy to overestimate the contribution of the coach, thereby minimizing the value of great athletes. Some coaches have gone so far as to say that winning is 90 per cent outstanding athletes and 10 per cent coaching.

2. SUPERIOR CONDITIONING.   Regardless of the ability of the athletes, it is the coach's responsibility to insure that each individual is in the proper physical condition to play the game. Tired athletes are more injury-prone than those who are still fresh. The late and great coach Vince Lombardi often stated that fatigue makes cowards of us all, and that the harder an individual works, the harder it is to surrender. Consequently, one of the goals of every coach should be to condition a team well enough so that they are physically as strong at the end of the contest as they are at the beginning. Often the outcome of a game is determined near the end, and the team in better physical condition has the greater chance of winning.

3. FEWER MISTAKES.   High school athletic contests are games of mistakes. The team or individual that makes the fewest mistakes has the greatest chance of winning. The mistakes a team or individual makes in competition usually occur in direct proportion to the quality of instruction, mental frame of mind, discipline, attention to detail, thoroughness of preparation, and physical condition.

Mistakes will occur when youngsters are swept up in the excitement of a highly competitive situation — it is inevitable. The coach's job, then, is to prepare the team well enough so that mistakes are kept at a minimum.

4. SUPERIOR MENTAL ATTITUDE.   When people of similar ability compete, the difference in winning or losing usually depends on being ready, mentally. In high school competition, where talented athletes come in cycles and the league is fairly balanced, the coach who has the ability to prepare the players mentally will have teams that are consistently at the top of the league standings.

It is not so difficult for a coach to know when an athlete is ready, physically, to play the game, but it is extremely difficult to recognize mental readiness. Usually, this is not evident until the contest has begun, and by then there is little a coach can do about it. Preparing an athlete's or a team's attitude is one of the most difficult aspects of coaching, and one of the most important.

The following illustrates the importance of an athlete's mental preparedness:

Positive Thinking

If you think you are beaten,
    you are,
If you think you dare not
    you don't
If you'd like to win, but you think you
    can't
It's almost a cinch that you won't.
If you think you'll lose, you're lost,
    For out of the world we find
Success begins with a fellow's will,
    It's all in the state of mind.
If you think you're outclassed,
    You are,
You've got to think high to rise,
You've got to be sure of yourself before
    You can ever win a prize,
Life's battle doesn't always go
    To the swifter or faster man,
But sooner or later the man who wins
    Is the man who thinks he can.

Author unknown

5. SUPERIOR TEACHING.   The importance of a coach's teaching ability was discussed earlier. There is, however, one other phase of teaching to be considered, and that is the care a coach must take not to talk too much in the practice area. Most of the talking should be done in group meetings or team meetings, in order to be able to take advantage of all possible practice time. Drills or scrimmages should not be interrupted in order to talk with one player. If an individual is doing something wrong this player should be taken aside and corrected while someone replaces him and the practice continues. It is a tremendous waste of time when a coach stops a drill and takes time to

Photo by Laurie Usher.

correct one person while 10 to 40 others stand around and wait. Multiply these few minutes several times and a good portion of practice time has been lost.

6. SUPERIOR PLACEMENT OF PERSONNEL.   Whatever the situation, the level of competition, or the sport, there are always only five best, nine best, or eleven best athletes, depending on how many are needed on the first team. One of the first priorities of a new season is to determine who the best athletes are and then make whatever position changes are necessary in order to get these people in the starting lineup.

It is ridiculous to have a fine athlete on the bench when changing this individual's position or someone else's could get this player into the game. Not only is getting the best people in the game critical, but getting the best people in the right position is crucial, as well. A coach should not hesitate to place athletes in different positions. Even though an athlete should be willing to do this, the ability of a coach to "sell" the youngster on the value of the move, both to the player and the team, will do much to help the youngster make the transition. Being blessed with fine athletes is one thing, but utilizing them properly is quite another.

Ability to develop pride.   One of the goals coaches strive to achieve is to develop pride and tradition in the teams they coach. The pride the team feels also carries over to the individuals who compose the team. When athletes are proud of their team and its accomplishments, it makes being a member of this team a highly desirable goal and creates an atmosphere in which it is pleasant to coach. Pride, in this instance, can be used by a coach as motivation for the team, and the athletes become more susceptible to the methods the coach feels are necessary to prepare this group to compete.

Pride and tradition cannot be purchased or borrowed or established by edict; they must either be inherited or developed over a period of time. This can be accomplished by various means, such as outfitting a team in sharp uniforms, firm discipline, developing excellent facilities, or through hard work, self-discipline, or first-class treatment during a season; however, the primary means is through success (winning). Once pride and tradition are established, they become self-perpetuating, provided the team continues to experience more success than failure. A winning tradition not only solves a lot of problems but prevents many problems from ever arising. Obviously, inheriting tradition and pride makes a coach's job much easier.

Teams who have established this characteristic consistently dominate the scene, unless a down cycle of talent catches up to them; that is, an absence of great athletes, or an unusual amount of injuries during the season. Championship teams and championship athletes have always had great pride in their accomplishments, and as a result put up fierce struggles to maintain the pride they feel for themselves and the team. This quality is the one which provides the motivation necessary for proud athletes or teams to come from the brink of defeat, to victory. Tradition and pride sometimes take years to establish, but once they are a reality, their value to a team is immeasurable.

Ability to organize.   The ability to organize is another quality necessary for a good coach. First, coaches must be able to organize their own thoughts and ideas in order to determine the direction and goals for the overall program. Then they must be able to organize the coaching staff in such a way that the staff, too, will be aware of the head coach's objectives and can function efficiently to accomplish these. The head coach must then be able to organize the program in order to make it the kind that gives every athlete an opportunity to demonstrate individual ability, one that will be enjoyable, and one that will be a worthwhile educational experience for each participant.

This quality becomes increasingly more important as the size of a coaching staff increases and as the number of people on the team grows. Without this ability on the part of a coach, a tremendous amount of time will be wasted, there will be confusion on everyone's part, and the team will not be consistently successful. This can breed discontent within a coaching staff or on the team itself, which in turn has an adverse effect on a team's accomplishments.

In spite of the necessity for organization of pre-season, in-season, and post-season activities and plans, the coach must also remain flexible. Plans are intended to serve as guidelines, and guidelines should be altered or changed whenever the situation necessitates it. Coaches should be careful not to become so rigid in organizing a program that they either won't change, or cannot change. Flexibility is one of the criteria for growth, not only in a coach's ideas and goals but in a program as well.

The planning which has proved successful for a season or several seasons should never be looked upon as a panacea for all time, because people change and certainly the situation changes in high school athletics, year by year. Colleges can plan a program and then recruit people to fit these plans, but the high school coach in the normal situation must make plans to fit the cycle of people who come out for the team each year. Some classes may be gifted with a great deal of talent while others are not, and it is this kind of cycle which creates the necessity for flexibility in a coach's thinking and planning.

Language.   Since junior high and senior high students are at an impressionable age and because coaches teach by example, the language a coach uses in front of the athletes does not go unnoticed. It is a mistake for coaches to get down on the youngsters' level by using slang or other teen-aged expressions. Instead, all teachers should attempt to lift youngsters up to an adult level of speech, by requiring conventional usage of English. In reality, every teacher in a school is an English teacher.

There are coaches who believe that it is necessary to swear at youngsters because this is tough language, and therefore it creates a picture of toughness on the part of the coach. For the most part, all cursing does is demonstrate ignorance of the English language. All teachers are expected to have such a command of the English language that they are able to express themselves clearly, without abusing a youngster with curse words. A female coach who resorts to swearing at her girls does a great deal to destroy any image of femininity in sport, and this should be avoided at all times, since women coaches are generally working so hard at creating positive attitudes concerning interscholastic sports for girls, particularly in answering the concern with maintaining a feminine image. A more immediate consideration is that in many girls' leagues there is a rule stating that the girls will be thrown out of a game for swearing. Coaches can be removed from the bench for swearing also, and if this occurs, their team is declared the loser.

Regardless of how each individual feels about swearing, our society has developed the belief and expectation that teachers simply do not curse their students in the teaching process. The fact that a teacher of athletics teaches on a playing field, rather than in a classroom, does not alter this idea one iota. There is not one shred of evidence to prove that cursing a youngster helps that youngster learn quicker, better, or more. Nor is there any evidence to substantiate the belief that it makes any individual tougher, or a better athlete. The coach who believes that cursing will add to his or her stature as a model for youngsters to emulate, thinking it indicates toughness and courage, would do well to consider the possibility that there might be better ways to do this than by resorting to the language of the gutter which degrades a youngster. When coaches constantly rely on curse words they are demonstrating an undesirable quality of a coach — "phoney tough."

There are a lot of youngsters living in homes where their parents do not curse them, in which case they will resent a teacher who does. A coach can destroy a great deal of respect a youngster might otherwise have for him or her by resorting to swearing. Some people look upon swearing as a strong way to show a weak mind.

The following list should help coaches consider the effect cursing could have on the students as well as on their own image;

Eleven Reasons Why I Swear

1. It is a mark of being a real man or woman.
2. It is an example of self-control.
3. It pleases my family so much.
4. It is a sign of refinement and culture.
5. It shows how well educated I am.
6. It demonstrates my command of the English language.
7. It sets a good example for youngsters.
8. It shows how tough I am.
9. It makes me a better teacher.
10. It makes people respect me.
11. It adds dignity to my role as a teacher.

Moral standards.   Traditionally, one of the qualities expected of coaches is the possession of high moral standards. This is so universal that many people take it for granted, but coaches should not. This quality is important for any adult who is a teacher of young people, but is especially critical for the athletic coach. The special role an athletic coach fulfills in the lives of impressionable youngsters, and the fact that coaches do teach by personal example, necessitate a life guided by high moral standards. A coach should take great care to avoid hypocrisy in the eyes of the students — coaches should not teach a set of values verbally while practicing the opposite. This helps destroy the coach's credibility and will eventually impair that coach's effectiveness as a teacher, model, and leader of young boys and girls.

The concept of coaches doing whatever they like simply because they are adults, and expecting youngsters to do or believe only what coaches tell them concerning moral standards, is a gross error. Even though our society is experiencing great changes in moral standards and conduct, there are still basic values upon which to base right and wrong behavior, to serve as guidelines for coaches to live and to teach by.

There seem to be very few absolutes concerning moral standards today. Therefore, all coaches need to determine in their own minds what they believe is morally correct for themselves and the youngsters they teach. If these standards are not acceptable to administrators of a particular school, it would be better for everyone concerned if this coach taught in some other situation. Administrators have been given the responsibility of running the school and employing the kind of teachers they believe will provide the best possible education for all the students. If a coach's moral standards are the kind that do not fit the expectations the school administrators have for their teachers, it is their duty to dismiss this person or not hire this individual in the first place.

Honesty.   Honesty is another quality a good coach should possess and one that should be insisted on from everyone involved in a sport.

There are no shades of gray concerning honesty. An individual is either honest or dishonest, and there is no in-between. It is not possible to be just a little dishonest.

The author conducted an experiment several years ago, using several hundred high school girls and boys to test the thesis that youngsters who were involved in interscholastic sport would be more honest in situations calling for honesty than students who were not athletes. The assumption was made that more honesty was learned through participation in athletics than in everyday life. The test in this specific situation proved this assumption false. Therefore, if honesty is to be learned in athletics, it must be deliberately taught by the coach as situations arise.

Coaching provides unlimited opportunities to teach honesty, while at the same time it also provides unlimited opportunities to teach youngsters how to be dishonest and how to cheat. In fact it is probably easier to teach the latter! In spite of the claims coaches have made for years about the values of sport and the character building that occurs through participation, there is little or no concrete evidence to support any of these claims. It is possible that sport teaches little or nothing that is good, unless the coach makes a deliberate attempt to teach something more than the skills of the game. This includes honesty, and it cannot be learned by accident. It must be taught and demonstrated by the way a coach deals with the players, their parents, officials, and opposing coaches, by the coach's observance of the rules of the game, and by the coach's strategy of how to play the game. It is through these situations that a coach can teach honesty, or conversely, how to be dishonest.

On the surface, it would appear that there is little cause for concern in dealing with this quality, but in the heat of competition, with the ever-present desire to win, this factor does assume great importance. As long as our way of life puts such a premium on winning, and as long as coaches' jobs depend on winning, as they do in many high schools, the quality of honesty will be challenged constantly.

It is one thing to agree on the importance of being honest and to subscribe to the idea of fair play, but it is quite another to practice these concepts, when winning what might be a crucial game is concerned. To the coach who has a great deal of integrity, this would not make any difference and ideally all coaches, leaders of young men and women, would possess this high level of integrity. In sport there can be no justification for dishonesty; but human beings being what they are, this is often overlooked. There are coaches who will do almost anything to win, and then rationalize by claiming that their tactics were good strategy. These tactics can involve bending the rules, outright breaking of rules, or doing something personally to upset or outsmart an athlete on the other side. No high school game should ever be this important. If so, it has ceased being a game and has no place in an educational institution.

Dignity.   The dignity with which coaches conduct themselves will be noticed by all who know them. This is not confined to game situations only, but reflects conduct during school hours, at league meetings, and in the life of the community. Maintaining some semblance of dignity becomes very difficult at times, such as immediately after a disappointing performance by a team, or in the face of criticism from "grandstand quarterbacks," both of which are inevitable in coaching. It can prove to be very embarrassing to coaches when they lose their self-control, "pop off" in either situation, and then read their comments in the local newspaper the next day.

The loss of self-control on the part of a coach during a game or contest is painfully apparent to everyone present. This is particularly true in sports such as wrestling and basketball, where the crowd is close to the action, and a coach can lose control in the wild excitement of the contest, and the mob spirit this generates. The sight of an educated adult stomping, screaming, throwing things, abusing athletes or officials, and having a temper tantrum on the sidelines is embarrassing and certainly does little for the dignity of the individual or the profession. A coach will sometimes try to explain the actions by saying, "I hate to lose." This is not a reason but an excuse. No one likes to lose, but not everyone behaves like a spoiled child when it happens.

It is a rare occasion when a classroom teacher loses self-control and screams at the class, breaks a piece of furniture, smashes a watch, and puts on a real show of anger because a class didn't do well on a test. Contrast this with the actions of some coaches on the sidelines when things aren't going well, and the difference is incredible. There are many reasons for this difference, but one of the strongest is the degree of ego involvement on the part of the teacher in each situation. Classroom teachers are in their own little world of four walls and a closed door, while the coaches have their students on display every week, sometimes in front of thousands of people, and coaches know that, in the eyes of most spectators, the performance of the team is a direct reflection on their ability as coach. If the team loses the coach is poor, say the fans. Consequently, maintaining self-control during and after the excitement of a highly competitive contest is not always an easy task.

Courage of convictions

> . . . Last, but by no means least, courage—moral courage, the courage of one's convictions, the courage to see things through . . . it's the age old struggle—one struggle—the roar of the crowd on one side, and the voice of your conscience on the other.
>
> *General Douglas MacArthur*

Another quality all coaches should possess is the courage of one's convictions. In order to achieve this, each coach must first do some thorough introspection to determine what he or she believes in, and the reasons why. The coach must then demonstrate the courage to stand up for these beliefs, no matter what. When an individual begins to compromise these beliefs that individual is through. This quality is important to every phase of a particular sport, and if these convictions are not compatible with the situation, there are three choices a coach can make. The coach can compromise in order to satisfy the situation, begin to look

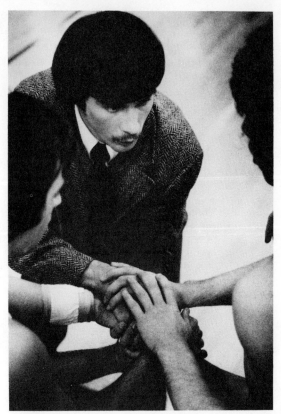

Photo courtesy of Jack Infield.

for another job if these convictions are absolutely incompatible with the situation, or compare what is taking place with what the coach believes in, to see if he or she is being unwise, unreasonable, stubborn, or unwilling to change because it would be an admission of being wrong and the coach's ego would not permit this.

If a coach is to be a true teacher and leader of young people, he or she will eventually have to take a stand on some issue which will require the courage to stand up and be counted. This is a trait not everyone possesses, but is an important ingredient in a coach's image. There are coaches who give a lot of lip service to this kind of courage but are nowhere to be found when the time comes to be counted. This can occur directly with some part of the athletic program, or in another phase of the school community. In an age when beliefs and convictions are constantly being challenged, a coach must use good judgment in clarifying principles, and then be willing to defend them when the need arises—and if an individual coaches for any period of time, the need will eventually arise from either the team, assistant coaches, administration, parents, or critics at some time in the career.

In his book *Chalk Dust on My Shoulder*, Charles Rousculp tells a true story of a situation in a high school, where an English teacher's job was in jeopardy because of some unfounded gossip in the community.

The classroom teachers' association voted unanimously to back the teacher. Later, one of the coaches came to this teacher and informed him that he had voted to back him, but that if it came to a showdown with the Board of Education, the coach would not take a stand, fearing the board would be unhappy with him, and he would lose *his* job.[1] This is a perfect example of an individual coach who obviously did not have the courage of his convictions.

The results of living and working with people who lack this kind of courage can also be illustrated by the following, paraphrased from a quote stressing the importance of speaking up for oppressed minorities.

When they came after the football coach, I didn't speak up because I wasn't a football coach. Then they came after the band director and I didn't speak up because I wasn't a band director. Then they came after the history teacher and I didn't speak up because I wasn't a history teacher. Then they came after the principal and I didn't speak up because I wasn't a principal. Then they came for me and by that time there was no one left to speak for me.

The message in this applies not only to teachers, or to minorities, but to people in every walk of life.

To know what is right and not to do it is the worst cowardice.

Confucius

Ethical standards.   Another challenge a coach frequently faces concerns ethical standards. Ethics in sports has been discussed, argued, legislated, and written about ever since sport was first developed, and is still of great concern today. A coach's personal philosophy also includes and dictates the ethical standards he or she will observe or not observe in coaching. If an individual's standards are high it sometimes takes a great deal of courage to observe them, particularly when opposing coaches use unethical methods to win.

Coaches will break rules deliberately and rationalize by saying that all their opponents do; therefore, they must break the same rules in order to compete with them. An example of this is practicing a high school team, or parts of the team, at a time when rules specifically state that it is a violation to do so. No matter what the rationale, this is unethical and serves as a poor example to all the athletes involved. Coaches should be strong enough so that no game is worth winning if they have to become unethical to accomplish this. If a coach does not believe this, he or she simply teaches youngsters that cheating can be justified if the other team is cheating also, and this is the only way there is a chance to beat them.

Good judgment.   Good judgment, which is the standard guideline for every decision a coach makes, normally develops through experience and maturity. One caution to be exercised is to avoid making snap

---

[1]Charles G. Rousculp, *Chalk Dust on My Shoulder* (Columbus: Charles E. Merrill Publishing Company, 1969), pp. 81–82.

decisions in anger, or issuing ultimatums to a person, especially in front of the team. This creates a confrontation, something a coach should try to prevent. Good judgment can do much toward solving potentially upsetting problems, as well as preventing some of these from ever arising.

Consistency.   Consistency in dealing with a team is something all coaches should attempt to establish. Consistency in enforcing rules, discipline, teaching techniques, expectations of the team, and in dealing with individual members of a team is important, because it helps prevent confusion, misunderstanding, and doubt from permeating the program. It also eliminates morale problems, by showing the athletes that there are no favorites on the team.

Being consistent in discipline is absolutely necessary. A coach should never make a rule that will not be enforced. When a rule is made, the athletes need to know that something will occur if they violate it, and they also need to know that no one on the team is immune. Possible penalties for breaking certain rules must be made clear, because without the threat of punishment, discipline soon deteriorates.

One of the things young people rebel against is inconsistency from adults, especially concerning discipline. They see a great deal of inconsistency in the way rules are enforced or not enforced; consequently, they test or challenge rules all the time to see how far they can go, and to see what they can get away with. When a team knows what they can expect from the coach, it prevents confusion and frustration from interfering in their attempt to accomplish their goals.

Fairness.   The ability to be fair and impartial involves treating all members of a team alike when it comes to determining who will play. Coaches should make every effort to insure that everyone trying out for the team gets an opportunity to show how well each person can play the game, rather than to predetermine who can perform well and who cannot. One of the traps a coach can fall into is to make certain assumptions about an athlete, on the basis of what an older brother or sister accomplished previously. This is unfair to a youngster, and also to other members of the team, and should be avoided at all cost. When a season is over, a coach should be able to honestly say that everyone on the team had a fair chance to prove their ability, so that any criticism about the coach being unfair, and not giving an individual a chance, cannot be justified.

Human nature being what it is, complete impartiality is extremely difficult to practice. Personalities vary and there will be people on a team whom coaches like more than they do some others, but great care should be taken not to give youngsters the impression that certain athletes are "teacher's pets."

Imagination.   Even though coaches are notorious copiers of other coaches' ideas, there is still a great deal of opportunity for imagination in coaching. Sometimes the coaches who exhibit the greatest imagination are the ones who are having losing seasons. Nothing seems to be working for them, so they use a lot of imagination to try to come up with some idea they haven't tried, or even heard about before, to give the team the extra edge they need to get into the win column.

Coaches who are consistent winners have less of a tendency to practice this because whatever they are doing is proving successful, and they are therefore hesitant to change anything. This is one factor which causes coaches to get into a rut, and stifles the imagination they might otherwise use to great effect. There are high school coaches who always look to the successful college teams and copy them as much as possible, rather than taking a chance and using their own imagination for their own unique situation. An imaginative coach is a creative coach, and generally this person runs a program in which monotony and boredom seldom exist. High school coaches sometimes sell themselves short when they reject an idea they have come up with because it didn't come from some famous big-name college coach. Being a high school coach should not put limits on creativity and imagination.

Sense of humor.   Another quality a good coach should show is humor, which relates back to a term previously used, "transparent realism." Everyone enjoys seeing or hearing something funny, and there are many funny things that occur in sport. When they do, a coach shouldn't be so firm and businesslike that these moments are squelched. Humor at the right time can do a great deal toward lessening tension, creating a good feeling within a group, and letting a team know that a coach can laugh also. Practices and meetings should never be so serious and businesslike that the opportunity for occasional good humor doesn't exist. After all, these are youngsters, and to them this is a game, and playing on a team should be fun. A good coach remembers this, and when the opportunity presents itself, the coach should be the source of the humor. Well timed and well directed, this can be a valuable tool in helping to create the pleasant atmosphere that should surround any high school athletic team.

Conclusion

Assuming that a coach is knowledgeable in a particular sport, probably the three most important qualities he or she should possess in terms of winning are:

1. The ability to organize;
2. The ability to evaluate personnel;
3. The ability to motivate youngsters.

DISCUSSION QUESTIONS

1. What is the best or right way to coach? Explain.

2. How can a coach earn respect?

3. How important is winning to you? Discuss.

4. What are the real reasons some youngsters go out for an athletic team? What implications does this have for you?

5. Why do some coaches win more consistently than others?

6. What does it mean to have "courage of your convictions"?

7. "Everyone wants to win—it's the individuals who don't want to lose who are the most successful." Explain.

8. "Show me a good loser and I'll show you a loser." What is your reaction to this statement?

9. What does this mean to you: "To know what is right and not to do it is the worst cowardice."

10. Is a coach's lifestyle anyone else's concern in regard to his or her position as coach? Support your point of view.

11. Is an intense desire to win a legitimate quality of a good coach?

12. How can challenge be used in motivation?

13. Discuss the concept of "peaks and valleys" in regard to athletic performance.

14. What are some ways you can think of to motivate athletes?

15. What are some of the cautions and concerns coaches should keep in mind when they attempt to motivate athletes?

Photo by Dick Brown, Centre Daily Times.

6

OFF-SEASON PREPARATION — A KEY TO SUCCESS

THERE IS NO DETAIL TOO SMALL.

The time to begin making plans for the next season is the day after your current season ends. Since the past season is still fresh in everyone's mind, it is an ideal time to sit down and think about what transpired in the preceding weeks and months. This is an ideal time to think about the good things that occurred, as well as the coaching mistakes that were made. In effect, this is the time for a thorough self-evaluation by both head coach and staff, if there is a staff. The results of this evaluation should set the pattern for next year's coaching plans. Coaches who decide to wait until the next season approaches to begin their planning have lost a great deal of valuable time, and will probably not do as good a job of organization as possible, as a result.

The initial step necessary in preparing for a new season begins with the head coach. Before coaches can provide the leadership necessary in organizing a staff, team, and program, they must be organized in their own minds so that they have a good idea of what needs to be done, as well as having general and specific guidelines that will provide direction for the whole program. This is not to say that a head coach should have all major decisions already made, thereby denying assistants an opportunity to contribute ideas. A head coach should not view assistant coaches who question ideas as Cassius is viewed in this excerpt from *Julius Caesar*, Act I, Scene 2.

> Let me have men about me that are fat;
> Sleek headed men, and such as sleep o' nights:
> Yon Cassius has a lean and hungry look;
> He thinks too much: such men are dangerous.

On the contrary, head coaches should encourage staff members to question and to contribute their own ideas; but, unless they themselves have certain ideas already well thought out, much time will be wasted in staff meetings, and firm decisions might never occur. Floundering around like this can be detrimental to athletic teams, particularly those that involve large numbers of athletes and several assistant coaches.[1]

1. The first point to be clarified in the minds of head coaches, in the off season, is a re-evaluation of their personal philosophy of athletics and coaching. It is important, especially today, when athletics are being challenged and questioned by so many people, that head coaches know exactly what they believe in and why. Coaches can take less for granted now than they could a few years ago; therefore their beliefs should be clear-cut, in their own minds at least, regarding all aspects of the sport they are coaching. This includes the special relationships the coach has with various people, style of play, ideas on training rules, practice sessions, cutting a squad, discipline, personal appearance, and winning and losing. This is essential, because if there are questions to be answered about any phase of the sport, it is the head coach who must come up with the answers, and this responsibility cannot be delegated.

This is important, too, because it is this philosophy which will provide the direction and guidelines for the conduct of the entire program the following season. It is in this area that the head coach has the greatest impact on the overall program. It is in this area, too, that the coach's attitudes and beliefs are reflected by the team he or she is responsible for coaching.

If a coach is aggressive, well disciplined, well organized, and believes in playing by the rules, the team will probably reflect this philosophy. If a coach is lackadaisical, disorganized, and believes in winning at any cost in any way, this philosophy will also be apparent in the way the team performs.

2. The next point to be considered by a head coach is the basic style of play the team will use, both offensively and defensively. If it is an individual sport, such as gymnastics, the coach still must come to some decision as to the basic style of the team. At the initial staff meeting, therefore, the head coach sets down these basic ideas. Then the staff goes to work debating, altering, working out the details, and finally, agreeing on what will be taught and how it will be taught.

There are as many ideas about offense and defense, or styles, for any kind of team as there are coaches, and many of them are quite successful. The point is that there is no one single best style or right way to run an offense or defense. Coaches or a coaching staff must teach what they know best. Too many high school coaches make the mistake of trying to copy something a big-time, winning college or

---

[1]Leon E. Smith, "Personality and Performance Research." *Quest* (January, 1970), p. 78.

professional team uses, without really understanding enough of the details to be able to do a good job of teaching. As a result, their teams normally do not execute well.

Basically, the two determining factors high school coaches must consider before settling this point are what they can teach best and what kind of athletes they have to work with. The latter point is crucial because nothing can be more frustrating than trying to make high school athletes fit a particular style of play, when they simply are not capable mentally or physically of handling it.

3. The next step in off-season planning is to plan a coaching clinic for the coaching staff, whether it be one other coach, or a dozen. During the course of a school year the various coaches attend clinics conducted by other coaches from all over the country. Hopefully, they will also have read articles or books about coaching or about a particular sport, and consequently, everyone on the staff has picked up ideas in the off season, some of which are good enough to adopt in the immediate situation. The quickest way to share these with the whole staff is to get all these ideas down on paper and then meet to talk about them.

It is not necessary for the staff to agree with or accept any of the items on the agenda; but by discussing all the ideas gathered over the off season, the staff will be aware of what other people are thinking and doing in their programs. It also helps a staff to reevaluate its own thinking regarding the program it is involved in. By doing this, the members of the staff either change their minds, or have their thoughts reinforced in light of the latest ideas of someone else. This is a good way for everyone to keep up to date in a sport, and sometimes an idea a staff rejects will trigger another idea which in turn is helpful to the program.

This becomes a useful tool especially when, for one reason or another, only the head coach is given the opportunity to attend clinics during a school year. Sharing all the ideas heard at these clinics helps the staff grow in their knowledge of the sport and eventually benefits the athletes they teach.

4. The next consideration is the organization of the staff. Obviously, this is no problem if the staff consists of one or two people, but in a large school system with a junior high program and possibly some involvement in the upper elementary grades there might be anywhere from three to fifteen coaches involved in a single sport. In this situation it is imperative that everyone know precisely what his or her role is in order to maintain some degree of efficiency.

The decision as to whether an individual will coach a freshman team, reserve team, or serve as a varsity assistant must be made by the head coach. Probably the soundest method of doing this (to prevent morale problems and still maintain a fine coaching staff) is to attempt to convince the superintendent of schools of the importance of hiring qualified high-level assistant coaches who have, or will develop, the qualities and knowledge expected of the varsity assistants.

In this manner, when a varsity opening occurs, everyone has the opportunity to move up if he or she wants to and the new person moves in at a lower level on the staff. Unfortunately, the hard reality of high school coaching shows very clearly that not all superintendents employ coaches in this way.

In far too many instances, superintendents do not involve head coaches in the hiring process. As a result assistant coaches are often hired to fill specific coaching vacancies without the head coach's knowledge, and this can create serious problems for that head coach.

This problem is probably more severe for women coaches than it is for men. In the first place, it is difficult to find that many women who are qualified and interested in coaching, who can also fill whatever teaching vacancy exists in the school. Secondly, it is difficult in many situations to find administrators who care enough about the girls' program to look for assistant coaches, let alone for qualified ones. Consequently, the task of persuading the administration to employ qualified coaches, while necessary, is frequently difficult.

It is also a fact that not every assistant wants to be a varsity coach. There are some who prefer to coach at the freshman level, for example, and they do a good job there. In a situation like this, varsity openings can sometimes be filled with the new coaches. There are two main disadvantages to this, one being that an assistant coach with no desire to move up can become too comfortable in that position and not put forth the effort the head coach would like to see. The other drawback is that hiring an assistant right out of college, regardless of that assistant's capabilities, usually means that contributions from this individual are limited because of a lack of experience. It is generally agreed among educators that it takes at least two years before a teacher begins to be a very effective teacher. During the first two years a teacher usually learns more than he or she teaches. Depending on the individual, however, it might not take that long for some coaches to begin making a significant contribution in athletics.

Since a teaching vacancy must exist in order to hire a new coach, it may be that the only individual who can fill it is not qualified to coach the phase of the team the opening calls for. In this situation the head coach will have to reevaluate everyone's responsibilities, do some realigning, and then take the area that is left and coach this personally. If the staff is a good one, and filled with people who are knowledgeable, this is not too difficult to do.

Some states have recently established coaching certification programs. They have also made it possible for school districts to employ part-time coaches; that is, individuals who are not members of a faculty, but who have earned coaching certification through an approved college program, may be employed for the sole purpose of coaching. Perhaps this will ease this problem somewhat.

5. Next, there will have to be some thought given to equipment issue. This is not too complicated for a swimming team, cross-country or golf team, for example, but if 150 people report for a team game like football, equipment issue can become a gigantic problem. If this hasn't been well thought out in advance it can assume chaotic proportions a beginning coach cannot begin to imagine. The four things that complicate equipment issue are (a) the time it takes for one individual to draw a complete uniform; (b) the necessity of everything fitting properly; (c) the fact that some youngsters, believe it or not, do not know the proper way to put on the various pieces of equipment; (d) and, finally, recording the number of each piece of equipment issued for each athlete's record for equipment control.

In order to solve all these problems and outfit a large number of athletes in an hour or less, the following method could be used. Lay out all the pieces of equipment in two lines down the gymnasium floor. The various items should be laid out separately, rather than in piles, and in the order in which an athlete would put on each article while dressing. As the youngsters walk down the line — varsity on one side, everyone else on the other — they put on each piece of equipment so that by the time they reach the end of the line they are completely dressed in full gear. At that point, a manager hands each athlete an equipment record card, and as the players undress in the locker room, they record the number painted on each piece of equipment and then turn the card back to another manager. All the while this is going on, the coaches walk up and down the line making sure the players are picking equipment that fits properly. This method is efficient, easy to control, and creates an atmosphere of careful organization and attention to detail which serves as an example to the team.

6. If there are to be team meetings at any time in a school classroom, arrangements should be made through the principal's office in plenty of time in order to insure that there will be no conflict in the use of the room, especially a room used to show films.

7. Another item in the off-season planning is the matter of mouth guards for the athletes involved in contact sports. There are two basic sources for these. Each student can purchase an assembly-line model at a sporting goods store for a nominal fee, or have one made to fit by a dentist. The latter method is expensive, unless there are several dentists in the community who would be willing to donate a few hours one night to make these for every member of the squad. This is not an impossibility, if a coach goes to work soon enough to see if it can be done.

8. Off-season is also the time to arrange for medical doctors to be present at home games, meets, or contests. In some sports, a doctor's presence is required by the rules. If this isn't the case, the head coach should try to arrange for the doctor's presence. Sometimes this will be taken care of for the varsity teams, while the junior varsity players or freshmen are neglected. This is not good, and it should be taken into consideration in the planning for a season. The absence of medical personnel or a qualified trainer at athletic contests poses a real danger both for the physical well-being of the players, and legally. Actually, this is the responsibility of the athletic director, but the head coach should double check to make sure this is being taken care of.

The medical considerations should include the following:

a. Every athlete participating in an outdoor sport where there is danger of a spike wound or similar injury should have tetanus shots up to date.

b. An emergency vehicle should always be present at every football game to save valuable time in an emergency. This vehicle should be parked as inconspicuously as possible, for obvious reasons.

c. Each athlete should fill out an accident card listing the family doctor, home telephone, and phone number of someone else to call in case the parents are not home. These cards should be kept on file near a telephone that is convenient to the practice area.

d. The telephone number of the local emergency service (normally the fire department) should be posted by this same telephone.

e. A reserved parking space should be set aside at the site of the game for the doctor. Sometimes a doctor cannot get to the game early and when he or she does arrive, there are no parking spaces left. This is a good idea, too, in case the doctor has to leave the game site for an emergency.

f. An athlete's physical examination should be given by the family doctor. The reason for this is that the family doctor knows the youngster's medical history and this is critical in determining whether or not he or she should be allowed to compete in athletics. Using one doctor to examine an entire team at one time is generally not recommended.

The easiest way to implement the last item is to mail each of the athletes a physical card before the season begins, have them arrange their own physical, and have the completed card ready to hand in when equipment is issued. Other possibilities would be to have students pick up these cards at the school office, or at various places in the community where youngsters congregate; or have the coaches carry a supply around for the asking.

9. Since the first few days of pre-season practice seem to involve a lot of collecting paper work from the athletes, record keeping can become a problem and a nuisance. This is particularly true when the number of athletes involved is large. A simple checklist, that a manager or assistant coach can be responsible for, will eliminate this problem and also remove one more chore from the head coach.

If there are a junior varsity team and a freshman team, it helps if they have their own checklists. It then becomes the responsibility of the coaches of those teams to see that each athlete has handed in the required material.

In order to prevent the problem of collecting forms throughout the season, it is a good idea to put deadlines on handing in each

NAME	PHYSICAL CARD	INSURANCE	ENVELOPES	ELIGIBILITY FORM

item. There really is no reason why this collecting couldn't be completed within two or three days after the start of pre-season practice.

There is one exception to this, and that is the physical card. No athlete should ever be permitted to begin practice without handing in a completed physical card. If coaches allow this to happen they are taking a tremendous risk of possible legal action against them. The simplest way to enforce this deadline is to refuse equipment issue to any youngster who doesn't hand in a completed physical card at the time equipment is being issued. In addition, these students may not begin practice, and perhaps some kind of penalty should be imposed for each practice session they miss. When coaches mandate this kind of policy, it can save them much aggravation in addition to preventing a possible calamity.

10. An area sometimes neglected by coaches is parent involvement. This should not be the case, since the people most concerned about the program, aside from the coaches, are the parents of the athletes. In general they are extremely anxious to understand the program in order to know what their son or daughter will be going through, what is expected of the youngsters, and what the coaches are trying to accomplish; they want to feel more a part of the experience their youngster is about to have. This is especially true with parents whose son or daughter is going out for a sport for the first time, or parents who have just moved into a new community.

In light of this concern, the head coach should plan to have a parents' clinic at the school sometime early in the season or during pre-season practice. The coach must clear the date and location of the meeting through the high school office, decide the agenda for the meeting, and duplicate the announcements. These can be sent home with the athletes, but as every teacher soon learns, notices sent home this way do not always get there. So rather than simply being given a note each athlete could be required to bring in a stamped envelope addressed to the parents. It then takes a manager a very short time to put the notices in these envelopes and in the mail. A meeting such as this serves a valuable purpose, too, in that it gives the coaches an excellent opportunity to meet all parents, while giving the parents a chance to meet the coaches. The only sure way to do this is for the entire coaching staff to be at the door or gate, so that each youngster can introduce his or her parents to each coach as they come into the meeting. The coaches might decide to include their wives or husbands in this receiving line so that parents can meet them as well. This all takes time but it is time well spent, and it also teaches some social graces to the athletes. This seems like a simple matter, but some youngsters will get so uptight that they sometimes forget the coaches' names as they introduce their parents.

1st ANNUAL PARENTS' CLINIC

   I. Where: High School Cafeteria
  II. When: Wednesday, August 31.
 III. Time: 7:00 p.m.
 IV. Why: A. Meet the Coaches
              B. Meet the Team
              C. Display of Equipment—Past and Present
              D. Explanation of our Program
              E. The Philosophy Behind our Offense and Defense for
                 this Season
  V. This is for parents of freshmen, sophomores, juniors, and seniors.
 VI. Here is your chance to learn, firsthand, exactly what your youngster will be doing this season and also a fine opportunity to have your questions answered.

                                      Hope to see you there,

                                      Coach

During this meeting the coach can bring the team up in front of the parents and have all players introduce themselves and their parents. As this is done, the parents should stand up so that other parents can see who they are, too. This can help eliminate unfortunate incidents during a contest, when a parent criticizes a player, only

Photo by Ken Kasper.

to discover that the youngster's parents are sitting nearby. If the parents at least recognize each other, they might be a little more careful in the stands.

There are other possibilities for bringing the parents together, too. For example, a swimming coach could invite the parents into the pool for some fun races, or a basketball coach could invite the parents down on the floor and have the players attempt to teach their folks some of the skills of the game through drills, followed by some short competition. This might help parents appreciate what their children are required to do in a sport. Sessions like these can be a lot of fun and they certainly won't hurt the program.

The parents' clinic is especially important to a new family in town. A gathering such as this can help them get acquainted quickly with a lot of people who have something in common — a son or daughter participating in athletics. People who have lived in the community for a long time, including the coach, often take it for granted that everyone knows everyone else. An exercise of this sort also helps parents feel more a part of the program, and this should be one of the coach's goals. When people feel a part of something, like an athletic team, and understand just what it is the coaches are trying to do, they are less apt to become critical as the season progresses.

Generally speaking, parents appreciate a coaching staff's taking the time to meet with them to brief them on the upcoming season. It is a great public relations gesture. The coaches are saying to the parents that they are a special group, and it is important that they have some inside information about the team. Mothers particularly enjoy meetings of this sort, since most women have had little chance to learn about the intricacies of what goes on in the more complicated high school athletic events, because of the scarcity of women's interscholastic athletic teams when they were in high school.

In the case of a girls' hockey team, for example, it may be that the father will get more out of the meeting than the mother, since field hockey remains an unknown to most men. He will be interested, too, to learn more about girls' interscholastic sports teams because his only point of reference is probably his own experience in high school athletics, and he might not be too excited about his daughter going through the same kind of thing. This is where women coaches can educate the families of female athletes. It is through this service that coaches can win a lot of support for their program by spelling out precisely what the objectives of the program are, and how they expect to accomplish them. Both father and mother should also know that participation in sport will not affect the feminine qualities of their daughter. This is necessary for parents, particularly if they grew up during the era or in an area in which competitive sport for girls was taboo. This could be a woman coach's most difficult point to make because of skeptics in the audience, but try she must, and her best aid in making the point will be the image she herself projects to these parents.

The following outline gives an example of an agenda for a parents' clinic.

AGENDA

PARENTS' CLINIC

1. Introduce coaches
2. Introduce coaches' wives or husbands
3. Introduce school officials
4. Introduce players (who in turn introduce parents to other parents)
5. Organization of various teams (such as Junior Varsity), and purposes
6. What do we expect of players?
   A. Promptness
   B. Hard work
   C. Respect
   D. Loyalty
7. What parents can do to help:
   A. Training rules
   B. Not allowing their youngster to quit the team
   C. Dating policies during the school week
   D. Morale — give a boost when needed
   E. *No coaching* on the part of a parent
8. What do we (the coaches) stand for?
9. Practice organization (times, dates, and so on)
10. Demonstrations

11. The selection of a student manager is something else that can take place prior to the beginning of practice and is not a chore to be taken lightly. A good, efficient manager is a valuable member of any athletic team. This individual can take care of many details in such a way that the head coach is free to concentrate on other aspects of the program. To insure getting this kind of youngster, a manager should be chosen rather than allowing someone from the student body to volunteer for the job.

The ideal arrangement is always to have a junior or senior, and at least one freshman or sophomore, as manager. In this manner, the younger students can learn about the job, and when the number-one manager graduates, there is always an experienced manager to take over. If the team has a lot of athletes, and is organized into varsity, J.V., and freshman teams, it is a good idea to have a freshman, sophomore, junior, and senior manager, with the senior in charge.

Basically, there are two methods of picking these managers. The primary source is the team itself. There may be someone who cannot continue as a player because of injury. There may be someone who simply does not have the ability to play. There may be someone who is so small that there is danger of serious injury and who should possibly be cut from the team. In such situations, if the coach is very tactful, that coach can suggest that this student consider becoming a manager, not as a demotion, but to fulfill an important function for the team in a capacity other than as a player. Surprisingly, youngsters often take this option willingly and enjoy still being a part of the program.

An important factor regarding managers is to impress upon the team that the managers are not servants or personal valets who are there solely to do the bidding of any member of the team. Instead, team members are to look at managers as people who are there to help in any way they can, and who are to be treated with the same courtesy extended to anyone doing someone else a favor.

Another source of managers is the physical education classes where a coach can get to know the students well. When the coach finds someone who displays the qualities necessary for a manager, the coach simply attempts to recruit this boy or girl for the position. Often these are students who have a great deal of interest in sport, but are not participating as a player for one reason or another. This gives them an opportunity to be an integral part of the team. Coaches of girls' teams, in general, seem to have a little more difficulty with this than do coaches of boys' teams. It seems that girls get involved in so many other school activities that they are often not willing to give the time required in being a manager.

One of the coaches on the staff should be assigned the responsibility for supervising the managers. In order to make sure the managers know what is expected of them and what their duties are, this coach should develop a checklist of things to do during the whole season, and post this in the managers' area. This also serves as insurance; in the excitement of game day, these youngsters are less apt to forget something if they have this checklist to refer to.

Another way to make managers feel an important part of the team is to recognize them at the banquet at the end of the season. In one situation the author knew well, the head manager always gave a very short speech at the banquet. One year he found an old leather football helmet that he mounted on a piece of fine wood. This outgoing manager autographed it and made a big thing out of passing it along to the next year's head manager, as a symbol of the authority of the position. This was a big hit at the banquet. This kind of thing is important to youngsters, and adds another dimension to the experience and fun of being a special part of a special group. Adults tend to forget how important small gestures like this are to teen-aged students, but it is upon these little things that tradition, *esprit de corps*, and high morale are built.

Good managers are worth their weight in gold, and after growing up through the system they begin to anticipate what the head coach wants done next and how the coach will react in certain situations. As a result, they are usually a step ahead of the coach most of the time. This helps make the coach's job somewhat easier.

12. Along about the same time, the head coach should carefully choose a student to serve as publicity writer or as a liaison between the coach and local newspapers. If the school is located in an urban area with many high schools all eager for coverage in the city newspapers, this is essential. In fairness to the sportswriters, they simply cannot cover every team in every high school regularly. So in order to make their job easier, and to make sure the team receives whatever publicity is due them, the coach makes an effort to feed information to the sportswriters through this student.

These youngsters should be chosen carefully, in the same manner as a manager, with the additional element of checking with the English teachers to get some possible leads.

The first rule for the student publicity writer is that the only information written or telephoned to any sportswriter comes from the coach and not the student. This is vital. The student is not to "free-lance" and become a source of information, but is rather to remain a liaison. Often, newspapers, radio, or TV stations pay these youngsters for calling in scores and other bits of material, so this can be an added incentive.

The coach must clear this procedure through the athletic director and sportswriters involved and if the student is conscientious about this responsibility, the newspaper people are very appreciative and rarely refuse to print any news item submitted to them. Incidentally, this method is a sure way for teams sometimes unfortunately labeled as minor sports teams to also receive their fair share of publicity. Many athletic teams often receive little or no publicity in the newspapers, and by utilizing this technique this can change, but the initiative rests with the coach.

The amount of time a coach spends in arranging for publicity is negligible when compared with the good it can do. The student publicity writer has two primary responsibilities. This writer is to call every radio and TV station in the city immediately after the game, meet, or contest to notify the sportscasters of the score and answer any questions they might ask, such as who scored, who pitched, were any records broken, or were there any gems of an unusual nature that sportscasters like to mention. As long as the information given out is fact, and not opinion, there is little cause for concern.

The second responsibility of the student publicity writer is to meet with the head coach the morning after an athletic event to write down any comments the coach wants printed concerning the game or, most importantly, the people who participated in it. This last item is an excellent way to publicize deserving youngsters, and a coach should try hard to get as many athletes' names in the paper as possible during a season. This does wonders for morale and it might be the only time in some athletes' lives that they will have a chance to see their name in the sports section of a newspaper.

This exercise is also a great way to publicize the contribution of an assistant coach, on not only the varsity level but J.V. and freshman levels as well. When an assistant deserves credit, it never hurts to give it publicly.

13. Another student assistant who can be extremely helpful to a coach is a student trainer. The filling of this position can be handled exactly like that of the managers. The students who are chosen for this position must be able to exercise good judgment and should be intelligent youngsters.

Some training room supply companies provide free correspondence courses for high school student trainers. The head coach should see to it that these students participate in one of these. Among the trainers' responsibilities are keeping the training room or training area neat and clean, caring for minor hurts like blisters, keeping an inventory of supplies throughout the season, and, eventually, taping ankles and applying first aid to minor injuries. All of this, of course, must be done under a coach's direct supervision.

14. Student statisticians can also be of great assistance to coaches. If a head coach believes that accumulating certain statistics on the team or individuals is valuable, carefully chosen students are very capable of performing this task. Statisticians should be chosen in the same manner as all other student helpers.

15. Prior to the opening practice, the coach must make it a point to meet with the athletic director or faculty manager to brief this official on the plans for the season, especially dates for pre-season scrimmages or practice contests, if the athletic director has to arrange for transportation. The athletic director should also be made aware of any special events, such as a parents' clinic, meet-the-team night, banquet dates, and so on. The athletic director has plenty of time to take care of the many responsibilities and can be of great help to the coach when it is known what the coach is doing or planning to do.

16. Off-season meetings can fulfill many purposes, one of which is to get a good idea of exactly who is coming out for the team. This information is useful in any pre-season planning, particularly when looking at depth charts by possible positions. This can be gathered, along with other pertinent information, through the use of a simple printed form such as the one that follows.

PLAYER INFORMATION

1. Name_____Class next year____ht.____wt._____
2. Home address_____Phone_____
3. Summer address_____Phone_____
4. Name of parent or guardian_____
5. Position last year: offense_____ defense _____
6. What position would you like to play next fall?
   offense_____ defense _____
7. List the name of one person in our school who is not out for the team who you feel could become a good player _____
   _____

8. List the five people you think will be our outstanding players next season:
   1. _____
   2. _____
   3. _____
   4. _____
   5. _____

This form provides a handy mailing directory, and can easily be divided by class or position. Item 7 is used only when one or two individuals' names appear on several of these forms. It may be that a potentially fine athlete has not attended the meeting, and the coach might elect to find out why. No coach should ever become so independent or callous that it is beneath his or her dignity to ask a youngster like this why that youngster missed the meeting, and to see if the youngster has any interest in trying out for a position on the team. It is possible that a small gesture like this can do a lot for a youngster, who in turn might become a fine athlete. In this case, the coach has done a great service for a boy or girl. This is not to be confused with coaxing a student to come out for a team. Coaxing should be avoided at all times.

17. If a coach is involved in a sport that begins in the fall or late summer, it often becomes necessary to correspond with all the members of the team over the summer months. This is the only sure way to get any pertinent information and materials such as physical cards to them and also to start them thinking about the sport before the first practice. This also serves as a method of keeping in touch with the youngsters over several months of vacation time and it lets them know the coach is thinking about them and the upcoming season. Letter writing is a good tool too for getting information directly to the parents. The following is an illustration of a letter sent to members of a freshman team to welcome them and to let them know what is in store for them. This letter could be adapted to any sport but is probably most critical for one that begins immediately after summer vacation.

TO: FRESHMAN (*SPORT*) PLAYERS
FROM: COACH

It won't be too long now until a brand new experience opens up for you as you begin what we hope will be a highly successful career as a (*sport*) player. Your class had more people sign up for (*sport*) than any other class in the history of this school, and we think this is a good sign. This will automatically create a great deal of competition among you and your teammates, but this is good, since competition usually brings out the best in you, if you are a competitor.

The number one goal of your coaches will be to try to determine as quickly as possible who among you is a "winner." By that I mean we are primarily interested in finding people who are real competitors. We can teach you all the skills necessary for you to become a good (*sport*) player, but you'd better bring a "fighting heart" with you.

Experience has shown us that incoming 9th graders rarely take time during the summer months to work out and toughen their bodies for the coming (*sport*) season, and when practice does begin, we generally find that they are in poor physical condition, and suffer because of it. Consequently, we are encouraging you to work out regularly during the summer to get your body in shape for the coming season. This also gives us a quick indication of just how much you want to play (*sport*).

I've enclosed a physical card. Have this filled out as soon as possible (your doctor might be on vacation later on). Bring this card, a pencil, and a notebook to the high school gym at 8:30 a.m. Thursday, August 17, for your first official meeting as a high school (*sport*) player. You cannot practice without a signed physical card, so be sure you have it with you. Practice begins Friday, August 18.

Our practice schedule is as follows: . . .

Welcome to the team, and I hope that you become the greatest (*sport*) player this high school has ever had.

Have a good summer,

[Coach]

The following letter is a sample of one that could be mailed to the sophomores, juniors, and seniors. Again this could be adapted to any sport.

TO: MEMBERS OF THE HIGH SCHOOL FOOTBALL TEAM
FROM: COACH

It won't be long until we begin working for a brand new football season, and one that will be a championship season for us. This is our ultimate goal as of this moment and if each of us dedicates himself toward this goal and is willing to give 100% effort all the time, we *will* become champions. From this moment on, as far as our team is concerned, we must think, talk, work, and play the game like champions, and to win the league championship must become a burning desire in your heart.

With this in mind, the coaches' first objective will be to pick out the boys who are "winners" and get them on the first team. We will try to determine as quickly as possible just how much you want to play the game, who are the real hustlers, the workers and the *hitters*. Once we find these boys we're on our way along "championship trail."

I've enclosed a physical card. Make sure you have this taken care of as soon as possible. Your doctor might be on vacation later on, and we will not issue equipment to anyone without a completed physical card. Make sure your tetanus shots are up to date also. Bring your physical card and a pencil to the gym at 8:00 a.m. Thursday, August 17 for equipment issue and squad meeting. Practice will begin at 7:30 a.m. Friday, August 18.

Our practice schedule is as follows: . . .

If, for any reason, you will not be out for football this fall, please let me know so that we can keep our roster up to date.

I hope you have been enjoying your summer and that you are looking forward to a great football season.

Sincerely,

[Coach]

The following are samples of letters sent to girls' hockey team members by their coaches.

Dear Hockey Player:

I hope you are having a good summer. I am having an "exciting" summer going to summer school. Actually, I am enjoying going to school instead of teaching for awhile. Going to the hills for a little camping has helped maintain my sanity. Just a few reminders before we take off for hockey camp:

Arrive at camp: Tues., Aug. 27 by 12 noon—lunch at 1 p.m., play at 3 p.m. Tues.

Remainder of fee due: $40.00

Address: The Hockey Camp, [address]

Bring: Bedding or sleeping bag, towels, rain gear, hockey stick(s), hockey shoes, lots of wool socks, at least 3 or 4 white tops to wear with kilts, Ben Gay, cards, monopoly.

NOW (TODAY!!!) is the time to start conditioning! Wear your hockey shoes. Jog lightly ½ mile for warm-up, sprint 25 yds., jog 100–200 yds., sprint 25 yds., and continue this until you get tired. You might put in a few yards of walking if you want. Then build up the amount of time and distance you jog-sprint so that you are jog-sprinting at least 30 minutes. In addition, running up steps and hills is great! Goalie conditioning: along with some of the above, running in your goalie pads, you need to sharpen your reaction and movement times by kicking (very quickly) a ball (hockey or tennis) into a backboard or wall. Also, sprint sidewards, front and back in a 12′x 12′ area.

Good luck! Get going on that conditioning! See you at camp.

Fondly,

[Coach]

Dear Hockey Player:

Believe it or not, the time has come to get ready for hockey camp. So here are a few reminders:

Camp: [address]

Dates: Leave from parking lot of the high school (by the gym) at 1:00 p.m. Sunday, August 17. Camp: Mon. through Fri.—Aug. 18–22 8:30 a.m. to 12:30 p.m. Return to town Friday, Aug. 22 immediately after camp, arriving, hopefully, by dinnertime. (If we plan properly, we should be able to return campers directly to their homes).

Lodging: [address]

REMINDER: $20.00 fee due for week's room and board.

Equipment: Sleeping bag
            Towel, wash cloth, soap, shampoo, etc.
            Neat clothes to practice in—no rags, please!
            Socks (preferably wool) and hockey shoes (or sneakers)
            Hockey stick
            Shin guards (you may buy your own, or borrow some from
               school on Sunday)
            Sweater (one) or sweatshirt for cool weather
            Some neat jeans or something to relax in—remember, we're
               staying on a farm
            Bathing suit
            Some spending money for snacks, lunch, and $3 each to pay
               for gas (that will cover the round trip)
            ONE ROLL OF ADHESIVE TAPE
               (All equipment except the sleeping bag and hockey stick
                  must fit into one small duffle bag or laundry bag. We will
                  not take any suitcases.)
            You may want to pack a deck of cards or a paperback book for
               evenings.

AND START RUNNING NOW! Put on your socks and shoes, and for the first two days do the following: jog ½ mile; then sprint 20 steps, jog 20 steps, for the remaining half mile. For the next two days jog ½ mile; sprint 50 steps, jog 50 steps, for the remaining half mile. For the rest of the days, jog ¼ mile; sprint 50 steps, jog 50 steps, for the rest of the mile.

REMEMBER: When we meet Sunday at 1:00, you will have four things with you: one hockey stick, one sleeping bag, one laundry bag full of what you need, and your money.

DON'T FORGET TO SHOW THIS TO YOUR PARENTS! Let me know if there are any problems — see you Sunday.

[Coach]

Sometime during the year, the high school head coach should have met with the upper grade of the junior high, middle school, or intermediate school to talk with the students who are interested in coming out for the high school team the following school year. This must be done through the various principals, and it gives the students a chance to meet the coach and have some of their questions answered.

This experience will be a big step for them, as well as an important one, and it holds some unknowns. Many parents are anxious to learn something about the program also. Consequently, it is worth considering writing to all the parents of these students to answer some of their questions, too — especially the question of a summer vacation falling about the time football practice begins or a trip over the Christmas holiday during basketball, wrestling, or swimming practice. The farther ahead parents know of these things, the easier it is for them to make plans, and they will appreciate the thoughtfulness of the coach in this regard. The following is an example of a letter to parents.

Dear Folks:

Last week we had a meeting of the 8th grade boys to sign up for high school football for next fall. We had 57 boys indicate that they intended to play football in 9th grade, which is the largest turnout we have ever had. Your son was at this meeting and expressed interest in 9th grade football. I hope that he does come out for the team, but before he does I believe you should have an understanding with him that once he decides to come out he cannot quit, and must finish the season. I think this is very important to the boy and you will be doing him a real favor if you make him stick to this agreement.

Practice begins on Friday, August 20, at 7:00 a.m. Every year problems arise because this conflicts with family vacations; therefore, I will try to explain our policy to you. If your boy is on vacation with you and reports late for practice, he can still come out for football, provided we have any equipment left. We do not save equipment for anyone, nor can we give it out early. In other words, it is first come, first served for the 9th graders, and while we think we will have enough for everyone, we are never sure how many boys will report the first day. One other factor to consider is that we practice twice a day, and each day a boy misses puts him that much further behind his teammates, and it makes it tough on him physically as he tries to catch up.

On Wednesday, May 19, at 7:00 p.m., the local dentists will be here at the school to fit each football player with a latex mouth guard. This is a mandatory piece of equipment, and we are fortunate to have dentists in our community who are willing to do this for us free. Make sure your boy is present. If he misses this, he will have to have one made on his own, and it could cost you $25.00 or more. Incidentally, he will need a metal nail file to spread the latex on the mouthpiece later.

As far as your son making the team is concerned, we want to have all the freshmen stay out for football the entire season. However, if we find that a boy is just too small, or in some other way cannot handle his body well enough to protect himself from taking undue physical punishment, we will cut him from the squad for his own physical well-being. The main reason for this is that football is a rugged game, and we certainly do not enjoy seeing a boy get hurt.

If you have any questions, please do not hesitate to call me.

Sincerely,

[Coach]

Later on, a second letter should be sent to the parents of every student planning on coming out for the team to bring them up to date on the latest plans for their information.

Dear Parents,

It won't be long until another football season gets under way. This is the time of year I look forward to, but I suppose some of you have mixed emotions about football. Some of you look upon it with anticipation, others with skepticism, and this is natural when you are concerned about your son's welfare.

I can tell you this — the "football fever" seems to be running high among the boys this year and to me this is a good sign. The interest is high, the competition will be keen, and this is what brings out the best in the boys.

Football, to many of our boys, is one of the most important phases of their high school career. This fills a great need for them — to be a member of a group, to be accepted by their friends, to have the respect and admiration of their classmates—and it is an opportunity for them to pit their courage against an opponent in a contact game. For football is a game which demands great physical courage on the part of a participant, and this is why I have so much respect for the boys who play this game.

Our practice schedule this year will be as follows:

7:30–9:30 a.m. — Practice

9:30–10:00 a.m. — Shower

10:00–10:30 a.m.—Light lunch

10:30–11:45 a.m. — Meetings

11:45–Noon — Dress

Noon–1:30 p.m. — Practice

This will get us done before the hottest part of the day, and you are all welcome to attend any or all of our sessions, but please — no coaching from the sidelines. You might show up the coach.

We are having our "First Annual Parents' Football Clinic" on Tuesday, August 31 at 7:00 p.m. in the high school gymnasium. We'd like very much for all of you to attend, if possible, so we can show you how and what we are teaching your son in order to help you enjoy our games more. You are welcome to bring along your whole family, if you like.

By the way, the season tickets will go on sale at the high school office, August 19–August 25 for you parents only, so if you are interested, you can have first choice of the best seats in the stadium.

Sincerely,

[Coach]

---

18. The next decision the head coach must make is whether or not to create a notebook for every member of the team. The first realization the coach needs to come to is the fact that writing a notebook, having it typed, duplicated, assembled, issued, collected, and revised every sea-

Photo courtesy of The Pennsylvania State University Still Photography Services.

son is a big undertaking, and extremely time-consuming. There is always the possibility, also, of a notebook being lost or stolen and ending up in the wrong hands.

On the plus side, however, is the fact that a tremendous amount of information can be put into a notebook and disseminated to a great many people, without ever taking a minute of valuable practice time or meeting time. A coach can provide athletes with much valuable information, such as training rules, coaches' phone numbers, sideline conduct, conduct in school, locker room discipline, practice procedures, injury prevention and care, care of equipment, and the coach's philosophy of offense and defense or of competition, all of which can be included for the athletes to read on their own time. This can save a tremendous amount of time during a season, and as every coach knows, time is of the essence.

19. Another valuable tool for the head coach is a checklist of things to be done prior to the opening practice. As a program grows in size and a coach gets more things to remember, a checklist becomes more important in organization. This is very simply a way to make sure that nothing is left undone when the first practice begins. The following is an example of such a checklist. The items marked by an asterisk apply to almost any athletic team.

THINGS TO DO—PRE-PRACTICE SEASON

*1. Check on condition of practice area
2. Plastic cover for dummies
3. Planks for board drills
4. Tires (pick up at local service station)
*5. Classrooms
*6. Accident cards in case of injury
*7. Phone (make sure it's in operation)
*8. Cafeteria—refrigerator for training room
*9. Socks—for sale to team
*10. Team pictures—date, time, place, rain date
*11. Notebooks
*12. Number equipment
*13. Clean training room
14. Scouting schedule for assistant coaches
*15. Parents' Club
16. Play cards for scout team
*17. Letter for parents' clinic
*18. Practice Labor Day at night
*19. Pictures of individual players for display in town
*20. Holiday practice plans
*21. Letters to athletes
*22. Pre-season meeting agenda
*23. Notify athletic director about pre-season practice games/meets/scrimmages
*24. Travel requests
*25. Officials
*26. Check in new equipment

The next section of the checklist should include every phase of the game or meet that absolutely must be covered, prior to the opening of the season. This information then is the basis for a master schedule. For example, a football coach would include items similar to these:

1. Kick-off
2. Return
3. Punt
4. Offense
5. Pass cuts
6. Quick kick
7. Defense
8. Huddle-cadence
9. Objectives of defense and offense
10. Pass defense highlight film
11. Offensive highlight film
12. Defensive highlight film

20. During the off-season planning the head coach has to consider the role of the school custodians, and what effect the beginning of a new season will have on them and their work at the school. Like so many other factors, this is of more concern to coaches whose season begins at the end of summer vacation or straddles a school vacation such as Christmas or Easter. The sports that begin prior to the opening of school in the fall can cause facility problems if the custodians aren't alerted in advance, because the school building and locker room areas are usually in great disarray as the custodians clean and prepare the building for another school year. Unless they are notified, field hockey practice or football practice can open in mid-August before the custodians are ready, and this can create real confusion when the athletes move into locker rooms that aren't ready for them. Unusual practice hours during winter holidays, when heat in certain parts of the building might be a problem, is another reason for keeping custodians informed of practice plans. The athletic director should take care of these details, but it still falls back on the coach to at least check to make sure this is done prior to the time when it is needed.

Custodians appreciate this gesture on the part of coaches, and as a consequence, are more than willing to cooperate and help in any way possible. Coaches should cultivate the friendship of the custodial staff to receive the kind of assistance from them necessary for the good of the program. If coaches treat these people as servants, rather than as friends and co-workers in a school, they will eventually run into problems that otherwise would never occur.

21. In any pre-planning, the head coach has to select, for pre-season scrimmages or practice meets, an opponent, location, and time and need for officials if it will be at home. In many states, the exact number of pre-season scrimmages is fixed, in which case the coach has no choice in this matter. After these decisions have been made, the athletic director should receive notice and then take care of all details at that point. In arranging these practice contests, care should be taken not to always schedule a weak opponent. The advantages to be gained from always playing a weak opponent are negligible and the team or individual players might get a false impression of how good they are. At the same time, a coach should not deliberately schedule a team that is too strong. In contact sports, this increases the chances of injury, and if the team gets handled rather easily, this could affect team morale to the point where the athletes lose confidence in themselves, their teammates, or their coaches. The idea that competing against strong competition will make a team better is true, within limits. The only time scheduling a weaker team for a scrimmage is justified is when a new coach is fielding his or her first team and is trying hard to sell him- or herself and a particular system to the team. If they do well, even against a poorer team, this will do a great deal of good in establishing confidence in the new coach. This is critical for a beginning coach in any sport.

22. Plans for the initial team meeting should also be formulated in advance. Since a meeting such as this generally occurs prior to the opening practice, time is not so critical. Therefore, this is an excellent opportunity to talk about many of the details of the program the youngsters need to be aware of, going into a new season. Communication is essential, and the better the understanding the athletes have of every facet of the program, the better the entire organization becomes. This is the time to give direction to the program and to let the members of the team known precisely what is expected of them, and, in turn, what they can expect of the coaches. The following agenda illustrates this point:

TEAM MEETING
PRE-SEASON

1. Meet coaches
2. Introduce manager-trainers and explain role
3. Insurance
4. Physicals
5. Registration cards for emergency in case of injury
6. Eligibility — double check with athletic director
7. Season tickets for parents
8. Socks, T-shirts, and so on, for sale through athletic department
9. Mouthpieces for contact sports
10. Two stamped envelopes — addressed to parents
11. Team pictures — date, place, time
12. Scrimmages against outside opponents
13. Meeting rooms for whole team or by position
14. Care of foot blisters
15. Salt intake
16. Scrimmage vests — what various colors represent
17. Hang up equipment, handle equipment problems
18. Training rules
19. Notebooks
20. Practice procedure
21. Seniors — meet later
22. Team clinic
23. Cutting the team?
24. Parents' clinic—date, time, place

Item 21 on the agenda, concerning the seniors, is an important part of a pre-season meeting. When the general meeting is over, the seniors should be asked to stay for a short while. After everyone else has gone, the coach should explain very clearly the role seniors must play on the team regarding leadership and attitude. This is crucial, because if the coach does a good job at this point, the problems associated with "senioritis" are lessened or eliminated. The main point to be made is that this is the last season these people will ever participate in at this high school in this sport, and for some it is the last athletic participation they will ever have. In light of this, then, it becomes important for seniors to attempt to provide the kind of leadership to the younger students necessary to insure a successful season. They also need to be aware of the fact that the performance of the team as a whole might have some bearing on scholarship possibilities. When senior athletes look at a season this way, they tend to approach it from an entirely different point of view.

In conjunction with the seniors on the team, one of the coach's concerns must always be that of "senioritis" — an undesirable frame of mind seniors sometimes adopt, in which they think they have it made and don't have to hustle like the poor underclass students who are trying to make the team. According to many women coaches, this is particularly true of female athletes in general. With boys this attitude is normally an individual matter, but with girls it often becomes a group problem. On girls' teams "senioritis" frequently manifests itself in the form of cliques. Sometimes the seniors think the team belongs to them, and they can become highly resentful if one of their group gets benched in favor of an underclass athlete. When this occurs, senior leadership has a nega-

Photo by Dave Shelley.

tive effect on the other people, morale will suffer, and the team will not reach its greatest potential.

Consequently, the coach must spend extra time at the beginning of the season creating a positive attitude in the minds of the seniors. One other reason "senioritis" develops is the fact that many seniors consider themselves at the end of their playing careers, which seems to dampen a certain degree of motivation in some athletes.

The Face in the Glass

When you reach your goal in the world of sports
And you have worked the big game that day
Just go to the mirror and look at yourself
And see what the face has to say,
For it isn't your family or friends or the coaches
Whose judgment upon you must pass,
The person whose verdict counts in your life
Is the one staring at you from the glass.
You may fool all the world down the avenue of years
And get pats on the back as you pass,
But your only reward will be remorse and regret
If you have cheated the face in the glass.

Author Unknown

In an effort to combat this particular attitude, coaches should encourage athletes who intend to go on to college to consider participating in athletics on the college level. Too many high school youngsters assume that they have to be super-athletes in order to participate in college athletics, and this just isn't so, except in the large universities. There are many smaller schools with fine academic standards and fine athletic programs, where good high school athletes can compete.

There are several ways to get youngsters to set higher goals for participation in athletics beyond the high school level. One possibility is to publicize the athletes from that school who have gone on to compete in college. This can be done by taking seniors to college games to see some of their former teammates perform, or by hanging framed photographs of former athletes in the locker room who competed in college athletics. These should be labeled by name and college, and normally are available through college athletic publicity offices; another possibility is to hang college banners or pennants in the gymnasium area, and place the names of those who are on the various athletic teams under the appropriate college or university.

This can do a lot toward preventing "senioritis" because this can be a great motivational tool for some athletes. Another benefit is that if a young person can be encouraged to go on to college and participate in athletics, this can make his or her college days more meaningful, more complete, and more enjoyable, in spite of what critics say about the evils of college athletics.

23. As a part of the initial team meeting, the head coach should also include a team clinic (item 22 on the agenda). This will enable the coach to deviate from the mechanics of getting a season under way and begin to communicate to the team his or her own personal philosophy of coaching. This also gives the coach the opportunity to go into detail concerning the goals for the season and to talk about the steps necessary in order to realize these goals. It is at this point in the initial team meeting that the coach can let the team know the decisions that have been arrived at by the staff regarding the style of play to be used during the season and the reasoning behind these decisions.

TEAM CLINIC

I. This will be a championship year, therefore we must:
   A. Think Championship
   B. Talk Championship
   C. Practice like a Champion
   D. Play like a Champion

II. How do we do all these?
   A. Work harder than our opponents
   B. 110% effort all the time
   C. Fewer mistakes than our opponents
   D. Superior physical conditioning
   E. Superior mental discipline
   F. Superior mental attitude

G. Superior technique
H. Superior desire
I. Superior defense ⎱
J. Superior offense ⎰ when appropriate
K. Superior organization
L. Pride in your team, teammates, school, and coaches
M. Loyalty to your team—make each other look good—associate with each other

III. You will make the team on how well you measure up to these criteria, your ability, and by showing the coaches that you are a winner.

IV. Mutual respect between coaches and athletes

V. The person listed as number two at a position is not necessarily the number one substitute at that position.

VI. Cuts (if cutting is a part of the program) to be based on:
A. Individual cases
B. Attitude
C. Effort
D. Hustle
E. Overall effect on the team

VII. Offense—objectives—priorities—(general picture) (when appropriate)

VIII. Defense—types of defenses and why (when appropriate)

When attempting to create positive attitudes within the team, the poem on page 176 could be very helpful.

It is a universal belief that when people understand why they are being asked or told to do certain things in certain ways, they are more apt to get the job done, or at least pursue it with a more positive altitude. This is the primary reason for a team clinic. The coach is really trying to create an attitude or frame of mind in the athletes that will make them want to give their best in whatever they are told to do during the season. Since this is usually a beginning coach's first official team meeting, the importance of this session cannot be overemphasized.

24. The budget is another off-season consideration, and in most cases has been prepared and accepted prior to or early in the beginning of a school year. Generally, the budget is prepared by the head coach. Basically every budget is based on the equipment inventory, number of students involved in the sport, travel expenses, replacement equipment, and officials. There might be additional items included, such as police and ticket takers, for example. The ideal situation to develop is one in which the equipment has been purchased wisely, so that each year it is necessary only to add small quantities to replace discarded gear, rather than to allow it to deteriorate to the point where a significant expenditure must be made to replace a large amount of a single item. Standardizing equipment styles, colors, and designs is a basic principle that will enable a coach to purchase replacement equipment in small quantities each year.

A general practice of many coaches is to pass old, worn-out equipment down to the junior varsity or freshman teams. This is a practice

Photo courtesy of Fellowship of Christian Athletes.

Like You

There are little eyes upon you, and they're watching night and day;
There are little ears that quickly take in every word you say;
There are little hands all eager to do everything you do,
And a little boy that's dreaming of the day he'll be like you.
You're the little fellow's idol, you're the wisest of the wise;
In his little mind about you no suspicions ever rise.
He believes you devoutly, holds that all you say and do
He will say and do in your way when he's grown up just like you.
Oh, it sometimes makes me shudder when I hear a boy repeat
Some careless phrase I've uttered in the language of the street;
And its sets my heart to grieving when some little fault I see,
And I know beyond all doubting that he picked it up from me.
There's a wide-eyed little fellow who believes you're always right,
And his ears are always open and he watches day and night;
You are setting an example every day in all you do
For the little boy who's waiting to grow up to be like you.

Author Unknown

that should be avoided. If equipment is not good enough for a varsity player to wear, and if it cannot be reconditioned, it should be discarded. Also, equipment originally purchased for varsity teams is generally too big for the younger athletes.

Worn-out, ill-fitting equipment can be conducive to injury, and sometimes coaches forget that when two 90-pound people collide in a contact game it hurts just as much as when two 200-pound people collide. It is all relative.

Added to this is the fact that athletes on reserve and freshman teams are not as highly skilled as varsity players. Therefore it becomes apparent that their need for protective equipment is just as great as, if not greater than, it is for varsity athletes. Providing adequate protective equipment is really a moral obligation of a coaching staff, and the head coach must see that this is done.

There is another consideration, too, and that is if freshmen, for example, are to learn the proper fundamentals of a game, they must have good equipment because poor equipment can hinder the process. This hindrance may defeat the primary purpose of freshman and junior varsity teams.

Providing proper equipment for every team within a program should be one of the head coach's primary goals. Finances are always a problem, but this should not be an excuse to outfit a team in cast-off equipment.

25. Basically, there are two ways athletic equipment is purchased in high schools. The head coach might be permitted to purchase needed equipment, or the head coach might be required to submit a list of equipment needs and specifications to a central purchasing agency in the school system. The purchasing agent, in all probability, would then proceed to ask sporting goods companies to submit bids.

Regardless of a school's purchasing policy, equipment should be ordered many months before it is needed, since delivery on athletic supplies is usually very slow. In fact, the time to prepare an equipment order for next season is immediately after the current one ends.

Normally, the best equipment to purchase is from a long established name brand company. As a rule, these companies will stand behind their products, whereas others might not. This is not to say that coaches should never consider purchasing lesser known brands from smaller companies, but the thing to remember is that the best bargain in cost might be the most expensive in the long term, if it doesn't hold up. And with the cost of athletic equipment rising all the time, coaches need to learn how to get the most for the least amount of school money.

The three guiding principles for purchasing athletic equipment, in order, are:

1. Quality of the equipment
2. Cost
3. Service (Will the individual who sold you the equipment provide prompt service to you in delivering, repairing, or replacing defective equipment?)

If the timing is not a problem, a good time to purchase athletic equipment is just prior to January, when many suppliers will reduce prices in an attempt to clear out their stock before inventory and tax time.

26. Whether or not to have team captains is another consideration for every coach. There are advantages and disadvantages to both sides of this question. The greatest advantage, which might outweigh everything else, is the leadership team captains can provide, not only during an athletic event but in every other aspect of a particular program, in-season and out.

Unless a coach is firmly opposed to the idea of captains, the decision should be left up to the players. They can decide if they want a captain or co-captains, whether seniors only should be chosen, and whether they want to vote or have the coach appoint someone.

The biggest danger is that this can become strictly a popularity contest. Popularity and leadership ability do not necessarily go hand in hand, and having captains who are not leaders can create additional problems which defeat the basic purpose of the whole concept.

27. Even though banquets usually occur after a season ends, decisions involving these affairs should be made prior to the beginning of a season. If the season is highly successful, everyone will want a banquet. If it is highly unsuccessful, a banquet becomes mandatory, in order to create some good feelings that will carry over into the off-season and into the next year.

Generally there are three basic kinds of banquets:

1. One all-sports banquet at the end of a school year,
2. Seasonal banquets involving all winter sports teams, for example, and
3. Banquets for each individual sport.

Banquets are usually held at the school or some banquet facility in the area.

The advantage of the all-sports banquet is that it is a one-time event, and theoretically creates unity among all the teams, both boys' and girls'. The main disadvantage is that if youngsters participate in a fall sport only, a banquet six months later means very little to them. A banquet seems to be most effective when it takes place the week after a season ends. There is also the problem of numbers of people and space.

The seasonal banquet is good because there is no danger of a major team having a better banquet than one of the so-called minor teams. The disadvantage is that of numbers of people and space, plus the fact that if a main speaker is contracted, that speaker usually ends up talking about one sport (the one he or she coaches), and the athletes on other teams have little interest in what is being said.

The specific-sport banquet allows far more flexibility, but can be the most costly if the school is financing these events. Of course, one way all of these banquets can be financed is by selling tickets to parents or to the community at large. One of the disadvantages in doing this is that there are families who cannot really afford to attend and it puts them in an uncomfortable situation.

The easiest type of banquet is one in which a civic organization sponsors the whole event. For the team involved it is usually very pleasant. The primary drawback is that normally only a few select teams in the school are so honored, and the rest are simply ignored. This sometimes causes hard feelings; therefore a coach should not actively encourage this outside sponsorship. However, when offered, a coach cannot afford to say no unless the school has a policy against banquets of this type.

The least expensive type of banquet, and a kind that every coach can organize with little expense for anyone, is a buffet at the school or the coach's own home if the team is small enough. This is the way it can be done. The coach figures how many team members, managers, coaches, coaches' wives or husbands, school officials, and parents will attend. The coach then takes this number and figures out a menu that is fairly simple to prepare, decides how much of each item is needed, and how many players will have to bring a dish for each item.

For example, a cake would have to be big enough for X number of servings, and in order for everyone to have enough for dessert, an athlete will have to volunteer to provide a cake of the correct size, and so on through the entire menu. This can be done in just a few minutes of a team meeting. To make sure there is enough to eat, the athletes usually bring a surplus of their contribution so that there will normally be more food than required. The author has never seen anyone go away hungry from a banquet like this.

To keep the coaches and their families from carrying the whole burden of planning and working on the banquet, the team captains' parents can work with them in making these preparations. To assist these parents and also to create continuity for the next year, the head coach can give them the names of some juniors' parents to help, and include the names of parents of the athletes most likely to be next year's captains. If there are no captains this simply means picking a few parents and asking them to help.

These parents then can take care of getting the food set out. To keep anyone from getting overwhelmed, another group of parents can be asked to decorate the tables. Each set of parents could be responsible for decorating one table. The number of tables there are dictates how many parents are needed to help. This provides a lot of variety, an opportunity to use imagination, and involvement without undue imposition on anyone.

Another idea that can easily become a tradition, and the highlight of a banquet, is the tapping of next year's captains as determined by team vote. The final event of the banquet could be to allow the outgoing captains a few minutes to talk about the season and what being captain has meant to them. As they finish their comments they begin walking among their seated teammates and, on a prearranged signal, slap the new captain or co-captains on the back (who up until that point were unknown to everyone but the outgoing captains and the coach) and bring them up in front of the group where their first official function is to make a short speech. When handled properly this ceremony is very effective and exciting. It adds another dimension to a very special event.

The next decision to consider in conjunction with a banquet is whether or not to have a speaker. If the decision is to have one, college coaches are often sought for this purpose, because the appearance of a college coach has become traditional, and it adds prestige to the affair. Usually, these people have a canned speech they change ever so slightly to fit a particular situation, and many times they spend a great deal of time talking about the sport at their particular university. Sometimes these presentations are very good and sometimes they are not.

If finances are a problem, an outside speaker is not necessary. Instead, a number of school officials and coaches, limited to about five minutes each, can talk about the team; some of the athletes can speak for a few minutes; the outgoing manager can pass on the symbol of authority to next year's manager; awards can be passed out and parents can be included as speakers also. For example, the mother of a player and the father of another player, one whose youngster played regularly and one whose youngster did not, can be asked to say a few words. One of the finest speeches the author ever heard at a banquet was given by the mother of a substitute who got into only one game all season, and then only briefly. The point is that there are a lot of people involved intimately in an athletic program who have a lot of talent and tremendous interest in the youngsters who participate. It sometimes seems like a waste not to take advantage of this and instead to bring in some expensive college coach who really couldn't care less about the situation unless there happens to be a prospective athlete there to recruit.

28. Filming athletic events also needs to be considered and decided upon. Normally when athletic events are filmed, 16 mm film is used. By using 8 mm film instead, the cost can be reduced significantly. Video tape is also very satisfactory. Filming can be an expensive tool, although an extremely valuable one, to an athletic team. When a coach is operating under a very limited budget and doesn't have enough money to film every game, this is not necessarily any cause for alarm. Some parents might be willing to take pictures of the events with their own equipment. Also, not every game has to be filmed. In most high school situations the crucial time of the season for teaching and learning is during the pre-season scrimmages, practice games or practice meets, and first few games of the season. This is when films are most beneficial. After this, films, in team games at least, serve primarily for the coach to see what happened in a game.

The advent of video tape has created a new dimension in filming athletic events. Most schools already own the necessary equipment and, as a result, coaches do not have to include money in their budget for this purpose. The other advantages of using video tape are that the tape can be erased and used more than once; since there is no developing time, the taped event is ready to view immediately. This is an excellent tool for teaching people in individual sports also, such as gymnastics, tennis, and golf.

High school athletic teams sometimes tend to improve to a point in a season and reach a plateau. Consequently, mistakes, poor technique, or poor habits must be corrected at the beginning of the season; otherwise these become ingrained and after a certain point in a season all the film in the world doesn't seem to make any difference. If a coach has enough money in the budget to film every game this is fine, but the chief advantage of filming late-season games is to use these films in the off-season in preparation for the next season.

29. The question of booster clubs is a concern only to a new coach who takes a job in a community where no such club exists. If a booster club is in operation already, a coach will have to live with it, because to try to disband it could create tremendous public relations problems.

If no booster club exists, a coach might decide to try and get one organized. There are three basic types of clubs. There is a community booster club, which serves many facets of the community, an athletic booster club that exists solely to support high school athletics, and booster clubs for specific athletic teams in the school.

Booster clubs can serve many useful functions and give a great deal of aid, especially when a school is attempting to establish a new athletic program or expand a program already in existence and funds are limited. The contributions of these clubs can range from outright financial support to providing banquets, transportation home after practice, and manual labor on the athletic facilities. At no time should booster clubs become a personal tool solely for the benefit of head coaches to provide them with money for clinics, Christmas gifts, or gifts of any kind, including a new automobile for their own use. This can breed many problems, including ill feeling among other coaches and faculty. Bad feelings can also occur when booster clubs exist solely to support one or two athletic teams, ignoring all the rest.

There is one important consideration for a new coach where booster clubs are concerned. Human nature being what it is, when an organization begins giving financial support to a team or coach, and starts paying some of the bills, eventually the people in that organization want some say, not only in how that money will be spent, but in how the program should be run, and, in time, who the coach should be. More than one high school coach has lost his or her job because the booster club became dissatisfied. Since the members of the club are taxpayers, and often leaders in the community, the influence they can exert over a superintendent or board of education is very powerful.

In order to help a booster club remain a group of boosters, the coach should take an active role in the club to help provide leadership, and to channel interest and enthusiasm in the proper direction. Not only do booster clubs get disenchanted with coaches and want them replaced, but they also resent a director of athletics or school administrators they believe are squelching the athletic program. It is in these situations that the coach must calm down the overzealous, and exercise the greatest diplomacy in order to prevent a wholesale purge that frequently creates factions in the community harmful to everyone concerned.

Booster clubs generally consist of four kinds of people. There are those who have a genuine interest in high school athletics; those who have a special interest — a son or daughter participating in sports; those who enjoy being on the fringe of athletics by associating with the coaches; and the sharpshooters who are frustrated coaches and attend meetings so they can challenge the coach. It is to the advantage of the coach to identify these groups as quickly as possible and to attempt to keep the boosters in their proper role and perspective.

30. Family summer vacations always create problems for pre-season practice that begins in August; Thanksgiving and Christmas vacation do the same for the winter sports, and spring vacation for the spring sports. Long before a season begins, the coaching staff should settle on a policy covering this problem. Then, when writing letters to athletes and parents before the season begins, they should spell out this policy to avoid misunderstandings later on. The sad thing about this problem is that it is the youngster who gets caught in the middle. On one hand, the coach says there will be practice, while the parents insist the youngster go with them because they will not go away and leave their child at home. Normally, some compromise can be reached, but the soundest procedure is to notify parents prior to the start of every season of the vacation practice schedule so they can plan accordingly. It is very poor policy on the part of a coach to wait until just prior to a vacation to announce a practice schedule. Not only is it unfair to the family, but it often creates ill feeling and this is something coaches should always try to avoid.

31. One of a coach's irritations occurs when the team is in the midst of a practice session and a newspaper photographer walks in and

Photo courtesy of Mike Sabock.

asks to take some publicity pictures. No matter how a picture-taking session is handled it interferes with practice. Not only does it disrupt practice, but the team usually has on its practice gear, which doesn't look very good in a picture. If a coach gives this matter some thought in pre-season planning, these interruptions can be avoided.

As the coach looks at the pre-season schedule, he or she simply picks a time when the team could use a break from the daily routine and monotony of practice, and selects that date for pictures. It is not necessary to cancel a practice session to do this; instead, practice is simply shortened so that the whole day is not lost for this purpose. After the date, time, and place (including a rain date for outdoor sports) have been set, the student publicity writer contacts every area newspaper, the yearbook photographer, television sportscasters, and the photographer for the game programs by telephone and by letter inviting them to come to the school at that time to take all the pictures they want. This should be done several weeks in advance for these people to fit this into their busy schedules.

When the day arrives, the athletes dress in their game uniforms, and the photographers take over. The team belongs to them and they are free to take as many pictures as they like of whomever they like. The youngsters really enjoy a session like this because it is a change in daily routine, and it has all the earmarks of a big-time operation. The photographers appreciate this, too, because they can plan on the date, the players can look sharp in their uniforms for pictures, and they don't have to interrupt practice.

This is a good time to invite parents and friends to come and bring their cameras, too. When these photographers are finished, the coach should arrange to have another photographer there to take individual shots of every member of the team. The school photography club can develop these into 8 × 10 photos which can be posted in a suitable display in store windows in the main section of town to create interest in the upcoming season. In many situations this is rare for athletic teams. There is no reason it has to stay that way. If coaches of any team are willing to take the initiative, this can change. Too many coaches sit in their office and complain that people just don't care, instead of doing something about it.

32. Obviously, the pre-planning of the head coach involves a great deal of paperwork, typing, and reproducing of forms, information, and letters. Most coaches do not have the time to do this, nor can they afford to hire someone to do this work for them. But there is a way to get this done quickly, efficiently, and without cost. Just as coaches recruit managers or student publicity writers, they can recruit student secretaries. The easiest way to do this is to talk with the typing teacher to find out who the best students are and to ask the teacher to recommend several students who could do the job. The coach then talks to these people to see if any of them would be willing to help during some of their study halls or during any other free period they have. Usually this request is quickly and eagerly accepted. When this student becomes a senior, the coach finds an underclass volunteer to begin working along as a secretary to learn about the job. This works very nicely, and when given specific duties and responsibilities, carefully chosen youngsters perform these tasks very well.

33. One other factor to discuss in preplanning concerns feedback from the members of the team concerning all aspects of the program. For obvious reasons, the best source is the graduating seniors at the conclusion of the season. This information is extremely useful in planning for the following year, and is an excellent method of evaluating a program. An example of student evaluation of a season follows:

SENIORS' EVALUATION
of (sport) at (high school)

In order to improve our (sport) program, we must take stock of the accomplishments, shortcomings, and objectives we have. We, as a coaching staff, will do this, while another source of evaluation is the seniors on the squad, whom we are now asking to help us. Would you please take the time to give us your frank and honest views and ideas? We'd really appreciate it. You need not sign it if you choose.

(evaluation continued on next page)

(If you need more space, use back for explanation.)

1. Did anything happen during the season to make you upset with your coaches, teammates, opponents, teachers, administration, student body, etc. in regard to (sport)?
2. Did you feel that you were ever called upon to do something for which you were not properly prepared?
3. List any personal criticisms that you think will be helpful to our team for the future.
4. Did you really enjoy the season? _____ Why?
5. Did you hear any comments by parents, fans, or others pertaining to the games or players that you feel would be helpful to the team or coaches?
6. How can we, as coaches, help our players to play a better game?
7. What was your opinion regarding our scouting reports?
8. How did you feel about our squad morale?
9. How can we improve our total program?
10. What do you think of our notebooks? (quantity, form, quality, clarity, etc.)
11. How did you feel about our equipment and uniforms?
12. What do you think of our film grading and sessions with comment sheets?
13. Are there any ways you feel we could better use our facilities? Any comments about these?
14. Any ideas regarding our total organization?
15. What do you think of our promotional ideas and activities? Do you have any other ideas along these lines?
16. What are your feelings about our pre-game warmup activities and organization?
17. Do you feel we were well drilled in fundamentals?
18. What about your comments regarding our training room and procedures there?
19. What about our practice planning and organization?
20. Regarding our younger team members: Who do you feel will be our best athletes next year?
21. Were there any players on the squad who you feel were playing out of position or should have played more and didn't? Was there any player who you felt should have played ahead of someone else?
22. What's your opinion pro or con about special awards?
23. Do you feel you were given a fair chance to show your ability?
24. What do you think about the scout team?
25. Do you think you were well prepared to play the game?
26. Did you study the scouting reports?
27. List any other points or ideas you feel would be helpful.

Thanks a lot for taking the time to help us evaluate our program. It has been a pleasure having you on the team.

Your Coaching Staff

Photo courtesy of The Pennsylvania State University Still Photography Services.

Off-season organization takes a tremendous amount of time, thought, and energy, but is crucial as a first step in a successful season and should not be overlooked by a head coach. There is an old Chinese proverb which states, "The longest journey begins with a single step." Off-season planning on the part of a head coach serves as the initial step on the long season ahead.

DISCUSSION QUESTIONS

1. What are some important points for a head coach to consider in organizing a staff, team, or program?

2. How does a team reflect the personality of the coach?

3. How can anti-discrimination laws affect your program?

4. How can you use film or video tape in coaching your sport? Will you allow your players to watch the film? When?

5. What do you view your role to be with the athletic booster's club?

6. Should every athletic team have a captain or co-captains? What are the advantages and disadvantages?

7. Should coaches encourage parent involvement in a sport? Are there limits?

8. How can "senioritis" affect an athletic team?

9. Are cliques more of a problem in girls' athletics than in boys'? How would you deal with this?

10. In what capacities can other students in the school become involved in the athletic program? How can they be chosen?

11. How could notebooks be used in your sport? What would you include?

12. Organize a parents' clinic.

13. Organize a team banquet.

14. You have set equipment issue or scheduled practice during school vacation time. One of your athletes calls to tell you his or her family will be going on vacation—therefore, they will be absent from your scheduled sessions. Discuss this from the athlete's point of view, the parents', and your point of view as coach.

15. How would you deal with the problem of a parent giving "coaching" advice to their youngster which is contrary to what you are attempting to teach?

Photo by Dick Brown, Centre Daily Times.

7

PRE-SEASON STAFF PLANNING

As a result of careful, well thought out off-season planning (Chapter 6), a head coach will have arrived at some basic decisions regarding the upcoming season. In spite of this, there will still be decisions to be made and questions to be answered in the few days prior to the first pre-season practice. This time will be less chaotic, however, because of the off-season decisions that were made.

When a head coach has no assistant coaches, obviously every decision regarding the new season must be made by the head coach. If, on the other hand, there is more than one coach involved, a staff meeting should be scheduled prior to the beginning of practice. Depending on the sport, the number of coaches, and how well the head coach is organized, these meetings could involve just a part of one day, or they could take the better part of a week or two.

At these pre-season meetings the head coach will set forth his ideas and plans and encourage the assistant coaches to question, challenge, present counter-ideas if necessary, and, finally, agree on what to agree on. Rarely, if ever, will everyone on a staff agree on every point; consequently, these sessions become a series of compromises within the staff. After everyone has had an opportunity to speak, the head coach must, by nature of the position, cast the deciding vote when a decision cannot be made by consensus. A good leader will tolerate uncertainty temporarily and then, must act. The democratic process is necessary and good only up to a point.

In spite of the fact that disagreements will occur and the head coach often must cast the deciding vote, the following is a set of guidelines every head coach can use in creating a good working relationship with assistant coaches.

A SHORT COURSE IN HUMAN RELATIONS

The 6 most important words are:
"I admit I made a mistake."

The 5 most important words are:
"I am proud of you."

The 4 most important words are:
"What is your opinion?"

The 3 most important words are:
"If you please."

The 2 most important words are:
"Thank You."

The 1 most important word is:
"We."

Author unknown

Assuming that there is more than one coach involved in a particular sport, the following would be appropriate to include in the first pre-season meeting.

The first point of order is for the head coach to reaffirm his or her personal philosophy of coaching to the staff. This serves as a review and reminder for the assistant coaches who have been on the staff and as guidelines for the new members. This also provides them with a sense of direction in everything they do in carrying out their coaching duties during a particular season. Understanding the head coach's beliefs is important, too, in that it provides boundaries or limits within which each coach must work, specifically in regard to the way coaches work with the athletes, the attitude toward winning and losing, the way the program will be run, and how coaches should conduct themselves at practice, to mention just a few.

Once this is clear the entire staff will feel more comfortable simply because they understand what the head coach believes in and the way the program is to be conducted. Each coach can then determine how best to carry out individual responsibilities within this framework.

Normally, a head coach will have the opportunity to attend more coaching clinics than the assistants will. The various members of a staff may possibly have attended different clinics, or come across different ideas in the off-season. In order to take full advantage of these ideas and thoughts of the whole group, the head coach should conduct a clinic for the entire staff at this point in preseason planning. In this manner all information is shared, and in reality, this session becomes an in-service workshop. This is particularly important when there are new coaches on the staff. This is when they learn about techniques, terminology, drills, and methods that will be used during the season. A session like this is good for returning staff members too, because it serves as a refresher course. This also eliminates confusion in practice because all coaches are using the same terminology, techniques, and ideas in their teaching, regardless of whether they are coaching freshman or varsity players.

The following agenda is an example of the kinds of things to be included in a clinic for a coaching staff. These points are in actuality an accumulation of ideas gathered at various coaching clinics which the author attended. Many refer to boys' football, but can easily be applied to almost any other sport. The important thing is that no item or idea is too insignificant to be mentioned in a meeting such as this, regardless of the sport involved. Whether or not a staff agrees with these ideas is immaterial. What is important is to know what others believe — especially if they are an opposing coach.

COACHES' CLINIC

   I. Don't take anything for granted in (specific sport) where youngsters are concerned.
  II. Characteristics of a winner (coach)
     A. Dedicated, organized, respected
     B. Strong disciplinarian
     C. Balanced game — all phases
     D. Teaches aggressive football — especially defensive
     E. Ability to improvise with ability at hand
     F. Ability to recognize and utilize talent on squad
     G. Doesn't beat him- or herself
     H. Hates mediocrity
     I. Precise in all aspects of the program
     J. Enthusiastic
     K. Willing to work
 III. Successful coaching —
     A. Well thought-out reason for everything you do
     B. Wise use of staff and time
     C. Know the difference between winning and losing:
        1. superior personnel
        2. superior conditioning
        3. fewer mistakes
        4. superior mental attitude
        5. better job of teaching (don't talk too much on the field)
        6. superior placement of personnel
 IV. Establish a tradition that only the most outstanding people play both ways.
  V. Pursuit drill done on live line, not sled
 VI. Emphasize rush rather than return on punts.
 VII. Take an athlete who is not a kicker—put him seven yards in front of a punter to see who has the guts to block a punt.
VIII. On tackling practice use "hamburger troops" to tackle — not the team members who play in the game.
 IX. Allow younger students to play everywhere and anywhere on team defense in early season to see if they have any special aptitude.
  X. Instill pride in interior linemen.
 XI. Build confidence in each athlete.
 XII. As long as a player is putting out on defense, don't get on him too hard and break his spirit — pick out something good.
XIII. Don't make all the work drudgery.
XIV. Make drills simulate game conditions, if possible.

XV. True test of coach is whether or not you got 100% out of the material at hand.

XVI. Get the best people in the game.

XVII. Being a member of the varsity is something they should aspire to — not get in the program and then see if they want to play.

XVIII. Why is this youngster out for (sport)?

XIX. The lower the athletes' ability, the greater their desire — the most skillful usually do not have the greatest desire. The winner is not necessarily high on skill, but extremely high on desire.

XX. Make your opponent play your style of game — slow down, hurry up, and so on.

XXI. Only happy people on the team — the starters.

XXII. Toughest problem is recognition of personnel — what an athlete does in the game — skill vs. motivation. This is all judgment on the part of the coaches.

XXIII. Game-type situations are best in rating players — not just drills.

XXIV. People play purely on their ability as athletes.

XXV. Smoking or drinking indicates poor mental discipline, poor attitude, lack of interest, no concern. No one was ever a better athlete because of smoking or drinking.

XXVI. Practice must be hard — overload principle.

XXVII. Pride in how well they practice is the mark of a good team. Look sharp. Test of morale is how a team practices. If practice is poor, send them in after you call them together once and tell them they aren't accomplishing anything.

XXVIII. Set a deadline when tryouts for the team end — a youngster makes it by then or else.

XXIX. As season progresses, cut down practice time, because an athlete is not going to get that much better but could go physically downhill.

XXX. How well can a coach create in practice what a player will face in a game? Repeat these situations until a player reacts through habit.

XXXI. Any sport is a game of mistakes, technique, and emotion.

XXXII. After every practice go over the roster and if a youngster had a particularly good day, tell him so — if he had a bad day, find out why.

XXXIII. Use youngster's whole name or nickname all the time.

XXXIV. Tell team members they are not allowed to get hurt — if they get knocked down yell, "Get up!" — if they stay down they'd better be hurt.

XXXV. Have faith in the athletes.

XXXVI. Use key words for coaches to yell — "faster," "quicker," and so on.

XXXVII. Clear-cut aims — remove doubts in athletes' minds.

XXXVIII. Togetherness in thoughts and actions

XXXIX. Good habits — do it right all the time — do it the way I tell you

XL. Regimentation — exactness (dress — calisthenics — everything)

XLI. Pleasure — laugh when it's warranted

XLII. Fear of losing — respect your opponent — fear none

XLIII. Don't get hit on defense — you do the hitting.

XLIV. Test players by having them draw plays and defense on board.

XLV. No backs ever get hit in numbers or on the ball. Use flipper.

XLVI. Get your hand over tip of ball.

XLVII. A great back runs with his heart — he can ignite the team with a single move.

XLVIII. Backs run all plays into end zone — every 10 yards. Put vests on the ground and he makes a cut at these.

Photo courtesy of Linda Huber.

Prior to the staff meeting, the head coach should have determined each coach's specific coaching assignment for the season. However, as the size of a staff increases, so does the necessity of clarifying additional duties and responsibilities for each coach. The first step is to make a master list of every item that must be covered. Each coach then can volunteer for these responsibilities or they can simply be assigned. This list should be put in writing and posted on the office bulletin board. In this manner there is much less chance of something important being left undone because everyone thought someone else was going to take care of it. The chart on pages 194 and 195 is an example of a staff of eight people, with coach A being the head coach, while G and H represent the newest coaches on the staff.

In column B there is an entry, "Staff scribe." This individual is to take notes at every staff meeting, reproduce them, and see that everyone on the staff receives a copy. This serves as a permanent record of what takes place in staff meetings and the decisions that were made. This is an important consideration for a high school staff where all the members of the staff are teaching a full schedule every day and have a lot of other things on their minds. The results of a meeting can be fresh in everyone's mind at the moment, but a week or two later there might be some confusion as to what actually took place. And since high school coaches do not have time to meet during the day or may not have a chance to see other members of the staff until practice, the minutes of these meetings serve as a reference for them if a question arises concerning some point made in one of the meetings.

COACHES' ASSIGNMENTS

COACH A	COACH B	COACH C	COACH D
Morale and discipline	Defensive game play	Offensive game play	Clinic notes
Offensive game play	Offensive game play	Defensive game play	Check-off List
Defensive game play	Clinic notes	Clinic notes	Public relations
Clinic notes		Check-off list	
Check-off list	Public relations	Accident and illness	Review periodicals
Scouting reports	Promotional gimmicks	Public relations	Physical cards
Public relations	Weight and isometrics	Film grading	Eligibility
Film grading	Film grading	Equipment issues	Old tires
Managers	Press box	Managers (tele. extra)	Practice plans
Brief scouts	Staff scribe	Checklist for managers	Orientation
Review periodicals	Review periodicals		Coaching clinics
Football notebooks	Coaches' pre-season		Summer Jobs
Statistics man	Picnic	Review periodicals	Summer conditioning
Team pictures	Office decoration		Cafeteria duty
Banquet	Personnel board		Classroom assignments
Parent night procedure	Practice plans	Practice plans	
Practice plans	Orientation	Orientation	Meetings
Film study room	Coaching clinics	Coaching clinics	Grade card check
Orientation	Summer jobs	Summer jobs	
Awards	Summer conditioning	Summer condition	Scout
Cheerleaders	Projectionist	Grade card check	
Pep rally			
Coaching clinics			
Summer jobs			
Budget			
Summer conditioning			

COACH E	COACH F	COACH G	COACH H
Check-off list	Clinic notes	Scout	Emergency file
Clinic notes	Check-off list		Sox salesman
Public relations	Public relations	Physical cards	Scout
Promotional gimmick	Drill file	Eligibility	Duplicator
Review periodicals	Library	Roster	
Training room	Review periodicals	Accident illness	
		Rep. to teachers' meetings	
Office decoration	Football notebooks		
Personnel board			
Music man			
Practice plans	Practice plans		
Orientation	Orientation		
Coaching clinics	Coaching clinics		
Summer jobs	Summer jobs		
Summer conditioning	Summer conditioning		
	Grade card check		
Grade card check	Scout		
Film exchange			
Eligibility, etc.			

Several items, such as public relations, are listed for every coach, because items such as this cannot be delegated, and are responsibilities of every coach. One coach should always be designated to attend faculty meetings during the season as a representative of the staff. This keeps the principal happy, and shows the faculty that coaches do care about what is going on within the faculty. If the staff takes the initiative on this point, they can avoid the possibility of faculty grumbling about coaches not attending faculty meetings. This can also eliminate the possibility of the principal's insistence that every coach be present at faculty meetings. Normally, as long as the principal is satisfied that the information is getting back to the coaches, this arrangement will be satisfactory.

Sometime during the days preceding the opening game of the season the coaches, and their husbands and wives, should set aside time for a picnic, progressive dinner, or other social gathering. This is an opportunity for everyone to get acquainted with the new staff members and to involve the spouses in the coaching family. If staff meetings take several days or evenings, a social event with the whole group is a good break in the routine just before practice begins. It is at this time, too, that after-game get-togethers can be planned.

In addition to the preceeding information, the following decisions and considerations must be resolved for every sport regardless of whether one coach is involved or fourteen. These decisions then must be made clear to athletes and coaches alike.

Practice Procedures.   This includes everything from the moment the athletes enter the locker room until practice is over and they have gone home for the day. Some considerations to be included are:

1. Practice times
2. Practice uniforms or dress
3. Length of warm up
4. Type of warm up
5. Equipment problems
6. Types of drills
7. Holiday practices
8. Excuses from practice because of injury or illness
9. Reporting late to practice
10. Foul weather practice procedures for outdoor sports
11. Use of bulletin boards for announcements
12. Conduct during practice
13. Visitors at practice
14. Injury care during practice — especially with only one coach
15. Athletes transportation to practice
16. Taping time
17. Protection of valuables in locker room
18. Excusing athletes from practice for other commitments
19. Where to report for practice after getting dressed
20. Squad meetings — time and place
21. How soon athletes should clear the locker room after the day's practice ends.

22. Use of training room
23. Language (swearing)

Agreeing on practice procedures is complicated only when the number of coaches and athletes involved is such that facilities and space become a problem. Practice procedures are rather unique for football, field hockey, soccer and cross country, since practice begins before the school year does. This creates a different set of problems for the coaching staff. Some of the problems that must be recognized as having an effect on two-a-day practice sessions in August are heat and humidity, family vacations, members of the staff attending graduate school, transportation for athletes in rural areas, and the work responsibilities of athletes who live on farms.

During the school year, practice times are not a consideration, as a rule, because they must be held immediately after school or in the evening. If a particular facility is overcrowded, a coach might decide to hold some practice sessions in the morning before school begins.

Acclimatization.   The concern with heat and humidity is a problem specific to any sport when practice begins in August. This needs to be considered very carefully when determining practice times, and is particularly crucial in football since the uniform itself is a heat trap.

These trouble signs mean to stop the activity.

Headache	Fatigue	Vomiting	Weak, rapid pulse
Nausea	Weakness	Diarrhea	Pallor
Mental slowness	Unsteadiness	Cramps	Flush
Incoherence	Collapse	Seizures	Faints
Visual disturbance	Unconsciousness	Rigidity	Chills

Remember that it is impossible to harm an athlete with water—external or internal. It is unforgivable to allow an athlete to lapse into heat illness due to inadequate fluid intake. Well hydrated athletes are alert and tireless, carry out assignments well and are, therefore, less injury prone.

HUMIDITY	TEMPERATURE	PRACTICE
Under 70%	under 80 deg.	no limitation
under 70%	80–90 deg.	full practice—water players watch weight loss
over 70%	80–90 deg.	shorts with minimum pads frequent rest
under 70%	90–100 deg.	change wet shirts
over 70%	90–100 deg.	exercise caution
any humidity over 95%	over 100 deg. any temp.	NO PRACTICE

F. C. Kelton, M.D. "Advisory Paper for Hotweather Athletics." *The Pa'thlete,* August, 1972, p.7.

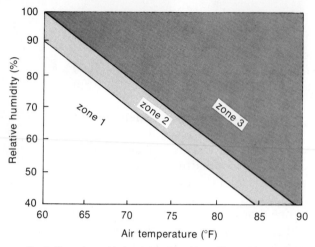

Football weather guide for prevention of heat illness. The combination of relative humidity and air temperature in zone 1 can be considered safe; for zone 2, use caution; and for zone 3, use extreme caution when practicing in full football gear.

Heat exhaustion and heat stroke are the only preventable catastrophes faced in athletics. Death from heat stroke is not a happenstance such as being struck by lightning. It is a totally predictable event, and it can occur at night, as well as during daylight hours.

The prevention of heat stroke begins in June when you meet your squad before summer vacation and indoctrinate them by impressing upon your squad the importance of running, drinking lots of liquids, and eating salted foods. This brings about acclimatization even before practice begins. Practice for the first seven days should be conducted in shorts and T-shirts. Acclimatization at the secondary school level should be well established at the end of this period.

If the wet bulb thermometer is above 70 degrees, practice should not be held — except early morning or late afternoon. Without psychrometers or other refined temperature taking apparati, check radio and TV weather reports. During practice there should be a rest and water break every half hour, with no limit on fluid or ice intake. Coaches should take liquids at this time also. Fluids may be plain water, ice, or any of the "ades" — and as a special treat on a tough day or tough practice — orange popsicles.

An adequate "ade"-type drink is:

1 Tsp. of salt
1 potassium tablet, purchased at drug store
4 quarts of cold tap water
Add sugar and flavoring to taste, such as any soft drink powder. Add ice.
Serve in paper cups.

Salt tablets, coated or uncoated, are valueless, and indeed harmful, taken without water. They can produce intense gastric and intestinal irritation and enhance the toxicity level of an incipient heat stroke victim. Alone they are not a preventative or a remedy for heat illness.

The apathetic, inattentive, uncoordinated athlete may be telegraphing impending heat illness. The big fullback, end, or interior linemen are particularly prone to disaster.

It is essential that weight levels be charted daily, preferably on graph paper. This should be done before and after practice. A 5-pound weight loss in one day is absolute top limit at the scholastic level, and each player should be carefully observed. With consistent, consecutive weight loss over two or three days the athlete must be removed from activity until weight is restored.

Training Rules. At one time in the history of sport, training rules were as much a part of the program as the equipment the team used. However, the trend in many locations of the country today is to water down the rules or eliminate them altogether. Many coaches do not establish training rules because such rules are difficult to enforce, and they might lose their best athlete by enforcing them. Furthermore, these coaches say that high school boys and girls are old enough to decide for themselves whether they should drink and smoke. In lieu of official training rules, some coaches will discuss the problem with their team, and hope the youngsters will refrain from using alcohol and tobacco, or at least be discreet about it.

On the other hand there are those who believe that coaches, regardless of their college major, are physical educators, and as such they have an inescapable obligation to teach youngsters how to take care of their bodies, and of the importance of maintaining a strong, healthy body. In light of this, to ignore educating youngsters about the harmful effects of alcohol, tobacco, and drugs, along with the importance of good nutrition, is to ignore an important obligation of coaching. The ease with which youngsters can obtain cigarettes and liquor compounds the problem; therefore, training rules, established and enforced, can do much toward preventing youngsters from developing these habits in their formative teen-age years.

If a coach, a staff, or the team decides to establish training rules, it is equally important to determine possible penalties for violation of these rules. They must also agree that any offender, regardless of position, ability, or any other factor, will pay some price for breaking a training rule. Without this, training rules are not worth the paper they are written on. Contrary to what some believe, observing reasonable training rules is not a sacrifice an athlete makes. When boys or girls learn to avoid habits that can be harmful to their health, this can hardly be classified as a sacrifice.

Some coaches have used the practice of checking on athletes to see if they are at home by certain hours, or of driving around town to see if any athletes are breaking rules. Coaches should avoid these kinds of actions because they imply distrust and a lack of faith, and can create resentment among athletes and their parents. Playing detective in this way can severely affect the coach's rapport with the team and eventually one's effectiveness with them.

More often than not, parents appreciate athletic training rules, because they provide them with another tool in their own efforts to prevent a son or daughter from drinking and smoking. And when parents feel this way, they see to it, as best they can, that the rules are followed.

The argument as to whether or not smoking or drinking hinders a high school student's athletic accomplishments is relatively immaterial. Prohibiting drinking and smoking is a matter of mental discipline and concern for a healthy body, both of which are important ingredients in sport and in life.

Discipline.   The reason for discussing this topic at staff meetings is twofold. First, the necessity of maintaining degrees of discipline involving all phases of the program where youngsters are concerned must be established; and secondly, every effort must be made to insure consistency on the part of each coach. In this manner, each member of the team knows what to expect from the coaching staff. Over-zealous disciplinarians and weak disciplinarians on a staff must be pulled toward middle ground by a consensus of the kinds of discipline necessary to insure that this will not become a disruptive factor when the season begins. This kind of agreement gives the staff solidarity and consistency in the eyes of the youngsters when discipline needs to be enforced, and lessens the chances of any coach being labeled as the iron hand or a soft touch.

Conduct of players and coaches.   This area of concern refers to the way coaches and players conduct themselves during practice sessions, in the locker room, pre-game, during a game, and while travelling to and from an athletic contest. This normally is a direct reflection of the head coach's beliefs, and is also another attempt to make sure all players know what is expected of them in order to help them do the best they can to make the season a successful one.

Very few head coaches fail to tell youngsters what is expected of them, but they often neglect to do the same with the coaching staff. When a head coach considers the fact that every coach on the staff brings a variety of experiences to the job, the necessity of clarifying the way coaches are to conduct themselves while involved in the sport season becomes apparent.

Coaches' appearance.   There are two schools of thought in this regard: (1) it is important for the whole coaching staff to dress alike for practice, and (2) it makes little difference what they wear as long as they get the job done. There is no known proof that one point of view is better than the other. This again becomes a reflection of the head coach's beliefs, or it might be determined by the staff as a whole.

The advantages of standard dress for practice are:
1. Unity in dress lends credibility to the belief that there is also unity in thought and purpose within the staff.
2. Attention to appearance makes it easier to impress the same thing on a team.
3. A neat, clean coaching uniform is an example of attention to detail which is a lesson members of a team need to learn in their desire to be successful.
4. It adds class to the coaching staff.

5. It gives a coaching staff a professional appearance.
6. When a staff dresses as a group of professionals, they have a tendency to act more professionally in their dealings with the members of a team.
7. It has an appearance of efficiency.
8. It enhances the image of the coach.

Drills. Since drills are an excellent way to teach various parts of a game, a lot of thought should be devoted to their use in the pre-season planning. For many coaches of team sports, drills are the basis of most practice sessions. The idea of every practice session being a full team scrimmage or practice game is not generally believed to be the best way to teach youngsters the fundamentals of any sport. Some coaches establish a file where drills are drawn up on 5 × 7 cards, categorized, and filed for the use of all the coaches on the staff. When several coaches are contributing to this, it can become very worthwhile, particulary to new coaches.

Basically, there are five sources of drills. They can come from a coach's own college playing experience, books or magazine articles, and clinics, from visiting college coaches, and finally, from a coach's own imagination.

Drills themselves can be classified into four distinct purposes: for developing agility, reaction, and conditioning and for teaching fundamentals.

In evaluating drills as to their suitability for use in your program, there are nine guidelines that should be considered:

1. Every drill should simulate a game condition.
2. When possible, every drill should accomplish multiple results.
3. Every drill should have a definite purpose and the athletes should know the purpose.
4. Drills should be kept short. This means anywhere from one minute to possibly a maximum of 15 minutes.
5. Drills should be of a variety in order to eliminate monotony and boredom.
6. Do not break the continuity of a drill to take time to correct one person. This is a tremendous waste of time.
7. Do not use your best athletes for "dummies."
8. Stack the deck. When teaching something new, arrange the drill so that the people who are to learn have a sure chance to succeed in the drill. Success breeds confidence, and ultimately, success.
9. Maximum participation — use drills that have a minimum of "standing around" waiting a turn.

One final thought and perhaps the overriding consideration in this regard is *"Repetitio est mater studiorem"* — repetition is the mother of learning.

Photo courtesy of Chuck Paschke.

Travel, dress, and conduct.   Every situation is different, but one common factor exists for every interscholastic athletic team, and that is travel to away games. If the trip is short, teams sometimes dress at school and travel to the game in uniform. For some sports teams, this is impractical, regardless of the distance, and so a decision must be made as to how the youngsters will dress for the trip. Some teams are provided with blazers, some are told to wear dress-up clothes, while others go dressed in blue jeans and sweat shirts.

Again, this usually reflects the personal desire of the head coach. But one point that should be remembered is that a team does represent a school and community, and their personal appearance is one of the ways they make an impression on people from another community. Because of this, many coaches prefer that a team dress accordingly.

Another potential problem a coaching staff needs to clarify is the way players are to conduct themselves on the way to or from a game. Nothing can be more embarrassing to a school than to have members of a team hanging out the windows of a school bus shouting wisecracks, obscenities, or just being obnoxious. Some coaches of girls' teams, especially male coaches, often think this will not be a problem with the girls because they will be "ladylike" in their behavior. This is a mistake because they can be just as obnoxious and foul mouthed as boys. The criticism in these cases always falls on the head coach, and rightfully so. Consequently, rules of conduct for away games must be established beforehand, saving embarrassment for everyone concerned.

Practice plans.   Every good teacher relies on lesson plans. For teachers of athletics, these are practice plans. A well thought out practice plan is a must for efficient use of time. This is also important when there are several coaches working with a team in order to coordinate the overall practice.

The best prepared practice plans are not worth the paper they are written on, if the time schedule is ignored. In order to insure that everything in the practice plan is covered, each coach must follow the plan to the minute. Coaches tend to ignore the time schedule when a particular part of practice is not going well, and spend additional time on that part of the activity. The trouble with this is that other facets suffer as a result, and in fact might not get covered in that practice. Normally, if something doesn't go well, move on when the schedule dictates, and that particular area is then re-scheduled for the next practice.

Practice plans should be prepared at least one day ahead of time, so that each coach can plan accordingly. A good time to do this is after practice, before the coaches leave for the day. These plans should then be posted so the athletes also know what is in store for them. Last minute planning should be avoided if at all possible.

The following guidelines should be helpful when writing practice plans:

1. The first team never loses in practice.
2. Practice plans should have a lot of variation.
3. Practice plans must be well organized.
4. Practice plans should provide for maximum participation.
5. Practice plans should provide efficient use of time.
6. Practice plans should take into consideration maximum use of space and facilities.
7. Practice plans should serve to teach new things, to review, to correct and to prepare for the next contest.
8. Practice plans should be adjusted in time and intensity as the season progresses.

It has been said that practice makes perfect. This is not true. Practice makes permanent. It is perfect practice that makes perfect. Therefore, the fundamental purpose behind every practice plan and practice sessions is to "habitize" the athletes, and to insist that whatever is done is done as near perfect as possible.

> Habit is a cable; we weave a thread of it every day, and at last we cannot break it.
>
> *Horace Mann*

SAMPLE PRACTICE PLANS—FIELD HOCKEY
(BEGINNING OF THE SEASON)

A. Objectives
   1. Develop endurance, strength, agility, speed
   2. Improve stickwork skills
   3. Determine players' game abilities
B. Situation
   1. Two-hour practice
   2. Adequate field space and equipment
   3. One coach

C. Practice
   1. 2:00–2:15 — running and agility drills
   2. 2:15–2:30 — stationary stickwork drills
   3. 2:30–3:30 incorporate drills for stickwork into running and agility drills
   4. 3:30–4:00 — half-field play — forwards against the defense (Those not playing continue to practice stationary stickwork.) Rotate players.
   5. End practice with several minutes of wind-sprints (which are gradually increased with each practice session).

All practice sessions prior to the season will follow the above plan with the following modifications:
   1. Gradual decrease in the stationary stickwork drills — an increase in the amount of time spent on moving and executing strokes, such as combining skills needed by backs and wings —players in these positions practice play patterns together.
   2. Gradual increase in the amount of time spent playing — go from one-half field to full field as soon as the group demonstrates enough endurance and proficiency in basic skills.
   3. Players for each position should be chosen well enough in advance to have the opportunity to learn to play together before the first game of the season.

PRACTICE PLAN — FIELD HOCKEY (MID-SEASON)

A. Objectives
   1. Maintain level of endurance.
   2. Improve weaknesses in individual skill and team play.
B. Practice
   1. Time for practicing skills or team play situations should be allotted according to need. Some examples are:
      a. Three inside forwards practice (one-half field) moving ball downfield and shooting from the edge of circle.
      b. Wing and inside forward practice centering ball and shooting.
      c. Back and wings practice clearing and carrying ball downfield.
      d. Forward line against the goalie.
      e. Plays for out of bounds, fouls, and penalty situations.
      f. Triangular passing forward line players.
   2. Entire practice may be devoted to play patterns if there are several days before the next game. A regulation game should be played at least two days before the next contest, with a shortened play period the day immediately preceding the game.

PRACTICE PLAN — TENNIS (BEGINNING OF THE SEASON)

A. Objectives
   1. Develop endurance, strength, speed, etc.
   2. Develop stroke competency.
   3. Improve game strategy, singles and doubles.
B. Situation
   1. Coach
   2. Two-hour practice
   3. Adequate courts and equipment

C. Practice
1. 2:00–2:15 — two per court rally — forehand crosscourt shot. Emphasis: ball control for good placement and recovering to middle of court after every stroke.
2. 2:15–2:30 — repeat "a" above with backhand crosscourt.
3. 2:30–2:45 — forehand and backhand crosscourt and down-the-ine shots. Player A sends ball crosscourt and recovers to middle; player B sends ball down-the-line and recovers to middle. (Ball kept in play continuously.) Alternate positions.
4. 2:45–3:00 — player A practices serves to right and left courts working on placement in outside and inside corners. Player B practices returning ball deep crosscourt and down-the-line.
5. 3:00–3:15 — player B serves, player A returns as above.
6. 3:15–4:00 — play pro set (round robin) to determine ladder positions. (This takes about a week.)

Mid-Season

Work with individuals on particular problems of each. May be done for two hours — or if near a match date, do for one-half of the practice period. Second half should be devoted to challenge matches.

SAMPLE WRESTLING PRACTICE PLAN

3:30–3:40	Calisthenics — announcements
3:40–3:50	Warm-up drills (reaction-spike drill)
3:50–4:00	Demonstrate new takedown and counter
4:00–4:15	Work on takedown and counter by the numbers
4:15–4:20	30-second escapes
4:20–4:35	Takedown tournament
4:35–5:00	Pinning combinations
5:00–5:10	Chain wrestling
5:10–5:30	One-minute matches — live

SAMPLE BASEBALL PRACTICE PLAN

3:30–3:40	Loosen up — throw
3:40–3:50	Pepper
3:50–4:00	Base running
4:00–4:10	Sliding — demonstration and practice
4:25–4:40	Shag flies sideline to sideline on the run
4:40–5:00	Outfield shag — infield practice
5:00–5:30	Hit (infield and outfielders continue)

SAMPLE FOOTBALL PRACTICE PLAN—OFFENSE

3:30-3:40	Calisthenics—loosen and stretch—reaction
3:40–3:50	Run tires, anti-fumble (backs and ends); seven-man sled (tackles, centers and guards)
3:50–4:00	Run sidelines (backs and ends); two-man sled (tackles, centers and guards)
4:00–4:10	Demonstrate new play to full team

4:10–4:25	Run plays — pass cut — line scrimmage
4:25–4:55	Full team dummy scrimmage — Red and White vs. Blue Shirts
4:55–5:00	Live punt
5:00–5:15	Full team live pass offense
5:15–5:25	Full team live scrimmage — goal line offense
5:25–5:30	Fun time (sprints)

Agreement on offense and defense.   Up to this point, the head coach should have given a great deal of thought to the kind of offense and defense (when appropriate) to use during the season. By doing this, the head coach is then ready to present these ideas to the coaching staff. It is at this point that every coach evaluates and questions what the head coach is proposing. Some ideas will be rejected, some accepted, adjustments will be made, but above all, when the debating has ended, every coach must accept the decision of the group or deciding vote of the head coach in order to do a good job of teaching. When these decisions are based on the personnel who will make up the team and who will have to play the game, it is easier to reach agreement.

Scouting assignments.   The pre-season coaches' meeting is a good time to make scouting assignments, too, when scouting is appropriate. This is one more item that should be gotten out of the way before the season begins, to make one less thing to think about later on. If the decision has been made to scout, the number of times each team will be scouted and which coach will scout which team should be put on a master schedule and posted in the coaches' office for the duration of the season.

Each coach is then responsible for finding out the location of the games to scout, and double-checking the date and starting time. If this is a sport where games are filmed, and a film exchange has been worked out with the next opponent, the scout should also be sure to make arrangements for the exchange. Scouting passes are normally handled by the athletic director or faculty manager.

Scouting forms (when appropriate) should be revised and reviewed during this time also. It is a good idea to keep these in a central file. In this manner each coach can get as many forms as necessary, whenever the need arises, without having to bother the head coach with yet another detail.

Cutting.   One of the most difficult decisions a coaching staff must resolve is whether or not youngsters should be cut from a team. The question is not so difficult when coaches feel little empathy for youngsters. But if coaches were to look at the question through their own eyes, assuming that it was their daughter or son who was getting cut, the issue takes on new meaning.

To youngsters who have grown up dreaming of the day when they could participate on the high school team, getting cut from the squad can be an extremely traumatic experience. The disappointment and sense of failure can be so severe that it sometimes affects the youngster's personality, behavior, and work in school. This phenomenon of athletic exclusion can have far reaching effects that we do not totally comprehend.

Ideally, no one should be cut from a team unless it is for disciplinary reasons. The ultimate in absurdity is a policy of cutting youngsters who try out for junior high school teams. This is the time to teach skills, and to create interest, rather than a time to pick the high school varsity. When cuts are made at this level, it is usually done for the convenience of the coach and for no other legitimate reason. Too many people, and not enough equipment or space, are not reasons for cutting at the junior high level — these are excuses.

There is no proof that daily practice sessions for junior high school athletes will make them better performers as seniors in high school. Likewise, there is no proof that a two-hour practice session in junior high school is better for a youngster than a one-hour session. Therefore, if space or equipment seems to be a problem, there is no reason why a squad cannot be broken down into small workable groups for practice purposes. In this way, several different groups could practice short periods of time each day after school or on alternating days.

The purpose of junior high school athletics should be to give every youngster every chance to participate in sport. Under no circumstances should junior high school coaches be permitted or directed to cut their squads. Winning is fun, but this should never become the number-one priority in junior high school athletics.

Young, ambitious coaches tend to be quick about picking out the best junior high athletes and cutting all the rest. They are eager to win in order to prove their superior ability as a coach. Consequently, the head varsity coach must make sure the junior high coaches know the priorities of their program. If the head varsity coach has several years of experience, that coach knows all too well that the smallest, meekest, and most awkward twelve year old youngster could well grow up into the finest varsity athlete of the senior class; that is, if the youngster is allowed to participate and mature without the threat of being cut during the ungainly growing-up adolescent years.

The junior high school coach who can look at a group of youngsters and predict with 100 per cent accuracy which ones will become varsity athletes has not yet been born. And when a junior high school coach cuts a squad, that is precisely what is being done.

On the high school level it would seem that the only justifiable reasons for cutting youngsters would be (1) serious disciplinary problems, (2) attitude problems that are having or could have adverse effects on the team, and (3) possibility of serious injury to an individual because of a gross lack of motor skills or size.

There is one other possibility to consider in cutting a team. When space, facilities and coaching are all limited, having a number of unskilled upperclassmen on the roster can be detrimental to the team. For example, a junior who never played tennis, and decides to try out for the team might fit this category. When these people take their turns in practice, they are using up valuable practice time for the highly skilled performers, thereby hampering the development of these individuals. Seniors who sit on the sidelines can become unhappy and this breeds problems, too.

Photo by Laurie Usher.

There does not appear to be a simple, clear-cut solution to the problem of cutting a team. As a general rule, if circumstances dictate a policy of cutting, it should not occur in junior high school, or on the freshman and sophomore levels. By the time youngsters become juniors, they have had several years to demonstrate that they possess some characteristics necessary to be an athlete. If they have not, and in the opinion of the staff cuts must be made, this would be the time.

In fairness to the individuals involved, a head coach should have the decency to meet individually with each youngster who is being cut, and carefully explain why this action is being taken. This is never easy to do, nor is it a pleasant thing to do. But the practice of putting a list on the locker room bulletin board and then retreating to the safety of the coach's office is cowardly, and is not consistent with the image coaches try to project.

Many coaches adopt the attitude that if practices are hard enough work, people will quit the team on their own, thereby eliminating the need of cutting anyone. There might be some truth to this. The biggest fallacy lies in the fact that an entire squad could pay the price of too much work over a long season because the coach cannot or will not make a decision regarding cuts. The whole question deserves careful thought and discussion on the part of the entire staff with the final decision based on a thorough consideration of all the ramifications and alternatives.

Evaluation of personnel. Of all the items on the agenda for pre-season staff meetings, none is more crucial than evaluating personnel. When evaluating personnel, certain principles should be understood by the staff. The first is that under no circumstances should people be played on potential alone. The saddest comments made by coaches are the ones which go, "If only he would do the job," or "Potentially she is a great one." More times than not the same statement will be made about this individual when the season ends. The important thing is that at a certain point in a season an athlete is either doing the job, or not. If not, this player should be benched in favor of someone who is, regardless of potential. Games are won by people who are doing what is expected, not by people who might do it someday.

This can be a source of great frustration to a staff. They should not fall into the trap of assuming that the next game is when a youngster like this will finally begin to produce, after he or she has already stumbled around for several games or contests.

The second principle of evaluating personnel is that players must be selected on the basis of desire and ability. High school athletes who rate high on desire will not necessarily rate high on ability. On the other hand, those who rate high on ability will not always rate high on desire. When an athlete rates equally high on desire and ability, this player is a super-prospect. Picking out this kind of athlete is easy. The difficulty arises after these people have been sorted out in trying to pick out other people who might be winners. The key to this is the degree of desire youngsters have in their hearts to play the game. Consequently, coaches must look for athletes with high desire, and get them into the line-up even though they might not rate too high on ability. These are youngsters who don't have much ability, but don't realize it, and while they might not be able to execute all the fundamentals properly, they know how to play the game.

The last choice in picking personnel is the individual with ability and little or no desire. These people are losers, and coaches who play this kind of athlete will also end up as losers, and the team will look bad in the process.

This principle can best be illustrated by the following diagram:

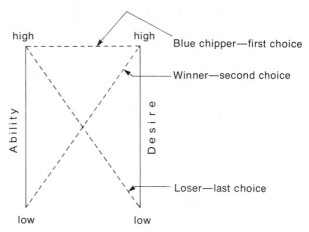

Photo by Laurie Usher.

The third principle is that coaches must establish priorities, according to what particular abilities they want in members of the team. For example, if a basketball coach decided he wanted shooters, then shooting ability would become high priority in evaluating prospects; if a field hockey coach determined that speed was her most important concern, this quality would become a high priority factor, while another coach might place a high premium on all around athletic ability. Predetermining specific priorities helps immeasurably in choosing a team.

The fourth principle of player evaluation is that, in the final analysis, players must be chosen on the basis of game-type situations. The best situation is an actual game or contest, and the next best is a practice meet or game with an opponent from another school.

Generally speaking, there are three kinds of athletes in regard to practice versus game or meet performance. First, there are those who look great in practice, and who also perform well in competition; there are those who do not practice particularly well but are great game time athletes; and finally, there are those who look great in practice but rarely if ever do well in competition. There is no way any coach can predict how an athlete will react in competition. Therefore, the ultimate test in evaluating personnel is the game, the meet, or the match.

This should be one of the primary purposes of interschool pre-season contests. This is the time to find out who the winners are, rather than worrying about which team is scoring all the points in an informal scrimmage. Coaches who go through these practice contests without filming or video-taping the entire session, and without giving every member of the team an opportunity to participate, are misusing one of the finest tools of evaluation in high school athletics.

Other methods of evaluating personnel should be discussed and agreed upon during these initial staff meetings also. Grading forms, to be used in player evaluation while viewing game films, need to be considered. Basically, the three kinds of forms are those that are used for a percentage grade, those that utilize written comments only, and a combination of these two.

Sociograms are a possibility to be considered in deciding on a starting line-up. Players sometimes see each other quite differently than the coaches do, and the use of a sociogram can point out discrepancies in this regard. This method is particularly useful in helping to create a feeling of cohesiveness on a team, simply because if the majority of a squad rejects a teammate for some reason, the use of a sociogram will quickly point this out. A coaching staff can use sociograms as a guide in making whatever changes they think necessary, and may also find them useful in counseling a youngster and in identifying specific problems.

Agility drills, time in sprints, quickness, and balance are commonly used methods in evaluating player personnel. But they must be used in conjunction with other criteria already mentioned, and with attention to player attitude.

Attitude can be described in many ways in sport, but generally it means that a youngster is teachable, cooperative, willing to abide by whatever rules are agreed upon, and is anxious to work hard to become a good athlete. Poor attitude problems can cause enough conflict on a team that, if left unchecked, can permeate the entire squad and literally destroy a season. This problem, if severe enough, can also carry over into the next season, and continue to create problems.

Another possibility for evaluating athletes is to initiate or develop methods by which individuals can challenge the person playing ahead of them. The main advantage in this is that it can do much toward eliminating grumbling by members of the second or third team. When people have a chance to challenge, they either succeed or fail, and in either case the results are their own doing, not that of a coach. Consequently, if they fail, the blame cannot be placed on anyone else and they are satisfied that at least they had a fair chance to show what they could do. This is an excellent way to recognize desire and also to keep the players on first team from getting complacent. Some coaches limit this to pre-season practice only.

Intangibles such as courage, desire, toughness, competitive spirit, and constant competitiveness (not giving up when losing is inevitable) are extremely important in evaluating athletes, but are very difficult to measure. Nevertheless, every possible effort should be made by a coaching staff to try to recognize these qualities, or the lack of them, in each individual on the team. Obviously, the sooner these unknowns become clear the sooner the best line-up can be determined.

Depth chart.   The use of a depth chart is a useful organizational tool, particularly when large numbers of players are involved. The first step in creating one is to write all players' names down beside the position they played the preceding season, or the position they indicate they want to play when filling out the brief questionnaire earlier (Chapter 6). The staff's next job is to create a depth chart making sure that every letterman is listed somewhere on the first team, if at all possible. This sometimes means changing positions for someone, and this is where player evaluation comes into play. But it must be done, otherwise some letter winners will be listed behind other letter winners, while another position will be assigned to an inexperienced player listed on the first team. Unless a coach is blessed with an incredible amount of material, this is a waste of talent and playing experience.

Since the staff has determined what the team will be designed to do, changing the positions of players to fit the overall scheme is not such a difficult task. When these changes are made, however, it is important that the head coach talk to each individual player involved, to explain why the change was made, in order to head off any possible morale problem.

As the depth chart is being filled in, the question as to who the best five, nine or eleven athletes are becomes the primary question confronting the staff. When this is determined, these players must be assigned a position on the first team immediately during this pre-season meeting. It makes no difference how many people sign up for a team — there will always be five best, eleven best, and so on. It is the coaches' job to try to determine who these people are before practice begins, at least in team sports where large numbers of participants are involved. After the lettermen have been assigned a position, the other positions should normally be filled by seniors who have game experience, then juniors, and sophomores.

The primary purpose of a depth chart is organizational. The players need to understand this at the outset, and their initial position or place on the team as listed on the depth chart is no guarantee that they will remain there. But the responsibility for creating changes in the line-up rests with those listed on the second or third teams. When they prove to the coaches that they are better than the players listed ahead of them they will be promoted at once. To insure that no one is overlooked or in the wrong position, every youngster on the depth chart should be evaluated by the coach or coaching staff after each pre-season practice session. The players should be aware that this continuous evaluation is going on also. This is important to the "down the liners," because they need to know they aren't being overlooked or forgotten.

Without organization of this type, initial practice sessions would be chaos, and would remain so until the team shakes down and positions are assigned. By creating a depth chart ahead of time, much valuable time is saved, and a great deal of confusion prevented.

Many coaches establish the idea that after letter winners have filled certain positions, the seniors who have not lettered get first chance at the open positions in the line-up. The reasoning behind this is that normally the seniors bring playing experience to the team, and generally a senior team stands a better chance of winning than one made up of underclassmen. Another reason for doing this is to give the seniors a fair chance to show whether or not they can do the job. In many cases they have been out for the team for several years, working hard, and now that they are seniors, they deserve this chance. Whether they make it or not depends on them and the person listed behind them on the depth chart. If a senior is a competitor, that senior will rise to this challenge and make a real contribution during the season.

Master practice schedule.   Once these important decisions have been made, the next bit of planning should be directed toward the actual pre-season practice schedule. The first step is to list every aspect of the sport that must be covered in order to get the players ready for the first game or meet. Each of these items should then be put onto a master schedule which includes every practice session up to the opening of the season. It is absolutely essential that this schedule be adhered to each day, regardless of the players progress, if they are to be ready for the opening of the season.

When coaches develop each practice plan based on the master schedule, the team will then have been exposed to every phase of the game necessary for the opening of the season. Naturally, the players won't master everything immediately, but by reviewing each day, and continuing to practice on all their shortcomings the rest of the season, these problems will finally be resolved. Most coaches find that trying to continue to teach many new things once a season has begun is not as satisfactory as doing the bulk of the teaching in pre-season. The rest of the season can be devoted to polishing the rough spots left at the end of pre-season practice.

In reality, this is nothing more than budgeting the limited pre-season time to make certain all the basics are covered. Sometimes coaches get concerned because the players aren't executing properly, and so they continue to teach that particular thing at the expense of some other phase of the sport. As a result, they begin to run out of time, and at the last minute attempt to concentrate a lot of teaching into a short period of time. This is poor planning, a poor teaching method and is never satisfactory.

Student helpers.   For the benefit of the coach responsible for the student managers, the duties of these youngsters should be clarified at this initial staff meeting also. It is possible to work this out earlier, but each coach should have a copy, in order to know what is expected of the managers.

The same holds true of the duties of the student trainer, and use of the training room space. These responsibilities, duties, and limitations must be clarified and supervised carefully, in order to prevent more serious problems from arising through the use of student trainers.

Pre-game, post-game.   Pre-season is also the time to decide on the procedures to be followed for pre-game warmup at home and away, halftime, for athletic events that have one, and post-game. The value of pre-game warmup is questionable, but it is traditional, and probably has a settling effect on a team. Whatever a staff decides to do prior to the beginning of a contest, it must be planned, to prevent last-minute confusion.

Halftime plans usually break down into getting to the locker room quickly and budgeting the time so that all needs can be taken care of. The actual conduct of a coach at halftime usually depends on the situation and is an area every head coach must give a great deal of thought. This includes what to say when the team is behind, ahead, tied, playing well, or playing poorly. Experience is the best teacher in this situation.

Post-game planning must include what to do when a team loses, and what to do when a team wins. Most coaches know what to do when the team is victorious, but give little thought to how to conduct themselves in a locker room gloomy with defeat. Numerous possibilities must be discussed and considered by all the coaches simply because situations in a locker room or on a bus on the way home after a loss vary, and a coach must be well enough prepared to know how to deal with them.

The staff should also discuss plans for the day after a game. If the game is played on a day preceding a school day, this is no problem. However, it is a different matter entirely when a game is played on a Friday or Saturday. Unless some plans are made to get the team together, the coaches probably won't see the team until after school on Monday, Consequently, two or three full days will have passed since the contest was played.

If the game was lost this means that the people on the team will waste a great deal of time brooding over the loss. It also means that if a player discovers an injury the morning after a game, the coach might not find out about it for several days. The time lost in treatment might prevent a youngster from competing in the next game.

Bringing a team together the morning after a game deserves consideration, because there are several advantages in doing this. Bumps, bruises, and other injuries can be cared for immediately, thereby saving valuable time in the healing process; if the team won, this gives them a chance to enjoy the win a little longer with their teammates; a relaxed, informal workout can be good for morale; if the game was filmed and the development service is good, the team can take a quick look at the game films; and most importantly, the coach can tell the squad some things about the next opponent, to get the team thinking ahead instead of celebrating too long or feeling bad too long, whatever the case might be. These workouts seem to make Monday practices a little easier, too, because it cuts down on the lay-off time between the game and Monday's session.

Pep rallies.   One of the questions that should be decided upon early concerns pep rallies and the role of the high school cheerleaders in relation to their involvement during the season. Traditionally this has involved coaches of football, basketball, and perhaps wrestling. In many situations there simply are no pep rallies for the rest of the boys' teams or any of the girls' teams. Pep rallies are not as integral a part of a season as they once were. In some sports, weekly pep rallies were as much a part of a season as the game itself, and were used to give the student body an opportunity to participate, to create an atmosphere of excitement, and to develop school spirit. The effect of a pep rally on a team has always been questionable, because they are usually held several hours before a game, and any positive emotional effects they have on a team usually wear off by game time.

On the other hand, some coaches prefer not to have pep rallies at all, because the emotional pitch can become so high that the players are emotionally drained by game time. It is generally felt that if a team is not being prepared mentally all week long, a short pep rally on game day will not help them anyway.

However, a coaching staff and the team must decide on whether or not they want pep rallies and, if so, how many. This information is important to the principal for scheduling purposes. When the dates are predetermined and publicized, the faculty appreciate this, too, so that they can plan accordingly.

If it were up to the cheerleaders, there would probably be weekly pep rallies all year long. This is particularly true today, because the role of a cheerleader has changed from that of a leader of cheers to that of a performer and entertainer of the student body. In spite of this, the head coach should work with the cheerleaders in the planning of these rallies, in order to provide some guidelines for creating the kind of effect necessary. This can be difficult for coaches of girls' teams, and some of the boys' teams as well, because the cheerleaders often, as stated earlier, confine all their efforts to two or three of the boys' teams only.

Oftentimes, members of the faculty resent time being taken from their classes in order to hold a pep rally. There is no way this can be completely avoided, but if the faculty can be shown that well-planned pep rallies are one way to create unity in a school, and to give the student body an opportunity to feel a part of an exciting school function, they might be more understanding and patient.

When a coach establishes good rapport with the cheerleaders, they can be of great assistance in helping to prepare a team mentally for an upcoming game. They can help by hanging signs and posters through-out the school, taping various materials on the players' lockers, and possibly helping to decorate the locker room for a special game. Nor-mally, they are most anxious to help in any way possible, and are very receptive to any suggestions in this regard.

Awards.   Another item on the agenda for the pre-season staff meetings concerns awards to be given out during the season and post-season. Some schools have adopted policies stating that the only awards granted to athletes are letters given by the school, based on playing time in the games.

In some situations awards are issued weekly as an incentive, while at other places various awards are given to individuals at the end of the season. These are given by the school to individuals the coaches choose, or they might be given by businesses or individuals in the community not directly connected with the school.

The decision of whether or not to indulge in different kinds of awards usually depends on the coaching staff. The important consideration is that, if this is done, the extent of the awards given must not assume proportions of absurdity. When this occurs the awards become gimmicks, their value is cheapened, and their purpose becomes suspect. For example, giving trophies or other awards to the most friendly athlete on the team, the athlete with the neatest uniform, the athlete with the best form while swinging a bat, or giving ten special awards to an eleven-man team seems ridiculous, and has little bearing on points put up on the scoreboard.

Allowing individuals in the community to pick certain players for awards has no place in high school athletics either. Often these awards are excuses for free advertising for a business while using the boy or girl, and the objectivity in these selections is always questionable. Instead of having a positive effect on a team, these awards often cause ill feelings among both the team and parents. There are enough problems in coaching, without adding to them by getting involved in promotional gimmicks such as these.

Recognizing an outstanding player or two every week on the basis of game films or judgment of the staff could be the extent of in-season awards. Awards should not necessarily be anything concrete or material, but rather a form of recognition for a job well done.

If athletes are properly motivated, their rewards will come from competing and playing well. Presenting a number of trophies and numerous other awards simply gives youngsters the impression that when they do something they are to expect some award in return. This should not be an objective in athletics, nor should it be perpetuated.

In this same light, coaches eventually are confronted with a request to establish or accept a memorial award or scholarship in memory of an athlete or coach. The thought behind this is certainly understandable, particularly when the present coaches knew the person to be honored. Normally, it falls to the coaches to select an athlete to receive this award and this always presents problems.

There are drawbacks to these memorial awards. Coaches get involved in singling out one athlete to be honored. This can become an unpleasant task because there are usually several outstanding people and to legitimately choose one as being the most deserving is often an impossibility. When new coaches join the staff, the name on the memorial award is unknown to them, and therefore the whole exercise has little meaning. Eventually, the coaches who permitted the establishment of this award will be gone, and so will all the students who knew the individual. This usually relegates the whole exercise to just another award that long ago lost its special significance. Instead of these awards, a permanent gift to the school with the individual's name attached or a self-perpetuating scholarship are two possibilities that could be considered.

It is easy to agree to accept the idea of special awards. But coaches must remember that once they are established, the athletic department will have to live with them for a long time.

Obviously, there are many important decisions a coaching staff must make before the season begins, if it values the importance of thorough organization. Staff meetings at this time will always take several days, or the better part of a week and are usually most beneficial just prior to the beginning of the season.

Team meeting.   The last organizational meeting to be held before the first practice is a team meeting. All the decisions and plans have been agreed on by the coaching staff, and at this point all the attention is directed toward the team itself. The team meeting can be held just prior to, or immediately after, equipment issue. In some states, there are definite rules stating when the first team meeting can be held and the coach should be aware of the ruling if it exists.

The primary purpose of this first meeting is organizational in nature, particularly when the head coach is new. This meeting should include the following:

1. Notebook issue (if there is one). Time should be taken to explain the purpose of the notebook, how to take care of it and a brief discussion of the contents.
2. An explanation of the roles of the captain or co-captains is appropriate at this time. These responsibilities should already have been discussed with the captains when they were elected. It is important that the team understand how the coach perceives the role of captains and what is expected of them.
3. Practice procedures must be clarified at this first meeting, including attendance and legitimate excuses for being absent. If this is made clear in the beginning, a lot of problems with cutting practice will be prevented. This is a potential problem area, and therefore the ground rules should be established immediately.
4. Rules that seem necessary in order for the team to have a successful year should be discussed at this initial meeting.
5. Training rules might exist or they might not. If they do they might be sport-specific and determined by the players themselves; the coaches might issue them by edict, or they could rest on policy created by an athletic board. The important thing is that the rules are sensible and appropriate and that the team understands why they exist. Parents should also know what these rules are. In this manner they can help see that they are not violated.

6. Insurance coverage should be discussed. Many schools make accident insurance mandatory for athletes and provide a policy at a minimal fee. Others offer a policy through the school but will accept evidence that the family has adequate insurance coverage themselves. This area of concern is normally school policy and the coach's role is merely to explain it and see that policy is observed.

7. All physical cards and eligibility information must be turned in at this time or at equipment issue. When athletes learn that no equipment will be issued without a completed physical card they will have them ready to hand in. By doing it this way, the coach has one less chore to think about during the season.

8. Seniors should be asked to stay after the meeting for a special session as described in Chapter 6.

9. Locker room discipline needs to be discussed before practice begins. It is a fact that many serious injuries have occurred in locker rooms, mostly through horseplay. This cannot be tolerated, for the athletes' own welfare. Some coaches put a time limit on how long athletes can spend in the locker room after practice. The sooner they clear out the less chance there is for fooling around and getting someone hurt. Injuries of this sort are inexcusable. Locker room discipline also includes hanging up personal equipment instead of letting it lie on the floor or on benches for the managers to take care of. Athletes should also be encouraged to make an effort to keep the locker room area free of trash. And under no circumstances should they ever bring glass containers into the locker room.

10. If there are cuts to be made, the team should know why and the criteria to be used in the decision.

11. A team clinic (Chapter 6) should be the final item on the agenda at this first team meeting.

After all of this has been accomplished, the fun begins with the actual practice sessions, and then, game time. With careful attention to detail and organization of the preceding items, a team and coaching staff has taken the first big step toward a successful year. At this point in time, the team and coaches are ready to go to work, knowing exactly what they want to do, what they must do, and the best way in which to do it in order to win. This is when the many long, tedious hours involved in pre-season planning begin to pay off.

The following 30 rules,[1] furnished by the University of Pittsburgh School of Business Administration, are based on the experience of scores of successful executives. They provide excellent guidelines for people in positions of leadership. Consequently, these are of great value to a head coach in dealing with a coaching staff and team.

---

[1]Air Force R.O.T.C., Air University Leadership Training, 1968, p. 32.

Photo courtesy of The Pennsylvania State University Still Photography Services.

THIRTY RULES FOR GETTING THINGS DONE THROUGH PEOPLE

1. *Make people on your staff want to do things.* Making people want to do things is a much more skilled and subtle process than selling them on doing it, and usually more effective.
2. *Study assistants and determine what makes each tick.* Most experts say that knowing one's personnel is the main tool of leadership.
3. *Delegate responsibility for details to assistants.* Delegating responsibility is the essence of leadership.
4. *Be a good listener.* Always give the other person the right-of-way when you both start to speak at the same time. A good leader must be careful not to develop the "executive syndrome," whereby he listens to an assistant for two minutes and then tunes him out.
5. *Criticize constructively.* Make sure all the facts are clear. Then suggest a constructive course of action for the future. Better still, have the person being corrected suggest his own corrective action. Constructive criticism should be preceded with praise when possible.
6. *Criticize in private.* Criticizing an individual in public will create resentment through embarrassment or humiliation.
7. *Praise in public.* Make certain that the praise is deserved, and that everyone involved is included.
8. *Be considerate.* Nothing contributes more to building a strong, hard-working, and loyal staff than a considerate boss.
9. *Give credit where it is due.* The leader who takes credit for the work of a subordinate is something of a tyrant. Credit for new ideas belongs to the person who developed them.
10. *Avoid domination.* The effective leader thinks of the staff as working with him, not for him. A dominant leader sometimes stifles people with initiative.
11. *Show interest in and appreciation of the other fellow.* It is a good idea to let an assistant know that you are concerned about him and that you appreciate the quality of his work. This will pay great dividends.
12. *Make your wishes known by suggestions or requests.* These can be dictated but there is less chance of resentment when using suggestions or requests.
13. *Be sure to tell the reasons for your requests.* People want to know both what they are doing and why they are doing it.

14. *Let your assistants know about your plans and programs even when they are in an early stage.* As a rule, the sum of the ideas of your assistants, plus your own, will ordinarily be better than yours alone.

15. *Never forget that the leader sets the style for his people.* If you are careless, late for meetings, or unenthusiastic, your assistants can be expected to follow suit.

16. *Play up the positive.* For most people, praise provides better motivation than criticism.

17. *Be consistent.* A leader who flies off the handle or gyrates wildly in mood, reaction, and manner bewilders his staff.

18. *Show your people that you have confidence in them and that you expect them to do their best.* People in general tend to live up to what is expected of them. At least, when goals and standards are realistic, most are able to do a first-rate job. If a leader shows that he has confidence in his staff and expects high standards of efficiency, that is usually what he'll get.

19. *Ask your assistants for their counsel and help.* This gets a staff involved. The goals of the group become their goal also. And people tend to consider their goals to be important. Consequently, they approach these in a more conscientious manner.

20. *When you are wrong or make a mistake, admit it.* No person expects a leader to be absolutely perfect. No leader loses face when he admits he was wrong — if he isn't wrong too often. By admitting mistakes, a leader gains the confidence of a staff in fairness and honesty.

21. *Give courteous hearing to ideas from your staff.* Even fantastic ideas deserve a full hearing. No idea should be disparaged or ridiculed.

22. *If an idea is adopted, tell the originator why.* If the originator knows why you approve of an idea, then his line of thought is reinforced. He is likely to apply it to other problems. If the idea is not adopted, tell him why, too. Ideas that are presented and never heard of again discourage additional ideas and produce resentment.

23. *Give weight to the fact that people carry out their own ideas best.* It is good tactics to deliberately plant seeds of ideas in the thoughts of others. Thus the person who executes the idea will feel that it is his own.

24. *Be careful what you say and how you say it.* You must consider the impact that words and voices have played in the life of the average person. Harshness and curtness, for example, are associated with anxiety, reprimand, disapproval, and hostility. Words can be spoken in an atmosphere of approval, even when you are criticizing an assistant. In any event, effective communication is a major tool of leadership and human relations. Carelessly chosen words, or an unintended inflection of the voice can breed unhappiness and misunderstanding. Words, forgotten the moment they are spoken, can cause unproductive days and sleepless nights for those who hear them.

25. *Don't be upset by moderate grousing.* In small doses, griping serves as a safety valve for letting off steam. When vicious personal griping is prevalent, this is another story, and can destroy a staff. In this case, it is up to the leader to find out the cause and correct it immediately.

26. *Use every opportunity to build up in assistants a sense of the importance of their work.* People like to consider their role in any job as an important one. Everyone likes to feel he is making some kind of contribution in order to function well. It is the leader's job to insure that assistants feel this way.

27. *Give your people goals, a sense of direction, something to strive for and to achieve.* In order to work more effectively, people need to know

where they are going, what the goals of the organization are, and why these are the goals.

28. *Keep your people informed on matters affecting them.* Whenever possible, let your staff know in advance. When people know what is coming and why, they are able to gear their thinking more realistically to the goal.

29. *Give assistants a chance to take part in decisions, particularly those affecting them.* When people have had a say in a decision, they are much more likely to go along with it enthusiastically. Even if they don't agree, they will go along, since they had a part in it; at least their views were considered.

30. *Let your people know where they stand.* Perhaps the most devastating work situation that can be devised is one in which a person doesn't know where he stands with the boss. He must know what you expect. The task of evaluating personnel is among the most difficult human relations problems with which any leader must deal. As a very general rule, evaluations that involve both praise and criticism are the most effective form of long-range motivation. But the criticism must be constructive.

DISCUSSION QUESTIONS

1. Many coaches feel that the best assistants should be coaching on the lower levels, to insure the teaching of sound fundamentals to young athletes. What is your opinion and why?

2. Should every team have training rules? Why?

3. What are your ideas of discipline?

4. Is your appearance as a coach important, and why? How about the appearance of your staff?

5. What is the importance of having a practice plan?

6. If you must, how will you handle cutting players? High school level? Junior high?

7. How important is team unity? How can you, as a coach, encourage and develop it?

8. What is the process of acclimitization? Of what value is it?

9. Which quality in an athlete seems most desirable to you, desire or ability? Why?

10. Why is the "game" the best way to evaluate an athlete; or is it?

11. How can coaches insure the right kind of people get elected as captains?

12. "Don't take anything for granted where high school athletes are concerned." What does this mean?

13. Interpret this statement: "the first team never loses in practice."

14. Give some examples of ways in which coaches can "stack the deck" in drills.

15. How will you expect your team to dress when travelling to an away contest?

16. What kind of awards would you give your team, if any?

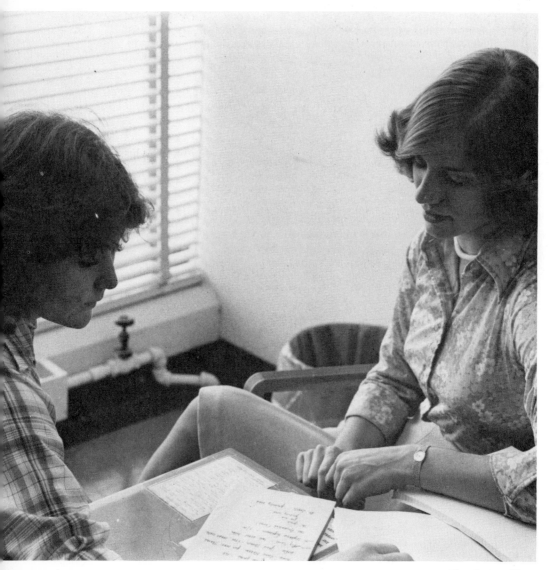

CHAPTER 8

Photo by Jean Dixon.

8

THE RECRUITING PROCESS

The relationship between high school coaches and college recruiters is one that deserves a great deal of consideration. It is important for high school coaches to understand the whole recruiting process. This process includes the youngster, the parents, the college recruiter, the guidance office, and finally, the high school coach. This understanding is necessary in order to provide the guidance youngsters frequently need when being recruited. As a rule, this facet of coaching is given very little thought by beginning coaches until they come face to face with a recruiting situation, and as a result, mistakes can occur.

In the past, the problems and concerns associated with recruiting have not mattered to coaches of girls' teams, since athletic scholarships simply were not available to them in most parts of the country. This has changed, and athletic scholarships for women are now a reality nationwide. Consequently, knowledge of the recruiting process is essential to coaches of all high school athletic teams if they are to assume any responsibility in the recruiting process.

Many people perceive recruiting as an evil in sport and imagine all sorts of illegal deals and promises in connection with the process. There is no question that there have been abuses, and little doubt that there will continue to be abuses. The important thing in this regard is that the high school coach doesn't perpetuate this by being a party to illegal recruiting practices.

On the other hand, the majority of college recruiters abide by the rules and make an honest effort to recruit an athlete through their own salesmanship, and not by under the table deals.

Since there are definite rules and regulations governing the entire recruiting process, every high school coach should have these at his or her disposal, and should be familiar with this material. The National Collegiate Athletic Association publishes a pamphlet titled *A Guide to the College Bound Student Athlete* which summarizes the rules and regulations governing recruiting, eligibility, and financial aid. This is available from the NCAA, P.O. Box 1906, Shawnee Mission, Kansas 66222. In addition, the Association of Intercollegiate Athletics for Women have spelled out their rules for recruiting female athletes in the *AIAW Handbook*. This material is available from AAHPER Publications, 1201 Sixteenth St. N.W., Washington, D.C. 20036. There are differences between the NCAA rules and the AIAW rules, but since these do change, these differences will not be listed here.

Every coach, at one time or another, will be confronted with recruiting, providing the individual stays in coaching long enough. Basically there are three attitudes a coach can assume when an athlete on the team is good enough to participate in college athletics: (1) the coach can take a "hands off" position, and allow the recruiter, the athlete, and the parents to handle the whole process; (2) the coach can participate in the recruiting process when asked; or (3) the coach can take the initiative, and contact college coaches to try and interest them in a prospective student athlete.

A coach's first responsibility to athletes is to take the time to educate them to the ways of recruiters. The pressure of recruiting is so competitive that many colleges are now beginning to make exploratory contact with sophomores in high school. Therefore, this orientation should not be confined to seniors alone. In the case of underclass students receiving correspondence from colleges, there is little a high school coach can do except to play it down as much as possible. This must be done in order to prevent youngsters from overestimating their ability, and possibly getting too sure of themselves because some college has contacted them. One sure way to do this is to remind the youngsters that if they are interested in competing in college and the possibility of getting a scholarship, the first step is to make the high school team. They need to understand, too, that the recommendation from the high school coach can be most influential, and if they don't keep their feet on the ground, develop a good attitude, and perform well in high school, the chances of an athletic scholarship are almost zero.

Another point high school coaches and athletes should be clear on is that a contact from a college coach is not necessarily a scholarship offer. This often creates a lot of misunderstanding on the part of the high school coach, the athlete, and the athlete's family. This occurs simply because they do not understand that college coaches make preliminary contact with many promising athletes. Therefore, youngsters and their parents need to know that initial contacts only mean that a coach or several coaches are aware that they have accomplished some special thing, and that they will be watching their progress throughout the rest of the season or the rest of their high school career. At that time the college coaches might or might not decide to actively recruit the youngster. Consequently, high school athletes should learn how to interpret contacts and not assume that a scholarship offer will necessarily follow. Instead, the high school coach could use this as a tool for motivating an athlete to further accomplishments.

The next point that should be made concerns the role of the recruiter. Athletes must understand that this individual is a coach who is also in the business of selling a particular university to the youngster and parents. The youngster should keep this in mind as recruiters extol the virtues of the various institutions. Therefore, the only way to really learn about a college or university is to visit the campus and talk with athletes and non-athletes already enrolled there. As a rule these people are not in the recruiting business, and will be quite frank about the college or university.

Sometimes a college recruiter will make promises to a prospect that cannot possibly be honored. The normal approach is to promise a youngster a starting position at least by the sophomore year, and suggest that there is also a good chance of playing as a freshman. Far too often this is merely dangling the bait of instant success before a youngster, but it is often taken as fact by the recruit. The only legitimate promise athletes should listen to is that the university can give them an education if they want one badly enough, and that they will be given a fair chance to make the team.

In order to provide some assistance to senior members of a team, a high school coach could begin by having each individual fill out a questionnaire such as the one on page 226.

Photo by Dick Brown, Centre Daily Times.

---

1. Name_____ Class Rank_____
   Height_____ Weight_____
   College Board Scores _____

2. Address _____ phone_____
   _____

3. Do you plan on going to college?_____

4. Are you interested in playing college *(sport)*? _____

5. Preference of school (large, small, conference, state):
   _____

6. What course of study do you plan to follow?_____

7. Will your folks need financial aid to send you to college?____

8. Are you willing to work while in college in order to help pay
   your expenses?_____

9. If you can, list your first three choices of colleges you would
   like to attend:
   1. _____
   2. _____
   3. _____

10. Do you want any assistance from this coaching staff in
    making arrangements to get into the college of your choice?
    Yes_____ No_____

11. List any individual honors you have received.
    _____
    _____
    _____

12. What is your best performance or season record (when
    appropriate)?
    _____

13. What athletic performance records do you hold?
    _____

The primary purposes of this questionnaire are to see if any of the seniors want to go on to college, to see if any of them are interested in participating in athletics there and to find out if they want any help from the coach.

Whether youngsters want direct assistance or not, the coach still has an obligation to clarify the recruiting process and offer some suggestions for the athletes' consideration. For example, the coach should:

1. explain the importance of choosing a college because it offers a degree in the field that is of interest to the athlete. An athlete should not choose a college solely on its athletic reputation, nor choose a school simply because of an offer of financial aid. If aid is offered, it is sometimes helpful for an athlete to ask the question, "Would I attend that college if no aid were offered?" It

might also help if the youngsters faced the question of whether or not they would attend a specific college if they couldn't participate in sport any more. A decision to attend any college based solely on financial aid, or solely to participate in sport, could be an unwise choice, and consequently, an unhappy choice.

2. discuss the size of school and caliber of competition which might offer the greatest opportunity for success. Most youngsters (and their parents) tend to overestimate individual ability in sport. This can create serious problems, especially with ambitious parents.

3. suggest that they consider several levels of colleges if they are unsure of what their own potential is.

4. encourage youngsters to give serious thought to the colleges they are interested in, and to attempt to narrow the possibilities down to just a few as soon as possible. In this manner, they are choosing the college rather than the college choosing them. This also prevents students from getting overwhelmed by recruiters from institutions that do not have what they want, academically or athletically. An approach like this is sound, and if a youngster is truly an outstanding athlete, this might eliminate some of the incredible pressure that great numbers of recruiters can exert on the athlete and the family.

5. discuss the location of the college and the implication this holds in choosing possible places to matriculate. While colleges in another part of the country sound exciting, athletes need to consider the cost of transportation back and forth; they need to consider how many times they will be able to get home during a year (if this is important to the student); and they should consider the fact that their family and friends might never see them play because of the expense of the trip. Student athletes should understand, too, that if they attend college in a state a great distance away from home, there is always the risk of competing for a position with an athlete native to that state, and if they are equal in ability, politics could enter the picture, and the local athlete will probably play first. This is often true when a youngster native to the state was sent there by an influential alumnus or front-liner who does a lot of recruiting for that school.

6. not attempt to influence an athlete in any way as to their choice of college, but rather give advice, if it is solicited. The final decision should be the youngster's and the parents, and not the coach's.

Unfortunately, there are high school coaches who do not hesitate to use an outstanding athlete to further their own ambitions. When this occurs, a coach will use every technique to influence an athlete's decision, because it might mean an opportunity to move with this prized recruit into a college coaching job now, or in the future. Some high school coaches will establish a "pipeline" whereby they see to it

Photo by Ken Kasper.

that their best athletes each year always end up at the same college. Again, the motive is often selfish, in that they hope this will provide them the opportunity to move to that same college someday as a coach.

There is nothing wrong with high school coaches desiring to move into the college coaching ranks, but they should be able to do it on their own merit, rather than as a package deal involving blue chip athletes. Coaches who operate this way are easily recognizable to recruiters, and in the long run it might prove more harmful to their ambitions than helpful.

The high school coach also has a responsibility to recruiters, since a recruiter often relies a great deal on a coach's recommendations. There are intangibles an athlete must possess that don't always show up on film, such as attitude, character, coachability and competitiveness, and this information has to come from the coach. Therefore, the coach must be honest and frank, not only for the recruiter's benefit but for the athlete's sake as well. There is no advantage in getting youngsters into a situation they cannot cope with. This sounds simple enough, but is violated repeatedly because of a tendency of high school coaches to overestimate and oversell their athletes. This happens because coaches are often biased toward their athletes, but another and deeper reason might be ego involvement on the part of the coach.

Helping an athlete get into college, possibly with an athletic scholarship, gives a coach a certain degree of pride and satisfaction, which is normal. All teachers enjoy seeing students go on to bigger and better things, and if they can feel that they played an important part in the process, so much the better. But when coaches see a student's success as a direct indication of their own ability as a coach, and as a personal accomplishment, this can lead to some maneuvering not consistent with the basic obligations of a coach.

One impression a high school coach should avoid making on a college recruiter is that of trying to sell an athlete. This impression can be fostered by a coach who takes the initiative in contacting a college to report the availability of a fine athlete, and then immediately asks what the college can offer. The same approach frequently occurs when the recruiter visits a school to see the coach. When a high school coach operates this way a scholarship possibility for a deserving athlete can be killed. This kind of coach can also earn an undesirable reputation as a flesh peddler among college coaches who recruit in that particular area.

Some recruiters resent coaches who have this attitude or use this approach, and unless the athlete is an absolute superstar, they will probably thank the coach politely and say they are not interested. There are enough good athletes available, and recruiting is a difficult enough job, without the recruiter having to put up with a high school coach who is selling athletes.

When athletes discover that their coach is using this approach, they sometimes develop a warped idea of their own potential as college athletes. They can also get the wrong idea of the whole recruiting process. Then, instead of youngsters choosing colleges because of the education they can get there, they allow themselves to be sold to the highest bidder. This is a sorry lesson for a high school student athlete to learn.

While attempting to sell an athlete in this fashion is to be discouraged, there is nothing wrong with high school coaches taking the initiative in contacting college coaches to let them know that one or several athletes are interested in attending that particular institution. If films or video tapes are available of the youngster in competition, the college coach should be made aware of this also.

There are many high school athletes who are intelligent enough to gain admission to college and who are skillful enough to compete in intercollegiate athletics. Normally, it is only the outstanding individual who gets most of the publicity or makes the all-star teams, and whose name is noticed by coaches of large colleges or universities. But every athlete does not have to compete in a big-time university athletic program. There are thousands of middle-size or small colleges throughout the country, where high school athletes can continue in athletics without being potential "superstars." Many of the smaller colleges have excellent athletic programs, but because of limited recruiting do not have the opportunity to scour the country for athletes as the large universities do.

In these situations, the college coaches appreciate having high school coaches write to them about good athletes who might be prospective students. At this point, the normal procedure is for the college coach to follow up this contact by getting in touch with the youngster, and possibly sending along some literature on the college. Hopefully, the youngster will also be invited to visit the campus at some later date.

Another possibility to consider is to see to it that the seniors on the team have opportunities to attend college games, particularly in the sport they are most interested in. This usually means that the coach will be transporting the youngsters in his or her own car. But this gives the athletes an opportunity to see college games and various campuses, and to meet some college coaches. Even if they choose not to go on to college, or if they do, but decide to give up participating in sport, the experience is a good one for them.

Prior to a campus visit, the high school coach should take time to advise the athletes concerning their visit. They should be encouraged to present a neat, clean personal appearance, and to wear suitable attire. Blue jeans and T-shirts might be appropriate dress in a high school, but they do little to create a favorable impression when visiting college officials.

Youngsters should be reminded that the coaches will be trying to sell them on the good points of the school. Consequently, they should have some questions fixed in their minds to ask the coaches. If possible, they should also try to visit with some of the athletes already attending the college.

Student athletes should also be cautioned about approaching the coaches with the attitude of "here I am, what can you offer me." There can be no argument as to the importance of finances in attending college today and the concern most families have regarding this matter. College coaches are well aware of this fact. Therefore, the conversation will eventually get around to college expenses, as well as scholarship possibilities or the availability of other kinds of legitimate financial aid. If this is not done, or if an athlete is not clear about this matter by the end of a visit, there is absolutely nothing wrong in asking for a clarification of the financial question, since this might have a bearing on a final decision as to where a youngster will matriculate. With the continued rise in the cost of a college education, this is a legitimate concern.

It is a good idea too, for high school coaches to establish a policy within their own schools regarding recruiters. The first ground rule might be that college recruiters are to leave a high school prospect alone during a season. If a student is truly an outstanding athlete, a coach sometimes has problems keeping this individual from getting too cocky and believing that he or she is indispensable to the team. In this situation, if college recruiters get to this youngster while the season is still going, the athlete might become impossible to live with the rest of the season. In addition, this youngster's self-image can become distorted and performance might suffer because the attention from the colleges has given the youngster a "swelled head."

Basketball coaches probably have more difficulty with this because their seasons runs well into the spring. If a recruiter waits until the season is over, the openings in the college are pretty well filled, unless a block of spaces has been reserved for athletes.

Certainly, coaches have no desire to interfere with an athlete's opportunities, but the fact remains that recruiters can be a nuisance during a season. A high school coach works extremely hard to get everyone on the team prepared mentally, and to get them to concentrate on the business at hand. This can be destroyed by having a recruiter walk in and tell one or several of the athletes that they are good enough to play on a certain college team next year. It doesn't take much to turn the head of a 17-year-old athlete, and publicity and recruiters probably head the list.

Consequently, some coaches simply will not allow any recruiter to talk with an athlete during the season. Of course, if a recruiter chooses to write to an athlete or call the home, there is not much a coach can do except to try to play this down, so that the student doesn't get too excited too soon.

Most college recruiters have learned that the first step when visiting a high school is the principal's office. The coach should have an understanding that the office personnel are to direct the recruiter to the

Photo courtesy of Dan Bowersox.

coach or some other designated person, and not to the youngster the recruiter came to see. This is one way a high school coach can maintain some degree of control over the recruiting process. There could be several reasons why a high school coach wouldn't want a recruiter talking to a member of the team at that moment. It could be that the sought-after youngster is developing an attitude problem; it could be that the athlete has already made a decision, and doesn't want to talk with any more recruiters; or it may be that the youngster doesn't want to talk with anyone from a certain college.

Another problem the high school coach should work out with the school principal is the question of pulling an athlete out of class to talk with a recruiter. Sometimes, a recruiter drops into a school without any prior notification. If there is a good prospect there, the recruiter usually wants to meet the athlete and talk for a few minutes. At first glance this doesn't appear to be a concern at all. But when a number of recruiters begin to show up to talk with the same student, this presents a serious problem. Classroom teachers often object to having their classes interrupted, and the youngster can miss so much time that grades begin to suffer.

As a rule, a principal will not object to allowing an athlete to leave class once in a while for this purpose. But if this is abused, the only alternatives are to get the athlete and recruiter together between classes, during the lunch hour, or after school. The coach should take the initiative and bring this question of recruiting to the principal's attention, in order to avoid an embarrassing confrontation later on. Most school administrators will be agreeable to some reasonable solution to this problem, but if they find out by accident that recruiters are interfering and disrupting classes, they can be quite disagreeable. The tendency then is for them to over-react and issue an edict that is quite unreasonable, and possibly unfair. Another solution to this potential problem area is for the high school coach to let recruiters know the best time to visit the school. It is also a good idea for recruiters to have a coach's telephone number both at home and in school. Recruiters are busy people too, and they appreciate knowing the best time to visit, so they can do what needs to be done and move on.

In order to assist recruiters, there are a number of things a high school coach can prepare ahead of time. The following represents a list of factors recruiters are interested in, and will save everyone a lot of time if the high school coach prepares this material prior to a recruiter's visit.

1. Team list
2. Individual player's athletic ability
3. The level of competition each individual could be successful in
4. Grade point for each athlete
5. Class rank of each individual
6. Test scores (P.S.A.T./S.A.T.)
7. Academic ability of each athlete

8. Course of study in high school
9. Possible major in college
10. Films or video tape

Because of the timing of recruiting, many recruiters believe this information should be gathered mid-way through an athlete's junior year in high school.

It is very helpful to both the recruiter and athlete if the coach can arrange to film a game, meet, or other athletic event, in order for the college coaches to see the athlete perform. It is not necessary that this be done in a competitive situation, and in fact, the youngster might participate in a sport where no films are ever used. There is no reason a coach couldn't arrange to film or video tape an athlete performing their speciality in practice. The main point is that the college coaches can see the athlete in action.

High school coaches should also be familiar with the types of scholarships and financial aid that are available. Not only could the coach answer questions a student athlete might have, but also help parents of athletes understand the differences. Basically, there are: (a) athletic scholarships, which can pay for some or all of a student athlete's education, and (b) grants based on financial need, as determined by a parent's confidential financial statement. Additional information on grants is normally available through high school guidance offices.

Coaches can also assist in their advising by learning as much as they can about various colleges. This can be accomplished by reading college bulletins, or visiting different campuses when the opportunity arises. Coaches can also learn some things about colleges by talking with athletes who have visited campuses either on their own, or as part of the recruiting process.

It is also helpful if high school coaches learn what kind of athletes different colleges are looking for. This can best be learned through experience, and by talking to recruiters when they visit the school.

Another way to learn what colleges are looking for in athletes, and to get an idea of the relationship between athletes' abilities versus the level of competition, is to ask college coaches to comment on game films when they return them. This might also prove valuable to the coach personally, as far as actually coaching the team or individual is concerned.

As coaches gain experience with recruiting, they will discover that there are basically two kinds of recruiters. There are members of a college coaching staff visiting schools to see if there are any prospects available, and there are bird dogs, or front-liners. The latter usually are graduates of some particular college, or have taken it upon themselves to adopt a college even if they never attended it. They might be recruiting for a college because they were asked to, or they may be doing it on their own. The one thing they all have in common, though, is that they get their "kicks" out of recruiting athletes.

Sometimes these people can be of great help to a college coach, and sometimes they can become nuisances. They can be a great help to a high school athlete, or they can cause problems for the high school coach. When a high school coach has problems with a recruiter, it is usually the bird dog. The reason is simple enough. In their eagerness to funnel local athletes into their alma mater, real or adopted, they violate rules of etiquette or procedure in dealing with public school people. Frequently, they bypass the principal, guidance counselor, and coach and go directly to the athlete because they don't understand that there is a correct procedure to follow.

When high school athletes start listening to promises that unofficial recruiters sometimes make, or listening to the flattery that goes along with recruiting, they can become awfully hard to live with, and to coach. After all, they have just been promised a full free ride somewhere. What possible reason could there be, they ask themselves, for getting all excited about a few high school games?

It is very difficult for some youngsters to cope with this kind of attention, and the coach knows this better than anyone. The bird dog doesn't know this, and probably doesn't care. This recruiter's primary concern is to get the athlete on campus, and if the individual makes the team, so much the better. Then the bird dog can stand tall and say to everyone, "Look what I did for this school." When a coach discovers a bird dog operating in the area, the coach must get to this individual in a hurry to let this person know how the recruiting process works in his or her school.

Photo courtesy of the Pennsylvania State University Still Photography Services.

One of the problems college recruiters experience occurs when they have an athlete highly recommended to them by the youngster's own coach, and they don't feel they want to offer this person a scholarship. They know that some coaches take this personally and become upset with the college. Some will get so upset, they vow that this particular college will never again get any athletes from their high school. Often this feeling comes about because of the tremendous ego involvement of the high school coach. The high school coach sees this as a, rejection and, therefore, an attack on the quality of the athletes being turned out. Instead of feeling this way, the coach should appreciate the frankness of the college staff in their evaluation of a youngster, based on their own situation. The college coaches might also be trying to keep a youngster from getting into a situation that is over his or her head.

The whole problem depends on the point of view. High school coaches naturally view this with tunnel vision. They see only the individual, and know that this is a good athlete. They also possibly feel that they have an obligation to help these youngsters get scholarships. Therefore, the high school coaches' attitude in this situation is understandably narrow.

On the other hand, the college coaching staff knows what they want in an athlete; they know what kind of personnel they have returning; they know what weaknesses have to be strengthened and, most importantly, they have the opportunity to compare a prospect with other outstanding individuals. In this light, one who appears to a high school coach to be an outstanding athlete, may be little better than average by comparison. College athletic departments do not have unlimited financial aid, and so they must pick and choose carefully.

It may be that an athlete turned down by one coaching staff will be accepted by another and perform well. To say that the first staff made a mistake is not necessarily true. It may simply mean that their needs were different at the time, or that the situation presented a different set of priorities for them in choosing high school athletes.

The point is that high school coaches need to be aware of and understand the problems of a college recruiter, and not become resentful when financial aid to an athlete is not forthcoming. If an athlete is determined to attend a specific college and participate in athletics there, the lack of a scholarship offer should not be looked upon as the end of the world. The student can still enroll there and get permission to try out for the team. If the individual can prove good enough to play, financial aid is still a possibility. If not, there are numerous opportunities for financial aid and loans in colleges today, over and above those that are given for athletics.

Not only does the high school coach serve in a guidance or advisory function in recruiting, but the coach also serves as a buffer between an athlete and recruiter. The high school athlete is rare indeed who can cope with the persuasiveness of a veteran recruiter. When a youngster is approached by several or many super-salespeople, the student's problems are compounded.

The pressure a recruiter can put on a youngster to commit to a particular institution can be overwhelming. The promises that recruiters sometimes make to an athlete and his or her family can be staggering. Recruiters can violate not only the rules governing recruiting, but rules of ethics also. It is in the latter event that high school coaches must use their prerogative as an interested party, to counsel the athlete before the youngster makes a decision that might be regretted later on.

Every high school coach should exercise caution in another regard involving recruiting. In his or her haste and desire to help an athlete get into a college, the coach must be careful not let the school guidance counselor feel any infringement on the counselor's function. If a coach has established a good working relationship with the guidance people, this will not be a problem. One way to do this is to work in cooperation with the counselor to help the student. The guidance office can provide information about any college in the country as to size, curricula, cost, location, and entrance requirements. Naturally, the guidance people have a great deal of information on file about the student and this is important to the coach also. When a coach seeks this kind of information from the guidance office, it fosters mutual concern for a youngster's benefit.

The recruiting process is a hard reality for a high school coach, and one every coach should be prepared to handle. The high school coach should emphasize the basic recruiting procedure for all concerned, so the situation does not get out of hand. The experience should be a very pleasant one for everyone concerned, and it can be, with some forethought, since the high school coach is the one to determine the policies regarding recruiting in each particular high school. One of the pleasant aspects of the process, other than seeing an athlete satisfied with a choice of a college, is getting acquainted with the college coaches who do the recruiting. In most instances they are fine people trying to do a job, with the least interference possible in the high school athletic program. When high school coaches treat these people with professional courtesy, and demonstrate personal integrity, it is not unusual to develop permanent friendships with these same college coaches. This will occur through a distinct feeling of mutual respect, which is the spirit that should prevail between professionals interested in a student athlete's welfare.

DISCUSSION QUESTIONS

1. Discuss the present impact of recruiting on girls' athletics.

2. Discuss the important suggestions you will make to your prospective college athletes.

3. Why is it important for a coach not to influence or pressure an athlete into choosing a particular college or university?

4. What responsibilities does the high school coach have to the college recruiter?

5. Is it possible for a high school coach to oversell an athlete? What does this mean, and what are the ramifications?

6. Why is it important for the high school coach to involve other members of the high school staff in the recruiting process? Who are these people and what are their roles?

7. What are the differences between recruiting procedures and regulations for girls and boys?

8. How can the ego of a high school head coach enter into recruiting?

9. Why should a high school coach establish recruiting policies?

10. What are the differences between athletic scholarships and financial aid?

11. What are bird dogs, or front liners? How can they affect athletes?

12. Discuss some of your own experiences with college recruiters.

Photo by Ken Kasper.

9

ETHICS IN COACHING

"THERE ARE NO DEGREES OF HONESTY"

An absorbing interest of the public and students has created an atmosphere not always purest. . . There has been evident improvement in the rules; what is needed most is to improve in the ethical standards of all persons interested in athletics. Conformity to athletic rules is too much of a technicality and not enough of a principle — athletics, like every other form of amusement or business, must eventually rest on sound ethics. It is unfortunate in the extreme that the public mind is so eager for amusement that it becomes indifferent to the ethical conditions surrounding the game — it is a manifest waste of energy to spend time in denouncing athletics; what is needed is efficient leadership by men to whom principle is dearer than anything else . . . . We shall never reform athletics simply by rules, we shall reform it only when we have inspired young men to cling to high ideals and to be governed by sound ethics.

(President Thompson, The Ohio State University, 1904).

Obviously, ethical behavior in athletics has been a concern of educators for many years. It is not some latter-day discovery or problem area. Human nature being what it is and American society being what it is, it would appear that ethical behavior will continue to be an area of great concern to many people regarding athletic competition and athletic coaching.

Unfortunately, most beginning coaches are so preoccupied with X's and O's and so worried about mechanical ways to teach youngsters to win, that they give very little consideration to ethics in sport as they prepare themselves for the coaching profession.

Throughout the world of athletics, sportsmanship and ethics have become synonymous. These words are used frequently, but it would be hard to find one definition to which everyone would agree. Everyone has his or her own idea of what a good sport is, and what ethical

239

behavior consists of, remembering that ethics and good sportsmanship vary according to the sport. For example, what is considered ethical behavior in baseball might be unethical behavior in tennis.

There are many definitions of the word "ethics," but for the purposes of this chapter, Webster's Dictionary offers four definitions that seem appropriate for coaches:

1. The discipline dealing with what is good and bad and with moral duty and obligation.
2. A set of moral principles or values.
3. Principles of conduct governing an individual or group.
4. Conforming to accepted professional standards of conduct.

Ethical behavior on the part of a coach not only involves observing the rules of a particular game, but more importantly, it involves a level of conduct according to the true spirit of the game, or the unwritten rules that are also an integral part of every sport. These unwritten rules are normally concerned with the conduct of a coach or competitor, and have been established and observed through the years under the heading of sportsmanship.

For example, in golf it is not against the written rules to talk while an opponent is putting. However, it is expected that everyone will remain quiet at this time because it is in the spirit of the game to do so. A high school baseball coach should not yell at the pitcher of the opposing team to upset him — not because it is against the rules, but because it isn't part of the game. A basketball player shouldn't scream at an opponent who is in the process of shooting a foul shot in an attempt to cause the player to miss — it just isn't in the spirit of the game.

In all game situations, there are officials involved to see that the written rules are not violated. Observing the unwritten rules, as dictated by the spirit of the game in each particular sport, is quite another matter. This behavior is governed not by a rule book, but by each coach's personal philosophy of coaching, and standards of ethical behavior. There is a very fine line between game strategy and ethics. There are coaches who take great delight in studying a rule book to see how far they can bend certain rules without breaking them. Even though they often violate the true meaning of the rule, they justify their action by simply stating that according to the rule book, they have not broken any rules. In their minds, this is good coaching, because it involves the strategy of making the rule book work in their favor. In actuality, they are beating the rule, although technically they are not. This factor is one that is responsible for much of the ill feeling that occurs between opposing coaches. To some, strategy is clever coaching even though "the spirit of the game" is involved while to others it just isn't fair, because, in their opinion, some things have no place in high school athletic contests.

For years coaches have been claiming that sport is a builder of strong character and honesty in those who participate. Many people accepted this as fact and the claim remained unchallenged for years.

Sports have always had their critics, but they were usually people who were outside the realm of sports competition. During the 1960's a significant change occurred when criticism of sport began to come from people actively involved — the athletes themselves.

The late 1960's was the era of the exposé. This was the time when former athletes, whatever their motive, became highly critical of the values of sport competition, and decided to tell it like it was. It was during these years, too, that the coaches themselves were challenged along with the values they stated as being inherent in sport. These were the years when the phrase "desperate coach" seemed to typify many in the coaching profession.

The fact is that sport can provide one of the greatest opportunities in school for a youngster to learn how to be dishonest, how to cheat, how to be hypocritical, and how to be unethical. On the other hand, athletic participation also provides one of the greatest opportunities for a student to learn honesty, integrity, dignity, the need to obey rules, and ethical behavior. It is also a fact that ethical behavior is not inborn in children. They must be taught right from wrong, and in the athletic situation it is the sole responsibility and obligation of the coach to do so.

> Great as are the opportunities in sports . . . for education in general, they offer especially fertile fields for the discovery and development of moral and spiritual values. In many ways these are for the pupil the most vivid and appealing form of experience in the school. The situations involved in sports are particularly loaded with adjustment problems in which moral and spiritual attitudes, standards and behavior patterns are involved. These situations are real, immediate, and concrete and therefore, far removed from abstractions, generalities, and merely verbal precepts. They present action situations in which values are intrinsically involved. . . .[1]

For centuries, education has been concerned with the development of moral and ethical values in students. There is no invention or secret formula known to humankind, which can insure a good and solid society, if personal integrity, honesty, and self-discipline are lacking. These qualities are among the significant contributions athletics can make to the young people of our country. In sport, it all depends on the coach, and whether or not he or she makes a conscientious effort to teach youngsters the importance of high ethical standards by word, and more importantly, by example. If coaches can instill these qualities in young people through sport, then they can rightfully say that sport does build strength of character for those who have the courage to participate. These are the lessons that will be remembered long after the scores of the games have been forgotten. It is also this kind of teaching that enables coaches to live with the unhappy message the scoreboard sometimes carries because they know that the outcome of a single game is not the beginning or end of the world.

High school athletes are at a stage where they urgently need to feel

---

[1]*Delbert Oberteuffer, Physical Education* (New York: Harper & Brothers, Publishers, 1956), p. 183.

important to their peers. They need close personal friends and to feel themselves loyal members of a group for which they have real enthusiasm. This craving for excitement and adventure is normal; yet today's world gives a youngster fewer opportunities than ever before to satisfy it.

The drama and excitement of competitive sports, the demands for efficiency and excellence, for courage and self-discipline, meet many needs of adolescent boys and girls.

Plato said, "You can discover more about a person in an hour of play than in a year of conversation." Competition brings out both the best and the worst in people. Competition is our way of life, and we are surrounded by it from the day we are born until we die. The infant experiences competition vying for attention from the mother with brothers and sisters, and for toys with brothers and sisters, or playmates. School-age youngsters are surrounded by competition for grades in school, making the honor roll, drawing the best picture, or writing the best paper. In affluent communities, youngsters compete with each other by the kind of clothes they wear, and from there, go on to compete for girl friends or boy friends. Youngsters learn to compete in band, for parts in plays, for a place on a team, and for a teacher's attention. As they grow up, they face competition in choosing a wife or husband, and finally the fierce competition of earning a living. There is no escaping competition.

Wherever there is life, there is conflict, and life without rivalry, anxieties, and strains simply does not exist. As long as games are played, there will be a winner and a loser, and it is the lot of everyone to experience both.

All games and sports — bridge, parcheesi, boxing, tennis, etc. — spring from the same root, the aggressive component; it is the primary weapon in the struggle for survival. Although conditions of life have eased since man lived in caves, this primary instinct must have exercise. And for this purpose men have devised sports and games which are mock struggles with artificial dangers. The ancestry of sport is written very plainly in the fact that the first games among all nations were simple imitations of the typical acts of warriors and huntsmen. The pleasure principle was not the motive of games, but rather a discovery stumbled on in the course of playing.

Life without struggle is monotonous, and sport became the substitute for fighting by tooth and nail . . . sports are a great and necessary catharsis, indispensable to civilized man — a salutary purgation of the combative instincts which, if dammed up within him, would break out in a disastrous way.

The whole human race has been benefited down the ages by this purgative effect of sports. Observe that the young child, the only natural and purely instinctive human being, has no sportsmanship and no generosity in his games. The child will take advantage of its opponent, and will wail and cry when it loses. To him the contest is grim reality, until advancing years, adult example, social pressure modify its reactions. That the contestant in a game or sport can forego an accidental advantage and the spectator cheer him for it — that the loser can smile and congratulate his vanquisher — these are among the major achievements of the human race.[2]

[2]Robert H. Boyle, *Sport, Mirror of American Life* (Boston; Little, Brown & Company, 1963), pp. 59–60.

Basically, problems in athletics regarding ethical behavior of coaches and athletes occur because of the concern for winning and losing. When the competition and desire to win are great, how will youngsters or coaches conduct themselves? In many cases, questionable acts committed in an athletic contest are explained away simply by saying, "I hate to lose." Some people will use every trick in the book to try to win a game or a race, and are often admired because they are labeled real competitors.

Americans have come to believe that winning is the whole object of any game, and the coach or athlete who won't do everything possible to win will never become a champion. Building character is something a coach does when teams lose, but the primary purpose of the team is to win.

Can ethical behavior be learned through sport? The answer is yes, but it is not automatic; nor can it be assimilated through osmosis. Ethics must be taught by the coach. There is no other way. To teach ethics, a coach must be an ethical person. The coach, for example, who holds illegal practice sessions before the rules allow is teaching dishonesty, plain and simple.

There are no degrees of honesty. A coach cannot be just a little dishonest or a little bit unethical. A person is either honest or dishonest, ethical or unethical. There are no shades of gray where honesty is concerned. The coach who speaks about adherence to the rules only to violate them himself is advocating cheating, not by what the coach says

Photo by Laurie Usher.

but by what the coach has done. When a coach says one thing and does another, the students will disregard these words and assume that the coach's actions are a greater indication of his or her true beliefs. All the words in a coach's vocabulary will not change this fact.

Coaches have been heard to say that they do not want to violate any rules, but feel they must because their opponents do. Therefore, in order to compete they have to cheat also. This is not a reason, nor is it good logic. It is simply an excuse to break the rules. Coaches who actively practice this kind of reasoning do so for three reasons: (1) they are ambitious and anxious to be able to move up the coaching ranks on the basis of their team's won-lost record, (2) they are afraid for their jobs, or (3) they are dishonest. Whatever the reason, behavior of this sort is unethical. It is conduct like this that makes a mockery out of the claim that sport builds character. Sport by itself can neither build personality traits nor tear them down. It all comes down to the coach, and what is taught by that coach's actions. Talk is meaningless, when contradicted by actions.

Athletics can create a fertile field for the development of ethical behavior. There are situations in games which demand that a youngster or coach react to, or make decisions involving, honesty and ethics. Many of these situations are not covered by a rule book, but challenge the spirit of the game. The following situations are examples given to illustrate this point.

1. Two undefeated football teams met in mid-season to determine first place in their particular conference. These teams had been rivals for many years. During the game team A attempted a field goal, and the kick was good. Because the game had been a rough one, the officials were so intent on making sure the game didn't get out of hand that none of them was in a position to rule on the field goal.

The players from the other team, sensing the confusion of the officials, immediately began to shout that the kick was no good. After some deliberation the officials ruled that the field goal did not count. The week after the game the referee wrote team A a letter of apology, because he had since been told that the kick was good and should have counted.

Obviously, this was a situation involving ethics on the part of one team. Were they correct in insisting the kick was bad? Should they have remained silent? Should their actions have been influenced by the score? Suppose the officials had asked the opposing team if the kick was good — what then?

2. In a girl's softball game, a runner trying to steal second base was called out. The second baseman dropped the ball, but recovered it quickly. However, the umpire did not see this, being blocked out by the runner and the dust. The runner told the umpire that the second baseman dropped the ball. The umpire then asked the second baseman if she dropped the ball.

This raises two questions. The first one is, should the umpire have asked the second baseman the question? The second question is, since she did ask the girl, how should the youngster respond?

3. Prior to a high school wrestling tournament, the participants were required to weigh in before lunch on the day of the competition. All the contestants lined up and weighed in as their names were checked off a master list. One of the host team's wrestlers had just made weight and gone home to eat lunch. He was so close to the weight limit that there was no way he could make it if he ate lunch. After everyone weighed in, the official noticed that this boy's name had not been checked off. The official interpreted this to mean that the boy had not weighed in, or if he had, he didn't make weight. His coach knew that he had weighed in and made weight; but he also knew that the boy had gone home to eat and couldn't make weight if he had to weigh in again. In this case, he would forfeit and this would cost his team valuable points. The other coaches and wrestlers were well aware of the possibilities also.

In desperation the coach decided to ask some of the wrestlers from other schools if they had seen his wrestler weigh in, and if so, would they verify that he had made weight. The boy whose name was next on the master list for weighing in was in the same weight class and had been beaten earlier in the season by the wrestler in question. The wrestler whose weight was being questioned probably stood between him and the championship of his weight class in the tournament.

Can there be any question about how the second boy should react in this situation?

4. In a high school softball game the home team was ahead by one run and the visitors had a runner on second base. The batter hit a ball to the outfield and the runner from second tried to score. The outfielder threw the ball to home, the play was close, and the runner was called out. The game ended with the home team winning by that one run.

As the catcher was taking off her equipment, she told her coach that she missed tagging the runner at home and the umpire blew the call. She wanted to know what she should do. What should the coach tell her?

5. This incident took place many years ago, in a football game between Iowa and Michigan. Iowa had the ball on Michigan's four yard line, with time left for one more play. Michigan was leading 7–6, and the winner would be the Big Ten champion. Iowa's best back and captain was Nile Kinnick, and everyone in the stadium knew who would carry the ball on this last play.

The ball was snapped to Kinnick as expected, and he plunged into the mass of bodies at the line of scrimmage. He burst through, but got hit at the goal line and fumbled the ball. The game ended as the ball rolled uncovered.

Both teams surrounded the referee. Michigan claimed the ball was fumbled before he crossed the goal line. Iowa insisted he had scored before he dropped the ball. Because of the pile-up of players, a definite decision was practically impossible. First, they called the captains, and then the players, into conference. The officials told them that the only one who knew what really happened was Kinnick himself. The referee asked both teams if they would accept his statement as to when the fumble occurred. The players agreed to this.

The pressure on Kinnick must have been incredible. There was pressure from both teams, pressure from the fans, and most of all pressure from his own desire to win the championship.

There are several questions that might be debated at this point. Should an official put an athlete in this position and, if so, what is the athlete to do, assuming the athlete knows the answer to the question the official raised? The fact is that the official did ask Kinnick a direct question, which required an honest answer in return. If he lied, only he would know, but he would live with that lie the rest of his life. In his heart, he would always know that he cheated, and the question in his mind must have been whether or not winning was more important than his own integrity.

As the entire stadium froze into an eerie silence, Nile Kinnick hesitated only a moment, and looking the official in the eye, told him that he had fumbled before he got over the goal line. And then, as if to convince himself of its meaning, he added that Michigan had won the game.[3]

One of the questions this raises is whether or not a game official should ever ask a participant a question like this, or any other for that matter? And if the question is asked, should an official expect an honest answer? Is a youngster obligated to give an answer in a situation like this? Or is the solution simply for an athlete to tell the official that it is the official's responsibility to make the decision, and then refuse to answer the question?

Nile Kinnick lost his life in World War II, and in 1972 the football stadium at the University of Iowa was named in his honor.

6. The field hockey coach of a certain team consistently teaches her players to go for the girl, and not the ball, to run over other players, instead of going around them, and to do anything possible to score. The officials in her area are not too competent, and as a result, her teams usually get away with very rough play. The other teams in the league are trying to play within the spirit of the game, using stickwork and skill to win.

The rough coach intimidates the other teams. Her teams usually end up the season in the top three in a league of 11 teams. When confronted with her violations of the spirit of the game, she responds, "I know we're rough, but we usually win, so what's the difference?"

Is this a matter of good coaching, or a violation of the spirit of the game?

---

[3]*Speaking to American Youth* (Louisville, Kentucky), October, 1959, p. 1.

7. In a high school baseball game, team A was losing, and had a rally in the making by loading the bases with no one out. Their next batter hit a ground ball to the shortstop, who threw to the second baseman, who, in turn, threw to first for the double play. Time was called and the coach of team B went out to talk with his pitcher. While he was on the field, the second baseman came over and told the coach he thought he had stepped off second base before he had the ball, but the umpire called the runner out anyway. Then he said, "Coach, what should I do?" How should the coach respond?

8. Sometimes high school baseball games are played with one umpire. Naturally, this puts the official at a great disadvantage, because of the position in relation to close plays at the various bases. In one game, a boy attempted to steal second base and was called safe.

As the players went back to their positions, the base runner began to walk off the field. His teammates shouted to him to go back because he was safe. He kept walking and said, "No, I wasn't safe. The second baseman tagged me with the ball, but the umpire couldn't see it from where he was standing." Was the boy correct in his action?

9. During a high school football game, with the score tied, one team's quarterback dropped back to throw a pass. His pass protection broke down, and he was forced to run with the ball. He took off toward the left sidelines and saw there was no place to go. He reversed his field, and ran almost the entire width of the field. About this time players were scattered all over the field. The quarterback spotted one of his ends downfield, and threw him a pass, which was completed for a substantial gain. This put his team in scoring position. As they formed the huddle for the next play, an official walked up to their captain and asked him if any of the linemen had gone downfield before the ball was thrown. If so, the play would be nullified, and a penalty assessed. How should the captain have answered the official?

10. In a high school baseball game, team A had a runner on third base. As the pitcher began to wind up to pitch to the next batter, the batter stepped out of the batter's box, and the coach (who was coaching at third base) yelled, "Hold it." The pitcher instinctively stopped in the middle of his delivery, whereupon the coach at third immediately charged the umpire, yelling, "Balk." The umpire so ruled and the runner from third was allowed to score.

After the game the coach of team B was angry, and accused the other coach of poor sportsmanship. The coach of team A simply replied that he had broken no rules, and besides, strategy was part of the game. He said the pitcher should know better anyway. The fact that he personally used a tricky tactic to outsmart a 16-year-old boy and score a run for his team was good coaching, in his opinion. Is this true in high school sports?

11. The score in a women's field hockey game was 0–0 when a player from Northwestern broke loose down the field and flipped a shot into the lower corner of the net. The officials signaled a goal, whereupon the players on both teams moved to mid-field, to line up for the face-off.

The girl who had scored the goal went up to an official and said, "It wasn't a goal. I hit the ball off the back of my stick." This is illegal in field hockey.

The startled official thought about it for a minute, reversed her decision, declared no goal, and gave the ball out of bounds to the other team at their end of the field.

When questioned about it after the game, the girl said she knew the official hadn't seen it, and she thought it wasn't right that her team should have the goal counted.

How would you react if you were that girl's coach?

12. During a girls' district playoff in softball, team "A" was losing 7–1. The plate umpire, a woman who had officiated many of this team's home games, went to the coach of team "A" and told her she could protest the game because the other team's batting helmets were not legal.

The coach of team "A" immediately jumped up and protested the game. The coach of team "B" then countered by saying that one of the girls on team "A" was not wearing a proper uniform.

A heated argument followed between the two coaches and the umpire, while the girls watched and listened. After a lengthy debate, it was finally decided to continue the game without protest. In the next inning team "A" scored seven runs, and won the game and district championship.

The coach of team "B" was outraged, since she felt some ethics were violated and that the ensuing argument unsettled her girls to the point where they blew the game. What do you think?

13. The following situation occurred in a collegiate baseball game during the playoffs for the championship. Team A had a catcher with a sore arm. He could not throw to second very well, but the opposing team was not aware of this. In order to keep the other team from stealing second every time they got a man on first, the coach devised a plan that worked like this: when their opponent finally got a man on first base, he attempted to steal second base on the third pitch. Instead of the catcher trying to throw him out, he simply tossed a high lob to the shortstop. The catcher's teammates began yelling, "Go back, go back." The base runner, upon hearing this, looked up in time to see the shortstop catching what looked like a pop fly.

He thought his teammates were the ones yelling for him to go back so he turned around and sprinted back toward first base. The shortstop had an easy throw to the first baseman, who then tagged the runner out. This happened three different times during the game, and in every case the runner was tagged out. Team A won the game and championship. The coach said the victory was due in part to this clever strategy. The opposing coach was furious at what he considered poor sportsmanship.

This raises two questions: was this good baseball strategy, or did it involve coaching ethics insofar as the spirit of the game was concerned?

14. A high school sophomore went to his football coach to tell him he was quitting football, and would not report for the first practice. In questioning the youngster, the football coach discovered that he was quitting because the cross country coach had told the boy he was too small for football, and that his best chance for athletic success was as a distance runner in track. He also told the boy that it was mandatory for outstanding distance runners to participate in cross country, in order to be ready for the spring track season. He hinted too that he might be able to get him a college scholarship in track, but that if he went out for football he could ruin his chances for a track scholarship.

Recruiting athletes within a school is not an unusual practice, unfortunately, and it can breed tremendous conflict between coaches. Is this a matter of ethics or does it involve something else?

15. A slam is illegal in high school wrestling because it is a punishing and dangerous maneuver. If a boy is taken down on the mat and the official calls it a slam, and the wrestler cannot continue because he has been injured, he is awarded the match by default due to injury. In an eight-team tournament a wrestler from team A was paired with the top-seeded wrestler in his weight class. He had little chance of winning, and had already lost to this boy twice during the season. In the first period, the top-seeded wrestler got called for slamming the boy from team A, and was penalized one point immediately. As the wrestler from team A started to get up off the mat, his coach jumped up from his chair and shouted, "He's hurt." When he said this, his wrestler sat back down on the mat, and the official called time to check the boy. His coach came out onto the mat and repeated, "He is definitely hurt and cannot continue to wrestle."

The doctor in attendance could find nothing wrong with the boy but the youngster said that his coach was right — his back hurt him, and he didn't think he could continue. By this time the coach of team B was arguing that the boy was not hurt. He insisted that the other coach was using this as an excuse to win by default due to injury and was abusing the rule.

The official stopped the match and awarded it to the boy who had been slammed. The top-seeded wrestler was out of the running for the championship at that point. The other boy, who said he had been injured, came back later in the tournament to wrestle two more matches as he advanced to the finals, and eventually won his weight division.

A question of ethics, strategy or a quick-healing injury?

16. The final event of the girls' dual track meet was a relay. As the anchor runners from both teams crossed the finish line, the second girl yelled to the starter that the other team had passed the baton out of the exchange zone. If this was true, the winning team would be disqualified and lose the race.

Due to an oversight, there was no inspector at the exchange zone. Consequently, the starter called the third and fourth runners of the winning team together and asked them if their exchange was in the zone or out.

If the official was justified in asking the question, what kind of response should the two girls give?

17. There are specific rules in some states which state very clearly when high school football practice may begin and when the season officially ends. This rule is violated constantly by coaches who take their players into the gymnasium to run plays and other drills during the school year, when it is against the rules to do so. This rule is violated, too, by coaches who conduct illegal practices during the summer months, before the official starting date. The ways in which this rule is violated are too numerous to mention. The fact that it is done is the important consideration.

Almost without exception, every coach who does break this rule rationalizes. He explains away his dishonesty by stating that everyone else is doing it; therefore he must do it, too, if he hopes to have a fair chance of competing with the coaches who are cheating. Is this really so, or is it merely a case involving dishonesty and a lack of coaching ethics, or is it an example of an unreasonable rule that should be eliminated?

18. In his junior year in high school a boy suffered a shoulder separation in football. He played quarterback, and was a gifted athlete. The team he played on was not a good one, and he took a lot of physical punishment prior to his injury. His father was also very ambitious for the boy. They discussed this injury constantly, and the possible effects it might have on the boy if it didn't heal properly.

By the time football season began in his senior year, his doctor had given the boy a clean bill of health. However, after just a few days of practice, the youngster complained of pain in his shoulder. Upon further examination, the doctor could find nothing wrong. It was discovered later that he had complained of pain in order to be able to take pain killers which helped him overcome his anxiety about further injury.

Before each game, every boy who had been given permission to take the pain killer was to take just one pill on his own. This youngster was taking three. Late in the season, he got hit very hard during a game, but seemed to be O.K. Later that night, after the effects of the pills had worn off, the boy was in great pain. His family took him to the hospital, where it was discovered that he had suffered another shoulder separation and required surgery.

The whole question of drugs, steroids, and the use of drugs to deaden pain in an injured athlete involves two factors — physiological and ethical considerations. Can any high school athletic contest ever be important enough to jeopardize a youngster's health and physical well-being through the use of drugs?

19. This situation involves two girls' intercollegiate junior varsity basketball teams. Team A was from a smaller college, where one of the main courses of study was physical education. Team B was from a larger institution, where physical education was also offered, but where inter-collegiate sports competition was not emphasized.

Team A was obviously keyed up for the opportunity to beat the girls from the larger university. In order to do this, they employed a full court press. Team B couldn't handle the press and they collapsed. By the end of the first quarter the game was a rout but team A continued to press. They pressed the entire game and the final score was 90–8. The girls from team B were humiliated.

Team A was definitely the better team, but it was the press that turned the game into a rout. When the coach allowed her team to use the press all four quarters to run up the score, was this good coaching, good sportsmanship, poor ethics, or an insult to the other team?

20. During an intercollegiate football game at West Virginia, the score was tied 7–7 in the third quarter. Team A punted to West Virginia, and the safety man fumbled the ball near the sidelines. There was a mad scramble for the ball as it rolled out of bounds. The ball was awarded to team A.

A player from team A who was given credit for the recovery said, after the game, that he didn't get near the ball (he wasn't in the game at the time), but thought he talked the officials into giving it to his team. He said he started on the field to play defense, since he thought it was West Virginia's ball. But when he heard the officials arguing about the decision, he decided to get in on the act and said to one of the officials, "It's our ball, right?" One of the officials said no, but the referee said the boy was right — his team had the ball.

Later, the player said he thought the ball should have gone to West Virginia. His coach said he didn't know whose ball it was, but it had to be the turning point in the game. Team A scored quickly, and went on to win by a substantial margin.

Was this a question of ethics on the part of an athlete or quick thinking?

21. A college quarterback was 13 yards short of breaking the existing career passing record of a great former passer. However, it was the last game of the season, there were only 70 seconds left in the game, and the other team had the ball. When the ball was snapped to start the next play, his teammates, who were on defense, dropped to the ground and allowed the ball carrier to score, untouched.

After the kickoff the quarterback was put into the game and he completed two quick passes to establish an all-time passing record for college football. At this point, the opposing coach was livid with anger. He branded the action a disgrace to football, a lack of class on the part of the other coach, and a humiliating experience for his team.

It is not clear who told the defense to collapse. No rules were broken. Was the spirit of the game violated and, if so, did it involve coaching ethics?

The preceding examples of situations in athletics involving ethics and honesty are only a tiny sample of the vast number of similar incidents that occur in the whole realm of sport. This list could be multiplied many times over by anyone who has coached any kind of interscholastic team for any period of time. The point is that situations demanding ethical decisions on the part of a coach or player do present themselves in sport, and they are inevitable.

When a coach has not been completely honest or ethical in these instances, that coach cannot expect a youngster to exhibit these qualities in similar situations — especially during the excitement of a highly competitive contest. This is one area in sport where the opportunity for character development is particularly great. But the youngster must be taught by the coach; an athlete will not automatically learn from the situation itself, or if the youngster does, he or she might learn that dishonesty can be justified, if it will help win a game. Most would agree that the latter is not a quality of strength of character.

There are those who believe that character is caught rather than taught, and that each experience a boy or girl has at home, at play, or in school is shaping that youngster's standard of conduct, good or bad.

The coach who assumes that athletes will develop high ethical standards merely by participating in athletics is greatly mistaken. A coach who is truly concerned about helping youngsters develop strength of character and honesty must make a conscientious effort to teach honesty and ethical behavior by personal example.

PROFESSIONAL ETHICS

Another facet of ethics in the life of a high school coach involves professional ethics. Unlike game-type situations or coaching decisions involving honesty, professional ethics could be defined, in this context, as a coach's conduct in fulfilling the obligations of the position in relation to the people around that coach. Professional ethics for a coach can be specified in five distinct areas.

1. Coach to teacher.   This is a reciprocal responsibility among teachers. Examples of professional ethics in this category include having a student speak critically of a teacher to the coach, having a student speak critically of a coach to another teacher, or having a teacher or coach criticize a fellow teacher in front of a student.

Professionally, this is unacceptable. This can cause a great deal of friction and ill feeling within a faculty. Coaches are more apt to be involved in this than almost any other teacher in the school, because of the role they fill and the informality of their relationship to many students. A coach should not be outwardly sympathetic toward any student criticism of a fellow teacher.

2. Coach to parent.   Conversations between a parent and a coach should be considered privileged communication. When parents talk with a coach about some specific concern they have for their youngster,

Photo courtesy of The Pennsylvania State University Still Photography Services.

they usually preface their remarks with, "Don't tell my child that I talked to you about this or he will really get upset." Naturally, parents expect their requests to be honored. Even if they don't specifically state the desire to keep a conversation in strictest confidence, a coach should possess enough good judgment to know when to keep the conversation to himself.

Most conversations of this type come about because a youngster isn't playing in the games, or was, and has been, benched. Naturally, parents would like to know why, because of their interest, and because their youngster comes home every night feeling very discouraged. The youngster normally does not want the parents to go to the coach for fear the coach will get perturbed and take it out on him or her.

The author is aware of a case where a parent asked a coach why his son was benched, only to have the boy come home from practice the next day with tears in his eyes and ask his father, "Why did you call the coach?" The coach had called the boy in and said he definitely would not start the next game, simply because he had a policy that any time a parent asked him about their son's playing time, he would not start the boy in the next game under any circumstance. The boy was crushed and the father was infuriated that a coach would deliberately do such a thing.

3. Coach to student. This situation is similar to the one above, except this time, the student confides to a coach and asks that the parents not be told. As was stated much earlier in this text, students sometimes feel the need to confide in an adult other than a parent. The logical person is often their coach.

Young coaches are flattered that a youngster wants to confide in them and to ask for advice. But there is one caution that should not be ignored. That is the danger of agreeing not to tell a youngster's parents something, only to discover that the problem is of such magnitude that the parents ought to be aware of it. In this situation the coach has backed him- or herself into a corner. Unless the coach can convince the youngster to tell the parents, the coach must either keep quiet or violate a confidence.

Therefore, a safe approach to the opening statement, "Don't tell my mother or dad what I'm about to tell you," would be to say, "I can't promise that. Let's talk and then decide what is best for you to do under the circumstances."

4. Coach and administration. The responsibility for observing professional ethics in this relationship is reciprocal. In far too many cases, the obligations of a coach to school administrators is clearly defined, but the reverse is not true (see p. 26).

Basically, there are three areas of concern in this regard: honesty, loyalty, and support. The fact that coaches and school administrators deal with the public to a degree greater than most other teachers, makes the observance of these areas essential to both of them.

The implications for the coach are clear. A coach must be truthful in all dealings with an administrator, and while employed by that individual, must do the best job possible for that principal. Under no circumstances should a coach speak critically of a school administrator to the public. Some coaches feel frustrated because they believe a particular administrator is hampering part or all of the athletic program. In desperation, they criticize this person before people in the community, hoping that these people will bring pressure to bear on the administrator and get things changed.

Not only is this unethical, but it is potentially dangerous to a coach's professional career. In one or two instances, it might seem to work. However, even though the coach might have won a battle, the administrator will eventually win the war, and ultimately it could prove costly to the coach.

One of the areas involving honesty that school superintendents often violate concerns the procedure of interviewing applicants for a coaching position. Frequently, unless the interview was a disaster, an applicant leaves the interview having been told that he or she is a fine prospect and will be contacted in just a very few days about the position. The young coach may quite naturally assume that he or she will be offered the job.

If the prospect is not hired, this pattern usually follows. Days, and possibly weeks, pass by without any word. Finally, the applicant summons up enough courage to call the superintendent's office. The secretary does not put the caller through to the superintendent because she or he says the job was filled quite some time ago, and they were just too busy to notify the applicant.

This practice in the employment procedure could be classified as bait casting. Every legitimate prospect has the idea that the job is theirs. Each of them is kept on the hook until the employing officials find the person they want, whereupon all the rest are simply dropped. The fact that the superintendent promised to be in touch often means nothing, and this is dishonest.

Another violation in this area of professional ethics occurs when a coach has coaching responsibility taken away. In many states, since coaching is strictly an extracurricular activity, this assignment can be taken from an individual at any time by the superintendent of schools. There is no obligation to explain why.

Consequently, more than one coach has settled down at the breakfast table to enjoy a cup of coffee and the morning paper only to read in the sports section that he or she was fired the night before. More than one coach has learned that the coaching job is gone, by looking at next year's teaching contract and discovering that there is no coaching assignment indicated. And more than one coach has been dismissed without any explanation other than "We think it is time for a change." These are painful, but real, examples of a lack of professional ethics on the part of some administrators.

Photo courtesy of Jen Bednarek.

5. Coach to coach.   This last category of professional ethics includes coaches within a school, as well as coaches between schools. (Illustrations of this category appear earlier in this chapter.) Each individual must determine what constitutes ethical behavior in a particular sport, based primarily on the spirit of each specific game. Some have referred to this as the golden rule of sport, which seems to clarify the preceding point for many coaches.

Nothing will infuriate another coach more and stay with that coach longer than what seems to be unethical behavior by an opposing coach. When coaches begin to feud, this often changes the games into bitter grudge matches, which complicates the matter further. It is this lack of ethical behavior on the part of a coach that makes a mockery out of the claim that coaches serve as a role model for honesty and integrity for youngsters to emulate. Ideally, the winningest coach should also win the trophy for sportsmanship.

An example of this facet of professional ethics involves applying for another coaching position. In their eagerness to land that first head coaching position, assistant coaches sometimes apply for a job that rumor has said will be open. This should always be avoided because of the embarrassment it can cause the other coach involved. An application for a coaching position should never be submitted until the opening has been officially announced. It may be that coaches violate this rule of ethics more than any other teacher in similar circumstances. Head coaches are guilty of this, and so are assistant coaches.

Some time ago the Representative Assembly of the National Education Association adopted a new code of ethics as a guide for the teaching profession. Thousands of classroom teachers, school administrators, and members of college faculties helped prepare the code.[4] Since all teachers should be members of a united profession, the basic principles herein enumerated apply to all persons engaged in the professional aspects of education — elementary, secondary and collegiate.

First principle.   The primary obligation of the teaching profession is to guide children, youth, and adults in the pursuit of knowledge and skills, to prepare them in the way of democracy, and to help them to become happy, useful, self-supporting citizens. The ultimate strength of the nation lies in the social responsibility, economic competence, and moral strength of the individual American.

In fulfilling the obligations of this first principle, the teacher will:

(1) Deal justly and impartially with students, regardless of their physical, mental, emotional, political, economic, social, racial, or religious characteristics.
(2) Recognize the differences among students and seek to meet their individual needs.
(3) Encourage students to formulate and work for high individual goals in the development of their physical, intellectual, creative, and spiritual endowment.
(4) Aid students to develop an understanding and appreciation not only of the opportunities and benefits of American democracy but also of their obligations to it.

---

[4]Reprinted by special permission of the National Education Association.

(5) Respect the right of every student to have confidential information about himself withheld except when its release is to authorized agencies or is required by law.

(6) Accept no remuneration for tutoring except in accordance with approved policies of the governing board.

Second principle.   The members of the teaching profession share with parents the task of shaping each student's purposes and acts toward socially acceptable ends. The effectiveness of many methods of teaching is dependent upon cooperative relationships with the home.

In fulfilling the obligations of this second principle, the teacher will:

(1) Respect the basic responsibility of parents for their children.

(2) Seek to establish friendly and cooperative relationships with the home.

(3) Help to increase the student's confidence in his own home and avoid disparaging remarks which might undermine that confidence.

(4) Provide parents with information that will serve the best interests of their children, and be discreet with information received from parents.

(5) Keep parents informed about the progress of their children as interpreted in terms of the purposes of the school.

Third principle.   The teaching profession occupies a position of public trust involving not only the individual teacher's personal conduct, but also the interaction of the school and the community. Education is most effective when these many relationships operate in a friendly, cooperative, and constructive manner.

In fulfilling the obligations of this third principle, the teacher will:

(1) Adhere to any reasonable pattern of behavior accepted by the community for professional persons.

(2) Perform the duties of citizenship and participate in community activities with due consideration for his obligations to his students, his family, and himself.

(3) Discuss controversial issues from an objective point of view, thereby keeping his class free from partisan opinions.

(4) Recognize that the public schools belong to the people of the community, encourage lay participation in shaping the purposes of the school, and strive to keep the public informed of the educational program which is being provided.

(5) Respect the community in which he is employed and be loyal to the school system, community, state and nation.

(6) Work to improve education in the community and to strengthen the community's moral, spiritual, and intellectual life.

Fourth principle.   The members of the teaching profession have inescapable obligations with respect to employment. These obligations are nearly always shared employer-employee responsibilities based upon mutual respect and good faith.

In fulfilling the obligations of this fourth principle, the teacher will:

(1) Conduct professional business through the proper channels.

(2) Refrain from discussing confidential and official information with unauthorized persons.

(3) Apply for employment on the basis of competence only, and avoid asking for a specific position known to be filled by another teacher.

(4) Seek employment in a professional manner, avoiding such practices as the indiscriminate distribution of applications.

(5) Refuse to accept a position when the vacancy has been created through unprofessional activity or pending controversy over professional policy or the application of unjust personnel practices and procedures.

(6) Adhere to the conditions of a contract until service thereunder has been performed, the contract has been terminated by mutual consent, or the contract has otherwise been legally terminated.

(7) Give and expect due notice before a change of position is to be made.

(8) Be fair in all recommendations that are given concerning the work of other teachers.

(9) Accept no compensation from producers of instructional supplies when one's recommendations affect the local purchase or use of such teaching aids.

(10) Engage in no gainful employment, outside of his contract, where the employment affects adversely his professional status or impairs his standing with students, associates, and the community.

(11) Cooperate in the development of school policies and assume one's professional obligations thereby incurred.

(12) Accept one's obligation to the employing board for maintaining a professional level of service.

Fifth principle. The teaching profession is distinguished from many other occupations by the uniqueness and quality of the professional relationships among all teachers. Community support and respect are influenced by the standards of teachers and their attitudes toward teaching and other teachers.

In fulfilling the obligations of this fifth principle, the teacher will:

(1) Deal with other members of the profession in the same manner as he himself wishes to be treated.

(2) Stand by other teachers who have acted on his behalf and at his request.

(3) Speak constructively of other teachers, but report honestly to responsible persons in matters involving the welfare of students, the school system, and the profession.

(4) Maintain active membership in professional organizations and, through participation, strive to attain the objectives that justify such organized groups.

(5) Seek to make professional growth continuous by such procedures as study, research, travel, conferences, and attendance at professional meetings.

(6) Make the teaching profession so attractive in ideals and practices that sincere and able young people will want to enter it.

DISCUSSION QUESTIONS

1. Debate this statement: "There are no degrees of honesty."

2. Many coaches pressure or antagonize officials. What is your opinion of that type of coach?

3. Some coaches coach their players to bend rules and to attempt to upset their opponent. How do you feel about such tactics?

4. What would you do if your principal suspended a player from the team for causing a disruption during the school day?

5. What are professional ethics?

6. "You can discover more about a person in an hour of play than in a year of conversation." React to this.

7. Is going out on strike violating professional ethics?

8. Is it ethical to lose on purpose?

9. When do strategy and ethics come into conflict?

10. What is meant by observing "the spirit of the game?"

11. Can you give a personal example of a situation involving honesty and ethics in athletics?

12. There are five principles stated in the code of ethics adopted by the N.E.A. as a guide for teachers — Discuss how these relate to a teacher/coach.

Photo by Dick Brown, Centre Daily Times.

10

ISSUES AND PROBLEMS

In the long history of sport there have always been problems and issues associated with all aspects of athletics. There is little reason to believe that the future will be any different. Some problems and issues have been solved or resolved, while others seem to defy the best intentions of educators. It may well be that some of these are of such a nature that clear-cut solutions are not possible. In these circumstances, what is needed is for each individual coach to arrive at solutions to these questions, based on what is best for the students in a particular situation.

This chapter is divided into two sections: issues and problems. There will be no attempt to present solutions to all of these points. Instead, alternative considerations will be discussed, which can be debated by the reader. This exercise should prove helpful to a beginning coach in clarifying his or her thinking on each of these matters.

ISSUES

Drugs. Possibly the number one issue in sport at present is drug use and abuse. As is often the case in sport, new ideas and trends seem to begin in professional althletics, and world class amateur athletics. These ideas then filter into the college level, and, eventually, to the high schools. No one can be sure of the extent of drug abuse in sport, but there has been enough documented evidence to prove that it does exist. Along with the increase of drug use in athletics arises the inevitable confusion between fact and myth. For example, are certain pills harmful while others are not; do drugs really help increase athletic performance; do they cause liver and bone damage; and will they increase strength? Drug abuse has gotten so commonplace among world class athletes that victory in any international competition hereafter might be determined by which country has the best doctors, chemists, and pills.

261

An in-depth study of this area is more properly a function of physiology classes, health educators, and the medical profession. It is the responsibility of every coach and prospective coach, however, to make an effort to learn as much about this issue as possible, either as a part of classes taken in undergraduate school or through independent study. A coach's primary concern in this matter has to deal with the physiological effects of drug use and abuse on the human body, and should be an integral part of team meetings at the beginning of each season.

Much of the concern with this issue stems from the apparent increase in the use of androgenic-anabolic steroids, antifatigue and stimulant drugs, and psychic energizers and tranquilizers, without medical supervision.

Drugs are chemicals which produce changes in the body. These changes are intended to be favorable, but may often be undesirable, possibly poisonous, even fatal. They also produce changes in physical functions of the body and in mental states, and a person is always different in some way after taking any kind of drug.

Drugs can be classified into three major classes, according to their effect on the user: stimulants, depressants, and hallucinogens.

STIMULANTS.   Trade names in this category include Benzedrine, Dexedrine, Desoxyn, and Dexamyl. Among the common nicknames are bennies, speed, lid poppers, pep pills, wake-ups, hearts, dexies, eye openers, and copilots. Results of abuse include: (1) restlessness (2) involuntary trembling, (3) enlarged pupils, (4) dry mouth, (5) higher blood pressure, (6) sweating, (7) aggressive behavior, (8) inability to sleep, and (9) headaches.

The danger associated with stimulants is that such drugs can induce a false feeling of "all's well" when, in fact, the user is completely fatigued. It short-circuits feelings of exhaustion, requiring the body to use up its reserves. Finally, there might be sudden and total collapse.

DEPRESSANTS.   Trade names for depressant drugs include Nembutal, Seconal, and Amytal. The nicknames for these drugs are barbs, blues, yellowjackets, goofballs, peanuts, and red devils. The results of abuse are: (1) slurred speech, (2) staggering, (3) drowsiness, and (4) slowed heart rate. The danger associated with depressants is that persons taking large amounts lose control of body functions, become restless, hostile, and quarrelsome. Overdoses can cause death. Reality is distorted, and a user can easily take an overdose, not realizing the effect the drug is having.

HALLUCINOGENS are not associated with this issue in sport primarily because most youngsters do not believe that drugs such as LSD and marijuana will enhance performance, as they believe stimulants or tranquilizers will.

Dr. John Boyer has suggested two basic principles regarding every medical decision involving an athlete:[1]

---

[1]John Boyer, "Drug Use and Abuse in Athletics," *Amateur Athlete*, May, 1971, p. 20.

1. No athlete should be permitted to risk permanent disability by masking a symptom with drugs.
2. Drugs should be used only where a clear therapeutic indication exists, and not to alter the normal physiological processes.

A class of substances usually associated with good health, but now regarded as deleterious when used in massive doses, is vitamins. The gross abuse of vitamins and minerals is now quite common in athletics. Although there is a general lack of danger with large amounts of vitamin therapy, it is not without risk. Deaths have been attributed to excess vitamin intake by the intravenous route. Prolonged ingestion of excessive amounts of vitamins A and D are capable of potentiating serious bone and liver disturbances. As Dr. Daniel Hanley observed, "The unwise use of vitamins by amateur athletes is horrible."[2]

One of the occupational hazards of athletics is pain. Two general kinds of analgesic drugs are available: local anesthetics, such as procaine and ethyl chloride spray, and those that act on the central nervous system, like codeine. Problems can be associated with all of them, such as excitation, coma, convulsions, and possible interference with vision.

The biggest danger lies in the fact that the pain is relieved but the cause is not. Thus an athlete must be cautioned to limit activity even though there is a distinct feeling of relief. Otherwise, more serious damage can be done.

While considerable attention has been given to amphetamines, interest in the androgenic-anabolic steroids (synthetic male sex hormones) has been increasing. The use of steroids is particularly high among athletes who feel it is necessary to gain weight, which in turn will give them added advantage in their particular sport.

The true effects of steroids on an individual is an issue that has not yet been satisfactorily resolved. Research findings have been contradictory. However, the American Medical Association categorically condemns the use of steroids by athletes. Daniel Hanley, official physician to the United States Olympic team in 1972, believes flatly that steroids have zero effect on muscle strength.[3]

The American Medical Association Committee on the medical aspects of sports bluntly maintains: "None of the fads, fallacies, and quackery associated with ergogenic aids (pep pills and the like) is of any more assistance to athletic success than the superstition of never changing underwear during a winning streak."[4]

Dr. William Fowler, Jr. of the U.C.L.A. medical school conducted a 16-week test on 47 men using anabolic steroids. He found no increase in strength, motor performance or vital capacity.[5] Harvard Medical School researchers have determined that pep pills improved performance by only 0.59 per cent in swimmers and 4 per cent in weight lifters.[6]

[2]Theodore Irwin, *Pittsburgh Press Parade*, September 6, 1970, p. 5.
[3]*Ibid.*
[4]*Ibid.*
[5]*Ibid.*
[6]*Ibid.*

On the other hand, J. P. O'Shea of Oregon State University conducted a study over four weeks giving athletes 10 mg of Dianabol per
day. The subjects increased their body weight by 5 per cent. An
assumption was made that the weight gain was in the form of muscle
since the subjects, who were trained weight lifters, increased their
weight-lifting ability by 18 per cent. O'Shea concluded that it was
reasonable to infer that a nutritional and physiological basis exists for
the use of anabolic steroid agents for the purpose of improving physical
performance.[7]

Obviously, there is much confusion surrounding the true effects,
short and long range, of the use of steroids by athletes.

Common usage of steroids has not brought much enlightenment as
to the drug's effects, at least on normal physiology. There are those who
believe the effects are primarily psychological. The fact that there is
still much dispute over steroids is due to a combination of circumstances. The manufacturers of anabolic steroids do not assume any
responsibility for how the drug is taken because this does not come
under jurisdiction of the Food and Drug Administration.

Medical researchers have done comparatively little work on trying
to separate the psychological effects from the physiological effects. As
far as the governing bodies of sport are concerned the use of any kind of
drug is contrary to their standards of ethics, and that is where their
study of the question normally begins and ends. Users of steroids say
the use of stimulants might be unethical, but the use of steroids to build
body bulk is not. Consequently, coaches have another consideration in
this matter, and that involves ethics. Until such time as researchers
have settled the question of drug use on the physiology of the body, the
question of ethics looms perhaps even larger. In the true spirit of sport
competition, athletes are expected to participate to the best of their
natural ability, and to win or lose on that premise. To some, the use of
artificial aids, such as stimulants and steroids, violates this principle,
which in turn violates this basic code of ethics in sport.

Even though amphetamines and steroids are taken because athletes believe they will aid in their performance, both drugs also provide
a psychological lift. To this extent, then, they are no different from
marijuana, heroin and other drugs used by many members of society in
general.[8]

Because of the widespread knowledge of the fact that professional
athletes and world class athletes do use steroids and possibly other
drugs, this is an issue from which high school coaches will not be
immune. As in most matters where a youngster's health is concerned,
the outcome of an athletic contest should never become so important
that a coach would condone anything that might prove physically
harmful to that youngster. Obviously, much research is needed before
the medical considerations are resolved. Ethically, every coach has a
decision to make until myth becomes fact.

---

[7]Nicholas Wade, "Anabolic Steroids: Doctors Denounce Them, But Athletes Aren't
Listening," *Science*, Vol. 176 (June, 1972), p. 1402.

[8]*Ibid.*, p. 1403.

Drugs should be discussed frankly, honestly, and completely with athletes. It should be part of the same kind of counseling coaches give youngsters on alcohol, tobacco, sportsmanship, and other practices associated with athletic competition. While coaches can do an effective teaching job in this matter, there is some evidence that the most effective teaching is done by people, young and old, who have actually suffered through the agony of drug abuse.

Elimination of sports programs.   Another critical issue facing many coaches is the decision some Boards of Education are making to eliminate interscholastic sports. Presumably, this is being done because of the financial burden comprehensive athletic programs place on the overall school budget. The increase in the number of girls' teams, brought on by the enforcement of anti-discrimination laws, has added to this financial problem.

In areas where the athletic programs are financed solely by gate receipts (except for the coaches' salaries), this does not appear to be quite the threat it is where the school board pays the whole bill. Nevertheless, the warning signals are out and coaches cannot sit securely in their offices assuming that sports are an untouchable part of the school program. Nor can they assume that the people who make school policy believe in the values of a well-rounded interscholastic athletic program. Educators are now living in an era of accountability.

Photo courtesy of The Pennsylvania State University Still Photography Services.

Members of school boards often see dollar signs first and values of a program second. As a result, many of their decisions are based primarily on finances. If sports become too expensive, they have no compunction about wiping out an entire program involving thousands of youngsters, as evidenced by a decision made in the Philadelphia city schools during the 1970's. Another consideration is that adults who have had unpleasant experiences in high school athletics or physical education may end up as members of school boards. As a rule, athletic departments can expect little sympathy from these people.

The implications for coaches are clear. Some possible considerations are as follows:

1. Coaches cannot take the existence of athletics for granted.
2. With the tax burden increasing within communities every year, school programs have met, and will no doubt continue to meet, resistance from the people who pay the bills.
3. Coaches must take the initiative to convince the citizens of a community that athletics are not a mere frill in a school program.
4. Coaches cannot assume that everyone values athletic competition.
5. Coaches will have to emphasize the values sport can provide that are not possible for a student to obtain in any other part of the school program. This might not be such an easy task, simply because many people will not accept the old clichés coaches have been reciting for years concerning character building and sportsmanship. The time has come when coaches will have to demonstrate or give evidence that definite advantages accrue to those who take part in sport.
6. The image coaches create in the public eye will have its effect on a community's attitude toward a particular athletic team. The degree of influence this has on people and their attitudes is unknown; that it has some influence is a strong possibility.
7. Coaches in ghetto schools must show that participation in athletics is one positive force in the lives of blacks and other minority groups that will keep them in school, and perhaps provide other opportunities for them.

Politics in sport.   In recent years, high school youngsters have become much more politically aware regarding local, national, and international affairs. As a result, some athletes might elect to use an athletic contest as a stage to express their beliefs or opposition to an issue.

For example, protests have been staged during the playing of the national anthem, during awards ceremonies, and at halftime or pregame. It is possible for athletes to feel pressure from a group or groups either within or outside the school to stage some kind of demonstration at these times.

More than one coach, school, and community have been embarrassed because they assumed this would never happen and consequently never discussed this with the various athletic teams. This can be a very unpleasant situation, and coaches should make it clear to the athletes that high school athletic events are not political arenas.

An athlete and a team represent a school district and community. As a result, many adults feel these youngsters have no right, as representatives of these groups, to express personal political or social points of view while competing under the name of their school. There are other times and places for this. A high school athletic contest is neither the time nor the place.

Religion in sport. This aspect of high school athletics might or might not be an issue in various parts of the country at the moment. However, two factors could change this. First is the tremendous increase in associating religion with sport and second, federal law, which says that there must be separation of church and state.

Part of the reason for this phenomenon is due to three organizations, basically. They are Athletes in Action, the Fellowship of Christian Athletes, and Pro-Athletes Outreach.

It is the Fellowship of Christian Athletes (FCA) that becomes directly involved with high school athletes. This group uses coaches and college athletes to bring younger athletes to religion mainly at summer sports camps and in high school groups called "huddles."

Establishing a group such as FCA in a public school, either thru the initiative of a coach or the athletes, can become an issue. Some public school officials are intimidated by laws concerned with the separation of church and state. Because the FCA is a religious organization, it has been denied access to some schools. In other schools the organization has been forced out because protests have been lodged by a segment of adults in the community.

Another related factor that could draw criticism to coaches and their teams is prayer when associated with an athletic contest. It has become traditional for many coaches to require or to allow their athletes to pray before an athletic contest or individual competition. Sometimes this occurs in full view of the spectators. There are those who would argue that this practice has no place in sport, and certainly not where everyone has to watch.

Whether religion in sport is right or wrong is not the point here. The point is that every coach should be aware that these possibilities exist and that some in the community will heartily approve and some will not. Rather than make an issue out of religion and sport, it would seem appropriate to discuss this with the building principal and the athletes before the fact.

Girls' interscholastic athletics. This has been an issue for decades, and has received added impetus in the past few years. There has been a marked improvement in girls' interscholastic athletics in recent years. However, in most states, girls' athletics have been woefully underdeveloped. This is a result of a combination of things, most of which are carryovers of old-fashioned beliefs, myths, and attitudes toward girls' sports. This is typified by the verse written by Ogden Nash, "Lads don't make passes at athletic lasses."

The long-time belief that physical exertion could be harmful to girls has been dispelled. Now one of the biggest obstacles to the participation of girls in athletics seems to be the question of femininity and aggressiveness. There are those who believe that active participation in sport will destroy a girl's feminine characteristics. The main concern seems to center around aggression in sport.

The chief argument against this belief lies in the very definition of the word feminine. It seems that femininity and aggressiveness are not compatible in many established definitions of the word. While it may be that aggressiveness is, in fact, a trait inborn in women that manifests itself in traditionally acceptable ways, like protecting her family, it has been deliberately suppressed in a competitive situation like sport, because society has determined that it isn't ladylike. What is needed is a less restrictive definition of the word feminine. There must also be an awakening to the fact that sports are for girls too, and that aggressive behavior is every bit as much a part of the female psyche as that of the male. There is no concrete evidence that participation in sport causes a girl to be less "feminine."

Another issue affecting girls' sport is the sharing of facilities. Compounding the issue is the traditional attitude of many male coaches and principals, who regard girls' sports as relatively unimportant. Consequently, in most cases when there is a showdown over practice facilities, the girls lose. This has changed somewhat because of equal opportunity laws, but in too many cases the basic problem has not changed that much.

In fairness to men who coach the pressure sports, such as football, baskeball, and wrestling, some of their resistance stems from the knowledge that losing seasons can cost them their job. Generally speaking, this is not the case in girls' high school sports. Consequently, the priorities for practice are clear in the minds of the male coaches, at least.

What is needed, obviously, is more facilities. But this is not always possible. Therefore, the job of selling the value of girls' sports becomes a task for women coaches, and sometimes the greatest support will come from the families whose daughters participate. School administrators can and will ignore requests of individual teachers, but they are particularly sensitive to the same concerns when expressed by the people in the community who pay the school's bills — namely the parents.

Winning.   The claim that coaches stress winning too much is another issue raised by critics of high school athletics. Coaches sometimes add legitimacy to this criticism when they publicly announce their philosophy of coaching by saying such things as: "winning isn't the only thing, it is everything; losing is worse than death; if we have a losing season the whole year will be a complete failure" or, "If we don't teach winning, what do we teach, losing?"

Coaches are competitors, and they like to win. There can be little argument over that.

It is time for coaches to stop defending themselves over the matter of teaching youngsters to play to win. There is nothing wrong with this as long as winning does not become the sole purpose of sport.

It may be that the great concern coaches have about winning has been fostered not by coaches entirely, but by the people in a community who expect or demand that the high school teams win. In most instances a coach's overemphasis on winning is in reality a mirror of the expectations of the community in which he or she coaches. The coach knows that winning means job security. Therefore, the coach's competitive spirit to win is magnified by the reality that the community wants winning teams and the coach can lose the job if this doesn't happen.

In this light, it would appear that the criticism of coaches who seem to care only about winning may not be justified.

Junior high school athletics. Competitive athletics in junior high school and the upper elementary grades is another issue with no absolute answers. In some communities, school-organized competitive sport in wrestling, football, basketball, and gymnastics has been expanded to include not only junior high students, but elementary children also — sometimes extending down into the third grade. The idea is that the sooner youngsters begin in sports, the better they will be when they become seniors in high school.

Like many beliefs coaches have, this one is not based on fact. There is no proof that a youngster who begins competing in wrestling, for instance, in the fourth grade will be better as a senior than the youngster who begins at some other point along the various grades. Further, there is no proof that participation in competitive sport of any kind in the lower grades will make a better athlete in senior high school than experiences in a well-rounded program of elementary physical education and intramurals, where everyone gets a chance to participate and where there is probably less pressure to win.

Junior high school athletics are much more common than grade school programs, and the feeling of many varsity coaches is that the junior high program should be patterned after that of the varsity. The logical reason is that this provides continuity, consistency, and progression in the program, all of which are educationally sound. One of the biggest problems at this level is to find qualified coaches who will coach in junior high. Many head coaches believe that this is where the best coaches should be assigned. This is the key to a successful junior high athletic program.

Little League athletic programs. Activities of this type relate closely to the preceding point about organized competitive sport for elementary school children. However, there is one additional facet involved which creates an entirely different problem. These programs are usually organized outside the school by non-school personnel, and dominated by adults who are not trained as teachers. The first mistake these adults make is to assume little children are miniature adults, and this simply is not true. As a result the programs are organized from the adult point of view, with little or no regard to what these children need or want.

Often the adults involved in Little League programs insist they are qualified to coach because of prior personal participation in sport somewhere, sometime. The logic in this statement is comparable to that of an individual's claiming to be a qualified surgeon by having undergone a successful appendectomy at one time.

Many successful big-time coaches have denounced Little League sports. Joe Paterno of Penn State, for one, was highly critical of Little Leagues in his book, *Football My Way*. In Coach Paterno's opinion, youngsters sometimes get a distorted view of themselves and their ability because of the publicity they often receive through Little League sports.

This author agrees, and further maintains that far too often Little League athletic programs for both girls and boys are, in reality, adult recreation programs. It is the adults who make the rules, choose the teams, direct practice, choose who will play, get most excited over officials' decisions, determine when and how long practice will be, and get into fights — verbal and physical — over something that occurs when eight-year-old children are playing a game. The adults also choose all-star teams and organize banquets for these same children. The author contends that it is doubtful that any of this is of any real concern to an eight- or nine-year-old youngster, or of any value, for that matter.

Included in this issue is the desire of many townspeople, and some coaches, to establish tackle football programs for elementary age children. Some of the volunteer coaches believe this is how little boys learn to be tough. In reality this is how some little boys learn to dislike the game, because they find out that playing tackle football can hurt, and not many children enjoy playing any game that hurts. There is also the negative reaction of the medical profession to take into account in this matter.

For example, many doctors agree that pre-adolescent bone growth is more rapid than muscle development, so that temporarily the bones and joints lack the normal protection of covering muscles and supporting tendons. During this period, a youngster is particularly susceptible to dislocations of joints and to bone injuries, especially to the epiphyses, or ends, of long bones. Dr. C. L. Lowman polled 400 orthopedists on this point. Approximately 75 per cent of them agreed with the idea that athletic competition was not good for young adolescents, and that body contact sports should be eliminated for this age group.[9]

Many people in the medical profession have expressed concern over injury to the elbow associated with pitchers in Little League baseball. This usually occurs as a result of youngsters trying to throw hard curve balls.

---

[9]John L. Reinhart, *Competitive Athletics For Pre-Teen Age Children* (June 5, 1957).

There is some concern, too, that there are not only dangers to the physical well-being of a pre-adolescent involved in competitive sport, but emotional ramifications as well.

Dr. Muzafer Sherif, a social psychologist, conducted what has become known as the "Lord of the Flies experiment." He took a group of 11-year-old boys to an isolated camp and split them into two groups. They competed against each other every day in baseball, football, and tug-of-war. The entire emphasis was that the only thing that mattered was to win. What began as fun and games quickly turned to hostility. Onetime best friends were at each other's throats, even when brought together for meals and movies. The situation did not get better until they joined in cooperative efforts that served everyone's mutual benefit. His conclusion was that competition alone is not inherently antagonistic to human behavior, but where winning becomes all-important to children, watch out![10]

The key to sound Little League programs of any type is intelligent supervision, based on sound educational principles of physical education. Properly conducted, Little Leagues are not harmful. Improperly conducted, they can be dangerous.

Three recommendations pased by a White House Conference on Children expressed the following concerning Little League sports:

1. That adults avoid exploiting youth by pressuring them into highly competitive organized activities for which their minds and bodies are not adapted; that they recognize children as individuals rather than as projects in leisure-time pursuits.
2. That schools and communities cooperate in designing out-of-school programs to provide constructive leisure time activity consistent with sound principles of child development, and to counteract pressures for competitive athletics promoted by groups with good intentions, but limited knowledge of the physical and social needs of children.
3. That competitive sports for pre-adolescents . . . supervised by trained and qualified leaders . . . be further investigated as to their value for children.

It would seem that the main implication for a high school coach in this matter is to think carefully about all the ramifications before suggesting the start of a Little League program for a particular sport. If such a program already exists, the high school coach should attempt to provide some sound leadership, in order to keep the program, and the adults involved, from exploiting the children who participate.

The argument that "children will play the game anyway, so why not have adults step in to teach them the right way and make it more fun" is not valid. When children organize their own games, they set all the rules and limits to suit themselves. They know what they want and what they can do better than some adult, who might be looking for a vicarious experience through children for reasons known only to him- or herself.

Bad experiences in Little League athletics can hurt participation in high school athletics. If children learn early in life to dislike a game, for

[10]Ibid., p. 10.

any reason, they tend to give it up completely. In their minds it just isn't worth it to them, and so they look elsewhere for some other thing that will be more fun.

An alternative to this could be a Saturday morning program for elementary youngsters, organized by a high school coach. In this program, the members of the high school team serve as coaches with the only adult involved being the head coach. In this manner, a real educator can design, conduct, and control a great program for the youngsters, in which they hopefully learn to enjoy playing the game, whatever it may be. It would seem that the only legitimate justification for any kind of Little League sport would be to teach youngsters to enjoy athletics for enjoyment's sake. Fundamentals and strategy can be taught later. Since youngsters mature physically at varying rates, fundamentals and strategy should be a secondary concern. Some children are simply not ready to learn certain fundamentals. When adults keep insisting that they try, a feeling of failure and frustration can develop in a boy or girl which can turn into dislike for the game.

All-star teams. The selection of all-star teams is another issue involved in coaching that needs to be given consideration by members of the coaching profession. There are all kinds of all-star teams — league, district, sectional, state, area, and national. Members of these teams are chosen by coaches, newspaper writers, fans, civic organizations, and magazines. The existence of all-star teams is usually taken for granted; few educators, if any, ever question their purpose or value.

The reasons given for all-star team selections usually include the following:

1. They serve as recognition for outstanding athletes.
2. They might help some youngster get an athletic scholarship.
3. If coaches don't pick an all-star team, the local newspapers will.
4. Announcing an all-star team in the paper helps sell papers.
5. All-star teams serve as motivation for high school athletes.

As a matter of fact, it may be that all-star teams have simply grown to the point where coaches have learned to live with them, without really questioning the reason for their existence.

Unfortunately, choosing all-star teams can often be an unpleasant experience for a coach. Within leagues, hard feelings sometimes develop between coaches as they struggle to win votes for their own athletes. Some leagues choose all-star teams by a priority system, whereby the final league standings determine the number of youngsters chosen from each school. In this situation each coach then picks his or her own people and places them on the all-star team without any vote taking place. This method insures representation for every team in a league. Obviously this leaves a lot to be desired.

In choosing district, regional, and state all-star teams, politics really takes over. This is where coaches buy and trade votes, and enter

Photo courtesy of The Pennsylvania State University Still Photography Services.

into arrangements to push for certain athletes. These sessions take on all the appearances of a miniature political convention, minus the demonstrations. There is no doubt that many outstanding athletes are named to all-star teams. However, it is also true that there have been and will continue to be high school athletes who are named to various all-star teams primarily because their coach is an excellent politician.

Some coaches make it a practice to ditto short biographies of their best athletes and mail these all over a state with a request that each recipient vote for this youngster. Usually, the last sentence tells the reader that the sender would be happy to trade votes even without any idea for whom this coach might be voting. Undoubtedly, there are coaches who feel they have an obligation to athletes to push them for all-star awards. On the other hand there are also coaches who push their own people for all-star recognition for selfish reasons. The latter group are those who use this as a personal scorecard, as a reflection of their coaching ability. The assumption is that the coach personally created X number of all-star athletes, therefore the coach must also be superior.

There might be some truth to the claim that all-star recognition will help a youngster get an athletic scholarship. If an all-star basketball team was chosen, the question might be asked whether or not the athletes chosen sixth or tenth have scholarship opportunities hurt because they didn't make the first five? And what about those who receive only honorable mention? If all-star teams are to help youngsters, do they; or are more athletes hurt because of the final selections? In a 10-team basketball league, for example, only five people will be first team all-stars. That means that if there are a total of 100 athletes involved, only 5 per cent will be chosen as outstanding while 95 per cent will be tabbed as something less than this. Looking at the claim that all-star teams help youngsters, it appears skewed in a negative direction.

Theoretically, high school athletics exist in our schools because they have educational value. The existence of all-star teams in this framework is questionable.

All-star games. These special events have become a seemingly permanent fixture associated with high school sports, in many states at least. In some areas, all-star games between states are played regularly. Some state high school athletic associations have outlawed all-star games. Others have taken the easy way out by ignoring the games, especially if the all-stars are all graduated seniors, and if the game is played after the school year ends.

There are many reasons given for having these games. For the coaches involved this can serve as an honor to be savored or as an honor to keep on file when applying for that really big job. Some all-star games surround themselves with an air of legitimacy by using part of the gate receipts for various charities and scholarships. To some people, using high school athletes for these purposes is not consistent with the stated objectives of secondary school athletic programs.

Another reason frequently given for the existence of these games is that it will help youngsters get scholarships. If the game is played after a school year ends it would appear that a coach has done a poor job in helping a youngster get into a college, if the youngster has to wait that long for people to recognize this talent.

An additional factor associated with these games, that might be the primary basis for their being, is the financial gain accruing, not only to the promoters, but to the community where the game is played. This is one of the arguments opponents of all-star games use in their criticism of the event. They believe that youngsters should not be used for entertainment and profit.

The methods for choosing the participants in these games is not without a large share of politics, and participating in the selection process can sometimes give one an uncomfortable feeling of having prostituted the purpose of high school athletics. At the same time, some coaches feel a great deal of elation because they believe in all-star games, and have succeeded in getting one of their athletes involved.

Polls. State rankings of teams is another "fact of life" for many high school coaches throughout the country. There are states where a system of playoffs determines state champions in every sport. There are others where state championship games are held for some sports, while the state champion in football, for example, is chosen by a vote from a few selected coaches and sportswriters throughout the state. The origion of such a practice is unknown, but its existence is real.

Aside from the many obvious flaws in picking a state champion by ballot only, probably the worst practice this breeds is that it encourages coaches to run up a score whenever they get the chance. To coaches who attach a lot of importance of these ratings, beating someone by a huge score is the quickest way to attract the attention of those few who somehow have been granted voting privileges.

The fact that a lot of youngsters can be humiliated in the process seems incidental to the ambitious coach. But this factor alone should be enough to cause highly principled coaches to outlaw the existence of state rankings based on such a method.

An interesting aspect of these three latter issues is the role the high school principal can play in the situations. Not only are there ambitious high school coaches, but there are also many ambitious high school principals. These individuals see every aspect of the school program that is highly visible to the public as a personal accomplishment, since the principal is the educational leader of the school. In these situations, coaches sometimes find themselves under pressure from the principal to push youngsters for all-star recognition, and to work for representation in all-star games, and a high standing in state rankings.

If a coach feels the same way, and the principal will insure that the coach can organize a program in a way to become a power in the state, this is good. However, if a coach and principal do not see eye to eye on this matter, this can create difficulties for the coach.

Excusing athletes from physical education classes.   This is another issue that has been debated for many years, and it continues to be a source of debate in many schools. There are at least four schools of thought in this matter: (1) athletes should be required to take physical education, (2) athletes should be excused from physical education during the season in which they participate on an interscholastic team, (3) any athlete participating in at least two sports should be excused from physical education the entire year, and (4) athletes should take physical education, but be excused on game days.

Theoretically, physical education classes offer a wide variety of experiences for the students. If athletes do not participate in these classes, they miss out on a great opportunity to learn about activities other than the sport they complete in. Generally, this is the rationale behind the policy of having all athletes enrolled in regular physical education classes.

As a rule, coaches object to this policy because of possible injury to an athlete and because the physical education program might be woefully inadequate. For example, a baseball coach might have a legitimate complaint if the varsity baseball players spent the entire spring playing softball in physical education classes. Basketball coaches get upset when their best athlete has a wrestling match in class on the day of a basketball game.

At one time, excusing athletes from physical education classes was widespread. There now appears to be a distinct trend away from this. In schools where comprehensive physical education programs exist there really is no reason why athletes should be excused from class. Many physical education teachers have discovered that having athletes in class can be a positive influence on the other students. Some teachers

Photo courtesy of Mamie Rollins.

will use athletes as assistants to help teach skills they know well, or as officials on days when interscholastic games are scheduled.

The idea that athletes do not need physical education because they get plenty of exercise at practice is valid only if the regular physical education classes offer exercise only. Aside from concern over possible injury, the physical education teacher also needs to exercise caution so that the athletes do not dominate the class. This can happen easily, and in the process, youngsters who really need these experiences frequently move into the background and receive very little value from the physical education class. This is an unfortunate experience and can create a lot of ill feeling toward physical education in these same youngsters.

Soliciting funds. Money-raising projects for athletic teams are another source of debate in many school systems, particularly when the athletes themselves canvass a community door to door. Some school districts have definite policies regarding student solicitation of funds. In most communities, with the tax burden already quite high, boards of education are very much concerned about public relations. Numerous solicitations by student organizations can become a nuisance factor in the community. The parents of the athletes may also object to their children's participation in these schemes.

Some coaches believe that there is nothing wrong with the idea;

others do not believe that soliciting funds is a part of high school athletics. Other coaches will compromise when the need arises and allow youngsters to organize money-making projects within the school, such as dances, selling pins or pennants, car washes, pancake dinners, selling candy bars, and so on.

Prior to embarking on such a project, every coach should clear it through the athletic director and principal, in order to avoid any repercussions from school officials or citizens of the community.

Naturally, there are other issues in high school athletics, some of which were mentioned earlier in this text. Further, what appears to be an issue in one part of the country may not be an issue anywhere else; an issue in one sport may not be of any concern in other sports; an issue in men's athletics may not be an issue for women, and vice versa. Therefore, the preceding list of issues is not all inclusive but seems to be at the forefront of the most pressing ones facing high school coaches at present.

PROBLEMS

The problems and potential problems associated with inter-scholastic athletic programs are virtually without end. Whenever coaches believe they have seen them all, new and unexpected problems often occur demanding a solution or reaction.

It is possible that all coaches do not experience the same problems to the same degree, or view the same things as problems, for that matter. Circumstances and personalities, along with other factors, have some impact on what appears to be a problem in situation "A," but is not a concern in situation "B."

In order to get some feeling of what men and women high school coaches perceived as problem areas, an open ended questionnaire listing 16 problem areas was created and mailed to several hundred high school coaches, male and female, for their reaction.

The list of potential problem areas, and the coaches' reactions, follow.

1. Fan control
2. Finances
3. Administrative support
4. Discipline
5. Facilities
6. Equipment
7. Parental interference
8. Injuries
9. Lack of community support
10. Attitude of high school students regarding participation in sport
11. Lack of faculty interest
12. Criticism from fans
13. Pressure to win (from the community)
14. Officiating
15. Lack of professional ethics among opposing coaches
16. Legal liability

The top concerns of the women coaches were:

1. Attitude of high school students regarding participation in sport
2. Facilities and officiating (tie)

Down the list, in a tie for 3rd, were finances and lack of faculty interest.

These coaches made additonal comments, elaborating on areas of concern to them as individuals. The majority of the comments had to do with the attitude of the athletes. For example:

- "I feel that there is a problem with apathy in the school system of today. It is much easier to not accept a challenge than it is to strive to become a good athlete."
- "A personal concern is the lack of student interest in supporting teams and also in going out for a sport. The athletes do not seem to be as dedicated as in previous years. I don't see much extra effort being given — this is particularly true of the boys at this school."
- "Players, in my opinion, aren't willing to sacrific sufficiently in order to be the best athlete that they could possibly be."
- "Players today simply are not willing to give of themselves 100 per cent — 100 per cent of the time for the team!"
- "Students today do not value a varsity sport like they used to. There are so many other extracurricular areas to go into, which may lead to less dedication to a student's goal to make, or become a member of, the varsity squad. They do not try as hard — if they fail, they quit and go into something else, instead of giving it the second and third efforts! I just don't see that in today's athletes anymore."
- "Discipline of players, enforcing attendance regulations; trying to aid students in development of self-discipline and dedication."
- "The girls were appalled when I placed mandatory attendance at all practices. In the beginning, they felt tennis was an 'inferior' sport or a minor sport, not requiring as much 'athletic' ability."

Two comments reflected concern for specialization versus generalization:

- "The turn-out for varsity sports is less than in previous years — there are more sports being offered during one season; as a result, the students with athletic ability are being 'spread thin.' I've also found that the dedication toward one sport has decreased greatly."
- "Coaches are putting pressure on players to specialize, because some are making their respective sport an all-year activity. This is grossly unfair to young athletes who should have an opportunity to experience participation and competition in other areas. (Also refers to making athletes decide between, say, a sport and band or a play when they could easily do both.)"

And finally, the ever-present concern about finances:

- "Because of the forced addition of the girls teams, all at once, financially, most schools are having problems. This also leads to equipment and personnel problems, and needless to say, facilities are totally inadequate. So, cuts are being made, rather than more money appropriated; the quality of supplies is being sacrificed."
- "Boys have a much larger budget than girls; also the faculty on the whole doesn't support the students in school activities."

The top concerns of the male coaches were:

1. Attitude of high school students regarding participation in sport
2. Finances
3. Facilities

In a distant tie for 4th were administrative support, discipline, and officiating.

The male coaches offered these additional comments expressing their individual concerns. Again, the majority reflect concern for the attitude of today's high school athlete:

— "It is becoming more and more difficult to motivate the students to participate, due to the many outside forces pulling at them. They will take the time to be on the first team, but they feel it's not worth the effort to be a substitute."
— "I think the attitude of a great many athletes is going downhill. They don't mind losing enough. I don't advocate 'win or else,' but if you are not willing to do some things on your own to benefit the total team effort, you are really hurting the cause. Self-discipline is almost nonexistent. Discipline is looked at as a punishment, rather than as a requirement to make you a better athlete. No one really seems to want to push themselves to become better. If they participate, that is enough. I don't want an athlete who just likes to win. I want the one who doesn't like to lose and is not satisfied with himself — one who always wants to improve, and gives the sport much more than the sport gives him. I guess I don't think enough people are willing to earn the title of an athlete — they assume it is free."
— "Lessening of 'team' concept, in that many quit rather than be a benchwarmer. The selfishness of participants in immediate outward reward expectations for effort. Lack of deep enough interest or desire to work hard year-round to excel in more than one or two players."
— "The students want to win without paying the price that it takes to produce a championship team; they cannot discipline themselves to the extent that it pays off in a team effort; they are more worried about individual accomplishments."
— "Concerning discipline, here we are referring to self discipline of the athlete, his impatience with his inability for instant success, and his lack of willingness to drive himself and work out his shortcomings."
— "In the past six years as head coach I have found that the 'self-disciplined' athlete is harder to find. By this, I mean during that time away from the practice sessions and dual meets."
— "I see less and less total commitment and effort by athletes. I see more and more satisfaction with something less than the best young men are capable of accomplishing."
— "There seems to be a growing trend to not participate unless you are highly successful. There are very few 'pluggers' any more."
— "It no longer is an honor to belong to athletic teams; the kids seem to think they are doing you a favor."

Boys are also facing decisions regarding specialization:

— "Another problem in our district is coaches putting too much pressure on kids to individualize; that is, if you want to be a football player for me, lift weights after football season and be ready for spring practice. Or, you should play basketball all year round if you want to be good enough to play for me."

Financing for athletic teams was also a concern of both men and women coaches.

- "Difficult to separate finances and facilities, since they are closely connected. Since the onrush of girls interscholastic competition, facilities have become the major problem to me as a coach, and as a parent with children participating."
- "One of our problems (due to lack of turnover in the faculty; coaches salaries, and some others) is staffing our coaching positions, especially with assistant coaches."

These comments reflected additional concerns of the men coaches — but were not indicated by women coaches.

- "People of the community, especially parents of athletes, have what I call the 'every complex.' That is, every kid should play every minute of every game, but still, you should win every game."
- "Over-involvement of community, resulting in pressure to WIN—or you're fired."
- "Lack of professional ethics among opposing coaches."

It is interesting to note the number of comments that appear, dealing with "attitude". This point seems to be a common thread for both male and female coaches. It is also apparent that the word "attitude" means slightly different things to different people.

If this attitude problem is as great as it appears to be, it seems obvious that high school coaches, in general, will experience a great deal of frustration if they fail to recognize this particular frame of mind in today's high school athletes.

Ideally, people become coaches and remain in that role because they love it. Apparently this love of sport and participation in it is not always reflected to the same degree in some of the students who are to be coached.

Based on the limited information of this survey the following implications are suggested. High school coaches should:

1. make an effort to find out exactly why youngsters are out for a particular sport;
2. attempt to find out what the youngsters' motivation is, and what their personal goals are;
3. do a better selling job on the advantages of being on "the team";
4. create an atmosphere around their sport which makes it desirable and enjoyable to participate;
5. teach the importance of "sticking it out", versus the less desirable trait of being an easy quitter;
6. teach the quality of selflessness;
7. teach concern for others;
8. or — face the fact that not all high school students view any particular athletic team as the beginning and the end of the universe, as we coaches sometimes tend to do.

It does appear that there might be a real difference between the way high school coaches view participation in sport and the way the students perceive this experience. This difference, in turn, could create a great deal of misunderstanding, and cause problems that might otherwise be avoidable. The assumption that all youngsters come out for athletic teams solely because they like it is erroneous and could be a contributing factor to coaches' identifying students' attitudes toward participation in a sport as a problem.

In addition to these problems identified by coaches, there are several others that deserve attention.

Legal liability. Law suits seem to have become a way of life in today's society, and no one is exempt, including coaches. Rules, decisions and actions of coaches are no longer accepted without question, as they once were. Since there is an element of risk in sport, along with the everpresent chance of injury, coaches are particularly vulnerable to legal action.

When speaking of legal liability in athletics, one need only be concerned with the area of torts. A tort is a legal wrong that results in direct or indirect injury to an individual or that individual's property, and for which payment for damages may be obtained by court action.

Photo courtesy of The Pennsylvania State University Still Photography Services.

When an injury occurs in athletics, the plaintiff, or injured party, must allege that the injury was caused or aggravated as a result of the coach's negligence. Negligence in this sense can be either an act of omission or commision. The critical question that must be answered is, should the teacher, through reasonable prudence and foresight, have anticipated danger or injury to a pupil under the particular set of circumstances in question. If the answer to this question is yes, then the teacher has been negligent in the performance of his or her duties.

COMMON AREAS OF NEGLIGENCE

There are several factors that commonly give rise to negligence claims in athletics.

1. *The absence of protective measures.* The coach is expected to anticipate the hazards involved in any activity, and to take whatever steps may be necessary to protect the safety of the athlete.
2. *Poor selection of activities.* The coach must select activities appropriate to the age, size, and skill levels of the student. Failure to do so can lead to serious injury, and constitutes an act of negligence.
3. *Unsafe condition of facilities and equipment.* Before using any practice area, the coach should always examine it carefully to be sure it is free of hazards. Such things as broken glass or holes on playing fields often lead to serious injury. No athlete should be allowed to use a piece of equipment until the coach has examined it to insure its safe operation and freedom from defect.
4. *Inadequate supervision.* The question of supervision involves both a qualitative and a quantitative judgment. The coaches must be knowledgeable in the specific activity they are supervising, and must then provide supervision during the course of the activity. Under no circumstance should athletes be permitted to play or practice without proper supervision.
5. *Inadequate control measures.* Closely tied with the question of supervision is that of control measures. Under no circumstances should the actions of one youngster or a group create a hazardous situation for others. Horseplay not only impedes learning, it often leads to injury.
6. *Use of poor judgment.* The area of coach's judgment is rather broad, and encompasses a wide variety of situations in which the coach fails to apply common sense and prudent judgment and a student suffers harm as a result. Examples would be:
   a. asking a student to assume an unreasonable risk; for example, activities designed primarily to build "courage."
   b. failure to apply proper first aid, or exceeding the limits of first aid.

These are, in general terms, some of the areas which frequently give rise to negligence claims. While the list may appear formidable, remember that a good coach who has a genuine concern for the welfare of the students will rarely be found neglecting their well-being. A few minutes of careful planning and preparation are usually all that are necessary to insure safety.

DEFENSES AGAINST NEGLIGENCE

There are several defenses against negligence which can be employed in legal actions where appropriate. The best defense, of course, is providing the extra ounce of care which prevents an accident from happening in the first place. There are times, however, when despite the most conscientious efforts, an accident occurs. In such cases, the following defenses are often employed:

1. *Proximate Cause.* The element of proximate cause must be proven in any case involving negligence. It is not sufficient to merely allege that a coach was negligent in his or her duties, one must prove additionally that this negligence was the cause of the damage which occurred to the student.
2. *Act of God.* An act of God is an accident which is attributable to the forces of nature, such as lightning striking a student, or a limb of a tree falling on a student. If, however, a prudent person could have foreseen the likelihood of such an occurrence, then an act of God is not a valid defense.
3. *Contributory Negligence.* Contributory negligence attributes part of the blame for an injury to the injured party. It usually arises when a player was injured while doing something which he or she was clearly warned not to do. In some states, proof of contributory negligence constitutes sufficient cause for dismissal of a negligence claim. The courts are beginning to turn, however, to a concept of comparative negligence, whereby the youngster is liable only to the degree to which he or she caused his or her own injury, and the coach can still be held liable in part. In cases where student negligence is present, the coach is still liable for a settlement if some percentage of liability is determined by the courts.
4. *Assumption of Risk.* Anyone who participates in sports and physical activities assumes that there are certain dangers built into the very nature of the activity. Since the coach cannot protect the student from such built-in dangers, he or she cannot be held liable for their occurrence. The amount of risk which a student can be expected to assume varies with age and skill level. The wise teacher will be sure that the students are made aware of the dangers in an activity, as well as the techniques by which they can be minimized.

The danger of accidental injury is everpresent in the area of sport. While you can never completely avoid it, you can minimize it by taking a few simple precautions.

1. Know your athletes. Be aware of their abilities and health needs, and plan your practices accordingly.
2. Be sure your equipment is safe and well cared for. Also, be sure to secure all equipment when not in use, to prevent injuries through unauthorized use.
3. Carefully organize and supervise your team. The better the planning and organization the less likelihood of injury.
4. Provide thorough instruction in both performance and safety techniques.
5. Should an accident occur:
   a. administer first aid only — do not practice medicine;
   b. get professional medical assistance as soon as possible;
   c. keep an accurate record of the exact circumstances surrounding the accident. The latter is particularly useful in the event of suit, since memory tends to dim with time.

Coaching your own son or daughter.   One of the unique problems in coaching occurs when a coach's own youngster is ready to try out for the team father or mother coaches.

Two distinct possibilities occur at once: first, the parent bends over backward in an attempt not to show any favoritism, and in fact makes it tougher on their own youngster; or, second, the parent plays their son or daughter on the first unit if the youngster has any kind of athletic ability at all.

The first situation really can be unfair to a youngster, while the second instance can create morale problems on a team, and subject the coach to a lot of criticism. As a result, coaches sometimes decide this is a good time to give up their coaching careers. Basically, their thinking is to give their children a fair chance to make the team, without any pressure that could otherwise occur. Normally, this situation exists after an individual has been coaching for about 16 years, and for some this seems like a good time to "hang it up."

One coach summed up the problem perfectly when he said, "I hope my son is so good that it is obvious to everyone that he should be playing, or so poor that I couldn't possibly think of allowing him to play. But if he is average, I'm in trouble."

Crowd control.   Another problem that needs close attention in some areas of the country is crowd control. This can usually be narrowed down to the fans at football games, basketball games, and wrestling matches. Many city leagues have abandoned night football, as a way to prevent trouble during and after games. This usually cuts down on the size of the crowd, which also reduces the gate receipts, which in turn creates a financial problem.

Presented by Neil Dougherty, Rutgers University, to the Pennsylvania Department of Education Curriculum Conference. June 22–25, 1976.

There are many recorded incidents in which basketball teams played games in locked, empty gymnasiums because of fights and riots involving spectators. The excitement of combat between two wrestlers, and the proximity of the spectators to the action, can also create a dangerous mob spirit.

Normally, it is not the responsibility of coaches to maintain crowd control. This belongs to the school officials and other authorities, including the police. But coaches do have an inescapable responsibility for their actions during a game, with regard to their effects on spectators. There is no question that a coach who becomes a raving, screaming, violent individual on the sidelines can incite a crowd into becoming a mob. This probably occurs more readily in basketball and wrestling because of proximity. More often than not, the fans take their cue from the coach when the officials' decisions go against their team. As a matter of fact, so do the players on the team.

In a situation where spectators begin to get out of hand, a coach who has a lot of courage can do much to stop this and bring the spectators back to their senses. If a coach would stop the game, use the public address system and tell the fans to stop abusing the officials and the other team, or else watch the game be forfeited, a riot might be prevented and saner minds would prevail. Obviously, this would take a lot of courage, but courage should be a quality every coach possesses. Abraham Lincoln once said, "To sin by silence, when they should protest, makes cowards of men."

Pregnancy and marriage.   This is another problem that has increased rapidly over the past few years and concerns male varsity athletes who accept responsibility for a pregnancy, but still want to participate in sports; or girls who become pregnant and want to participate on a team before and after the birth of a baby. Along with this is the question of married high school students participating in sport.

In the past, many schools had a policy which prevented married students from participating in any school-sponsored extra-curricular activity. Recently, this has been challenged in courts of law in a few cases, and the policy was overruled as illegal. The safest course for an athletic department in this question would be to recommend a policy sanctioned by the board of education, so that one individual or department is not put in a position of having to defend policy in a court of law.

In the case where children are born out of wedlock, and the young people involved do not get married, another consideration arises and that concerns morality. It is interesting to note that many coaches will enforce training rules and punish offenders through some sort of disciplinary measure; but few, if any, printed training rules cover immoral behavior.

With today's changing attitudes about almost everything, including morals, some young coaches are apt to say that they have no right to pass moral judgment on an athlete. They claim that bearing illegitimate children does not have much to do with moral behavior. Rather, it is simply a mistake, and young people should not be penalized for this by being prevented from playing on a high school athletic team.

Others maintain that high school students who get themselves into this predicament should not be members of a high school team because of the influence they might have on their teammates, younger people on the team, or youngsters in the community who look up to athletes as models to pattern themselves after.

Once again, the coaching situation will have a great bearing on what action is or is not taken in such a case. The attitude of the community, school, administration, fellow coaches, and the individual coach all help to determine what seems to be the best course of action. There is no easy answer to this question that would satisfy everyone in every situation. There are many ramifications, whichever decision is made, for the school, the coach, and the youngsters involved; especially the health and safety of a pregnant female athlete.

It would seem prudent for every coach going into a new situation to investigate existing policy concerning this matter. If there is none, it becomes urgent to establish one before a situation arises that forces the establishment of such a policy.

Misconduct and discipline.   One of the disciplinary practices some schools employ is to declare a youngster ineligible for a particular game because of misconduct in school. Sometimes this comes from a principal; sometimes it comes from a teacher. Regardless of its origin, this kind of action usually infuriates a coach unless the youngster's behavior was so flagrant that the coach wouldn't let the athlete participate either.

Using athletic participation as a club to hold over a youngster's head is a questionable educational technique. Teachers who have come to dislike the athletic department or a particular coach can create tremendous problems if allowed to hold people out of a game because they misbehaved in class.

This is unfair to the young person; it is unfair to a team; and it is unfair to a coach. Keeping a youngster out of chemistry for misbehaving in math is unheard of. When a youngster misbehaves in athletics, there is no known case on record where discipline was applied by holding the youngster out of English. If athletics truly have educational value, a principal should never allow this educational experience to be denied a youngster because of something that occurred in some other educational experience in the school. Educationally, this is not sound. If a school principal does not believe this, a coach and athletic department have a selling job to do to convince the principal otherwise.

As was mentioned earlier in this chapter, there is no limit to the problems that are associated with an athletic department. Those presented here are ones that apply to all high school teams, in varying degrees, nationwide, and appear to be the most critical problems facing coaches at this time.

Photo courtesy of Mike Shine.

CONCLUSION

My first consideration shall be the welfare of the boys and girls. My leadership shall be wholesome, and contribute to cleaner living, better health habits, and a true respect for the rules of play, authority of officials, and consideration of, not a lone opponent, but all with whom contact is had.

My objective shall be to make competitive athletics truly a part of the educational program.

My personal conduct on the field, in the school and out, shall be such as to be truly worthy of imitation by the boys and girls whose welfare is my job.

My relationship with the players, fellow coaches, teachers, and school authorities shall be such as to develop mutual respect and confidence.

My objective shall be to win, if possible, to lose, if necessary, but at all times to have the conduct of all contribute to a fuller understanding and a keener appreciation of fair play.

I shall teach that Good Sportsmanship is Good Citizenship, and as such, is essential to individuals, communities, state and nation.[11]

Coach, you have picked an exciting way to earn a living. It is my sincere hope that the ideas presented in this text will help smooth out some of the rough spots all new coaches face as they begin a career in

---

[11]Unknown, "The Coach's Code," *The Physical Educator*, May, 1969, p. 67.

coaching. May coaching be everything you ever hoped it would be for you. Good Luck.

DISCUSSION QUESTIONS

1. How do you view Little League athletics? Support your opinion.

2. How would you attempt to convince a Board of Education that they should not drop inter-scholastic athletics?

3. Should an athlete's lifestyle or dress be of any concern to a coach? Why?

4. Should athletes be permitted to use an athletic event to demonstrate and express a protest of any kind?

5. When the sole purpose in sport is to win, a "game" becomes an all or nothing experience. Explain this.

6. Should girls be permitted to play on boys' teams, even if there is a girls' team in that sport? Should boys be able to participate on a girls' team?

7. What are some ways coaches can avoid the possibility of law suits?

8. Of what value are All Star teams? Why?

9. Do state rankings have any place in high school sport? Why?

10. Should an unwed, pregnant girl be permitted to represent a school as a member of an athletic team? A boy who accepts responsibility for a pregnancy?

11. Does religion have any place in sport? Explain.

12. The farther down in the grades boys and girls begin competitive sport, the better athletes they will be in senior high school. Do you agree with this statement? Why?

13. Has anyone in the class had their father or mother as a coach? Describe this experience.

14. If the attitude of high school students toward sports is a problem in your school, what could you, as a coach, do to change this?

APPENDIX

Sources of Official Rules

I. Official AAU Rule Books and Guides
AAU directory
AAU handbook
Junior Olympic handbook
Aquatics handbook
Basketball handbook
Baton twirling rules
Boxing handbook
Diving rules
Gymnastics handbook

Amateur Athletic Union of the
United States
3400 W. 86th St.
Indianapolis, IN   46268

II. NDGWS Official Guides for Women's Sports, Including Rules
Aquatics guide
Archery-golf guide
Basketball guide
Basketball rules reprint
Bowling-fencing guide
Field Hockey-lacrosse guide
Gymnastics guide
Outing activities and winter
  sports guide

Division for Girls and Women's
Sports
1201 Sixteenth St., N.W.
Washington, D.C.   20036

III. NAIA (Rules)

National Association of Intercollegiate Athletics
1205 Baltimore
In the Dixon Inn
Kansas City, MO   64105

IV. NCAA Rule Books and Guides
Baseball guide
Basketball guide
Basketball rules
Basketball read-easy rules
Basketball scorebook
Football guide
Football rules
Football rules interpretations

NCAA Publishing Service
P.O. Box 1906
Shawnee Mission, KS   66222

V. **Books and Guides for High
School Activities**
Baseball
 Rules
 Casebook
 Umpire's manual
Basketball
 Rules
 Casebook
 Handbook
 Officials' manual
 Rules simplified and
 illustrated
 Girls basketball rules
Football
 Rules
 Casebook
 Handbook
 Officials' manual
 Rules simplified and
 illustrated

National Federation of State High
School Associations
400 Leslie Street
Elgin, IL 60120

VI. **NRA and International
Shooting Union Rule Books**
NRA smallbore rifle rules
NRA pistol rules
NRA high power rifle rules
NRA 10 meter precision air rifle
and pistol rules
ISU constitution and general
regulations
ISU rifle: smallbore free,
 smallbore standard, air rifle,
 big-bore free rifle, big-bore
 standard rifle

National Rifle Association
1600 Rhode Island Ave.,
Washington, D.C. 20036

VII. **Additional Activities**
Baseball
Official baseball (non-
professional annual)
(annual w/rules)
 Baseball (copyrighted rules)
 (for professional, semi-pro,
 amateur and youth teams)

National Baseball Congress,
338 S. Sycamore
Box 1420
Wichita, KS 67201

Baseball
(constitution tournament rules)

All American Amateur Baseball
Assn., R. D. 5, Box 316A
Johnstown, PA 15805

Baseball (American Legion)

The American Legion
P.O. Box 1055
Indianapolis, IN 46206

Baseball, Babe Ruth (13–15)
rules and regulations

Babe Ruth Baseball
P.O. Box 5000
1770 Brunswick Ave.
Trenton, NJ 08638

Baseball, Babe Ruth (16–18) rules and regulations	Babe Ruth Baseball P.O. Box 5000 1770 Brunswick Ave. Trenton, NJ 08638
Baseball, boys 9–19 rules and regulations	National Hot Stove Baseball League, Inc. P.O. Box 273 Alliance, OH 44601
Baseball (Khoury League)	George Khoury Association of Baseball leagues, Inc. 10934 Lin-Valle Dr. St. Louis, MO 63125
Baseball, Little League	Little League Baseball, Inc. P.O. Box 1127 Williamsport, PA 17701
Baseball, Mustang-Bronco Pony-Colt	Boys Baseball, Inc. P.O. Box 225 Washington, PA 15301
Baseball – official playing rules	American Amateur Baseball Congress, P.O. Box 5332 Akron, OH 44313
Billiards (official rules and records for all pocket and carom billiard games)	Billiard Congress of America Frederick J. Herzog 717 N. Michigan Ave. Chicago, IL 60611
Bowling (duckpin bowling rules)	National Duckpin Bowling Congress, 711–14th St., N.W. Washington, D.C. 20005
Bowling, women's (tenpin)	Women's International Bowling Congress, 5301 S. 76th St. Greendale, WI 53129
Bowling (tenpin)	American Bowling Congress 5301 S. 76th St. Greendale, WI 53129
Deck tennis	General Sportcraft Co., Ltd. 140 Woodbine St. Bergenfield, NJ 07621
Fencing rules	Amateur Fencers League of America, 240 Eton Place Westfield, NJ 07090
Football – touch and flag	The Athletic Institute 705 Merchandise Mart Chicago, IL 60654
Football – flag football, intramural flag football	AMF Voit, Inc. 3801 Harbor Blvd. Santa Ana, CA 92702

Football (Junior League)	Pop Warner Junior League Football, 1041 Western Savings Bank Bldg. Philadelphia, PA 19107
Golf–*The rules of golf*	United States Golf Association Golf House, Far Hills, NJ 07931
Golf rules in pictures	United States Golf Association Golf House Far Hills, NJ 07931
Golf rules in brief	United States Golf Association Golf House Fair Hills, NJ 07931
USGA golf handbook	United States Golf Association Golf House Fair Hills, NJ 07931
Gymnastics	
Age group gymnastic workbook	United States Gymnastics Federation P.O. Box 4699 Tucson, AZ 85717
Code of points for men	United States Gymnastics Federation P.O. Box 4699 Tucson, AZ 85717
Code of points for women	United States Gymnastics Federation P.O. Box 4699 Tuscon, AZ 85717
Measurements and Dimensions	United States Gymnastics Federation P.O. Box 4699 Tucson, AZ 85717
Men's judging guide and course	United States Gymnastics Federation P.O. Box 4699 Tucson, AZ 85717
USGF men's rules for competition	United States Gymnastics Federation P.O. Box 4699 Tucson, AZ 85717
Modern gymnastics	United States Gymnastics Federation P.O. Box 4699 Tucson, AZ 85717

National compulsory routines, girls	United States Gymnastics Federation P.O. Box 4699 Tucson, AZ 85717
Rules and policies for girls	United States Gymnastics Federation P.O. Box 4699 Tucson, AZ 85717
Supplement to the men's code	United States Gymnastics Federation P.O. Box 4699 Tucson, AZ 85717
Indoor hockey	Cosom, 6030 Wayzata Blvd. Minneapolis, MN 55416
Platform tennis	General Sportscraft Co., Ltd. 140 Woodbine St. Bergenfield, NJ 07621
Racquetball (rules)	International Racquetball Association 4101 Demster St. Skokie, IL 60076
Soccer (rule book)	General Sportscraft Co., Ltd. 140 Woodbine St. Bergenfield, NJ 07621
Softball — rule book for 12″ fast pitch 12″ slow pitch and 16″ slow pitch	American Softball Association of America 2801 N.E., 50th Oklahoma City, OK 73111
Squash racquets (rules)	U.S. Squash Racquets Association, Inc., 211 Ford Rd. Bala-Cynwyd, PA 19004
Tennis (rules only)	U.S. Lawn Tennis Assoc. Publications 71 University Pl. Princeton, NJ 08540
Volleyball (rules and guide)	U.S.V.B. Assn. Printer P.O. Box 109 Berne, IN 46711

Tournament Scheduling*

One of the first and most important steps in organizing competition is selecting the tournament best suited to the sport. In many sports, only one particular form of tournament is suitable, while others may adapt to more than one system.

In the planning stages of every individual tournament, there are certain factors that will determine the type of tournament to be used. Among these would be the number of entries, the time alloted for playing the tourney, the facilities that are available, and the advantages and disadvantages of each tournament structure. Also, in each individual case there will be problems and situations that will arise and have some bearing on the choice of a tournament.

Seeding

The method of seeding, where it is possible, can play an important role in elimination tournaments. A team, or player, that is "seeded" is considered to be highly rated in skill and a definite contender for the championship. The purpose of seeding is to prevent the highly skilled entries from eliminating each other in the early rounds. This is accomplished by placing the seeded teams, or players, in separate brackets. Thus, the glamour and excitement mounts when the top teams are pitted against each other in the final rounds. The final goal is to have the championship round between the two best entries, the semi-finals between the four best entries, and so on depending on the size of the tourney.

Two of the main objections to seeding are (1) matching the inferior player with a superior player, which usually ends in defeat for the former, and (2) creating dissatisfaction and resentment on the part of those players who are paired with a seeded opponent. However, if superiority is evident among certain entries, these teams, or players, should be seeded to guarantee a better outcome of the tournament.

Generally, two out of every four entries are seeded. But, in many cases, the number of seeded teams will depend on the individual situation. When the method of seeding is not practiced, entries are played by drawing lots.

Byes

Whenever a team is awarded advancement into the next round without having to compete against an opponent he is considered to have received a bye. If there are seeded teams in the tournament, they should be awarded the byes. If the original number of contestants is an exact power of two (2, 4, 8, 16, 32, etc.), the use of a bye or byes is not

*Reprinted by permission of the Rawlings Sporting Goods Company.

required. But, when the total number of contestants does not balance out to an even power of two, the system of byes is utilized to make up the difference. If there were only 13 teams, which is not a perfect power of two, the number of byes to be used would be 16 minus 13, or 3. A team that is awarded a bye automatically advances to the second round.

In elimination tournaments, if there is an even number of byes, they are divided equally and placed half at the top and half at the bottom of the bracket. The position of byes as used in Round Robin tournaments will be taken up in the discussion on that type of tournament.

Preliminary qualifying rounds

Where there are a great number of contestants, it may be necessary to conduct preliminary qualifying rounds to cut down the field. The teams that play in this "pre-tournament" tournament are drawn by lot or chosen because of poor or unknown ability. The latter method of selecting prevents losing superior entries in the qualifying rounds. After the necessary number of rounds are completed to reduce the field to the desired number, the regular elimination tournament can be charted and scheduled.

Single elimination tournaments

This type of tournament is charted in bracket form on page 296. Being the quickest method of determining a winner, the Single Elimination tournament has the disadvantage of providing fewer opportunities for contestants to play.

The number of games to be played to complete the tournament can be figured simply by subtracting 1 from the number of entries. For example; with 16 entries, 15 games will be played ($16 - 1 = 15$). In determining the number of rounds required, this total should be the same number as the power to which two must be raised to equal the number of entries. For example; with 8 contestants, two must be raised to the third power, indicating there will be three rounds. In the case of Figure 1 in which there are only 13 contestants, this total must be raised to 16, the next highest power of two. Thus, as $16 = 2^4$, there will be four rounds.

To calculate the number of games to be played in Round 1, subtract the number of byes from the number of teams and divide by two (Figures 1; $10 - 3$ (10) divided by $2 = 5$ games). As explained previously, the byes are placed as such in Figure 1, with the seeded teams being awarded the byes.

If time permits, an interesting preliminary game to the championship contest would be a play-off for third place. This gives the losers in the semi-finals an opportunity to play again and allows more teams to participate in the placement laurels.

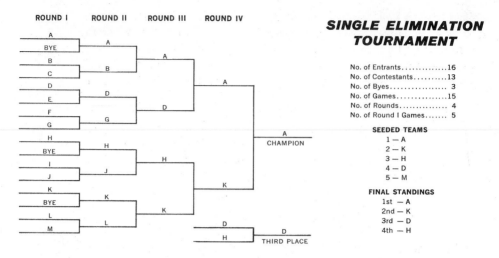

ROUND I ROUND II ROUND III ROUND IV

SINGLE ELIMINATION TOURNAMENT

No. of Entrants.............16
No. of Contestants.........13
No. of Byes................ 3
No. of Games..............15
No. of Rounds............. 4
No. of Round I Games....... 5

SEEDED TEAMS
1 — A
2 — K
3 — H
4 — D
5 — M

FINAL STANDINGS
1st — A
2nd — K
3rd — D
4th — H

CHAMPION

THIRD PLACE

Consolation tournaments

Aside from the regular elimination tourney, a Consolation tournament may be conducted with losers from the first round of play participating. This arrangement enables every entry to play in at least two contests. Weaker teams who may have drawn a seeded team in the first round and teams who have traveled long distances are given a second chance to compete.

The chart below illustrates the consolation bracket. In order to equally balance the total number of entries, three byes are used (8 entrants − 5 contestants = 3 byes). From this point, the tourney is conducted like a Single Elimination tournament, ending with a special consolation champion.

Double elimination tournaments

The Double Elimination tournament requires a much longer period of play than the Single Elimination. Each team must be defeated twice before being eliminated from further competition. As shown in the chart on the next page, the championship bracket is carried on in the usual manner, with the defeated teams dropping into the losers' bracket. The teams that win out in both brackets are matched for the championship.

If team "E" would have defeated team "G" in Figure 3, the tournament would have been over since team "G" had been defeated previously. With team "G" winning, team "E" suffers its first defeat and a rematch between the two must be held to determine the champion.

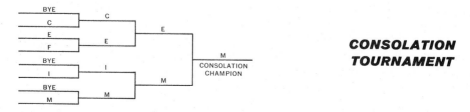

CONSOLATION CHAMPION

CONSOLATION TOURNAMENT

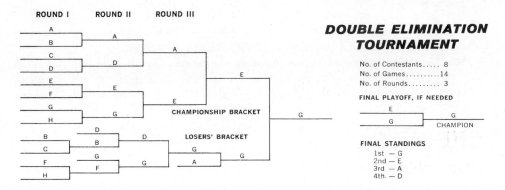

DOUBLE ELIMINATION TOURNAMENT

No. of Contestants..... 8
No. of Games..........14
No. of Rounds......... 3

FINAL PLAYOFF, IF NEEDED

FINAL STANDINGS
1st — G
2nd — E
3rd — A
4th. — D

CHAMPIONSHIP BRACKET

LOSERS' BRACKET

CHAMPION

The number of games to be played in a Double Elimination tournament is determined by subtracting 1 from the number of entries and multiplying by 2. Add one to this total for a possible championship play-off. If byes are needed in the losers' bracket, they should be arranged to avoid being matched with an entry which drew a bye in the championship bracket. Also, avoid pairing entries that have met in earlier rounds.

Round robin tournaments

Requiring a longer period of time for completion, the Round Robin tournament provides more participation for every contestant than any other type of tourney. Every player, or team, competes against every other player, or team, which stimulates interest throughout the playing season.

The final outcome of such a tournament is decided on a percentage basis. The winner is determined according to the percentage of victories, which is obtained by dividing the number of victories by the number of games played. The team with the second-best percentage is awarded second place, the team with the third-best percentage third place, and so on. As an added incentive during the playing season, team percentages should be posted from time to time. This tends to add to the competitive atmosphere of the tournament.

Before charting out a schedule, the total number of games to be played must be determined. This may be done by either of two ways:

(1) apply the formula $\dfrac{N(N-1)}{2}$ with N representing the number of entries or (2) record the number of entries (6, 5, 4, 3, 2, 1) and then cancel the highest number, adding to the remaining figures (5+4+3+2+1 = 15 games to be played).

There are many different methods of arranging and charting Round Robin tournaments. One of the most common methods is to arrange the teams in two vertical columns, as follows:

1-4
2-5   (Even Number)
3-6

With an even number of entries, the position of No. 1 remains stationary while the other numbers revolve clockwise or counter-clockwise until the original combination is reached.

In the case of an odd number of entries, a bye is used and placed at the top of the second column. With this arrangement, all numbers revolve with the first number drawing the bye or "open date" in each round.

SCHEDULES
Round Robin Tournament

4-Team Schedule

Field or Court

A	2-1	4-2	4-1
B	3-4	1-3	2-3

Field or Court **5-Team Schedule**

A	1-4	3-1	5-3	2-5	4-2
B	2-3	4-5	1-2	3-4	5-1

Field or Court **6-Team Schedule**

A	2-1	3-4	6-4	5-3	5-6
B	4-5	6-1	2-3	6-2	1-3
C	3-6	2-5	1-5	4-1	4-2

Field or Court **7-Team Schedule**

A	1-6	4-2	2-7	5-3	3-1	6-4	7-5
B	2-5	5-1	3-6	6-2	4-7	7-3	1-4
C	3-4	6-7	4-5	7-1	5-6	1-2	2-3

Field or Court **8-Team Schedule**

A	5-6	3-4	7-8	7-5	1-3	3-6	8-2
B	3-8	1-7	6-2	6-1	4-2	4-5	7-3
C	4-7	8-6	4-1	2-3	5-8	2-7	1-5
D	2-1	2-5	5-3	8-4	6-7	8-1	6-4

Field or Court **9-Team Schedule**

A	1-8	5-3	2-9	6-4	3-1	7-5	4-2	8-6	9-7
B	2-7	6-2	3-8	7-3	4-9	8-4	5-1	9-5	1-6
C	3-6	7-1	4-7	8-2	5-8	9-3	6-9	1-4	2-5
D	4-5	8-9	5-6	9-1	6-7	1-2	7-8	2-3	3-4

Field or Court **10-Team Schedule**

A	2-1	10-4	6-9	10-6	5-3	1-9	7-3	5-6	8-4
B	5-8	1-7	7-8	2-5	6-2	10-8	6-4	1-10	9-3
C	4-9	8-6	3-1	3-4	7-10	2-7	5-1	2-9	6-1
D	3-10	9-5	4-2	1-8	8-9	3-6	8-2	4-7	7-5
E	6-7	2-3	5-10	9-7	4-1	4-5	9-10	3-8	10-2

Field or Court **11-Team Schedule**

A	1-10	6-4	2-11	7-5	3-1	8-6	4-2	9-7	5-3	10-8	11-9
B	2-9	7-3	3-10	8-4	4-11	9-5	5-1	10-6	6-2	11-7	1-8
C	3-8	8-2	4-9	9-3	5-10	10-4	6-11	11-5	7-1	1-6	2-7
D	4-7	9-1	5-8	10-2	6-9	11-3	7-10	1-4	8-11	2-5	3-6
E	5-6	10-11	6-7	11-1	7-8	1-2	8-9	2-3	9-10	3-4	4-5

Field or Court **12-Team Schedule**

A	6-9	11-3	5-8	10-11	12-8	4-2	8-1	9-3	4-7	7-12	1-9
B	3-12	10-4	2-11	9-12	4-5	5-12	9-7	6-1	3-8	6-2	10-8
C	4-11	8-6	12-1	8-2	3-6	7-10	10-6	7-5	1-11	9-10	2-5
D	5-10	9-5	6-7	1-5	2-7	6-11	2-3	8-4	12-10	4-1	3-4
E	2-1	1-7	3-10	6-4	10-1	8-9	12-4	11-12	2-9	5-3	11-7
F	7-8	12-2	4-9	7-3	11-9	1-3	11-5	10-2	5-6	8-11	12-6

1-Bye
2-5
3-6   (Odd Number)
4-7

When teams do not have "home" fields or courts, a Round Robin schedule should be adjusted so that each team plays approximately the same number of games on each field or court.

Round Robin Tournament *(Continued)*   SCHEDULES

13-Team Schedule

Field or Court

A	1-12	7-5	2-13	8-6	3-1	9-7	4-2	10-8	5-3	11-9	6-4	12-10	13-11
B	2-11	8-4	3-12	9-5	4-13	10-6	5-1	11-7	6-2	12-8	7-3	13-9	1-10
C	3-10	9-3	4-11	10-4	5-12	11-5	6-13	12-6	7-1	13-7	8-2	1-8	2-9
D	4-9	10-2	5-10	11-3	6-11	12-4	7-12	13-5	8-13	1-6	9-1	2-7	3-8
E	5-8	11-1	6-9	12-2	7-10	13-3	8-11	1-4	9-12	2-5	10-13	3-6	4-7
F	6-7	12-13	7-8	13-1	8-9	1-2	9-10	2-3	10-11	3-4	11-12	4-5	5-6

14-Team Schedule

Field or Court

A	2-1	13-14	4-7	7-12	11-5	2-11	5-3	1-9	7-8	10-13	14-6	8-4	12-10
B	3-14	1-7	5-6	8-11	12-4	3-10	6-2	10-8	14-1	11-12	2-5	9-3	13-9
C	6-11	8-6	12-1	9-10	13-3	4-9	7-14	11-7	2-13	1-5	3-4	10-2	14-8
D	4-13	9-5	13-11	1-3	14-2	5-8	8-13	12-6	3-12	6-4	10-1	11-14	2-7
E	5-12	10-4	14-10	4-2	8-1	7-6	9-12	13-5	4-11	7-3	11-9	12-13	3-6
F	7-10	11-3	2-9	5-14	9-7	1-13	10-11	14-4	6-9	8-2	12-8	6-1	4-5
G	8-9	12-2	3-8	6-13	10-6	14-12	4-1	2-3	5-10	9-14	13-7	7-5	1-11

15-Team Schedule

Field or Court

A	1-14	8-6	2-15	9-7	3-1	10-8	4-2	11-9	5-3	12-10	6-4	13-11	7-5	14-12	15-13
B	2-13	9-5	3-14	10-6	4-15	11-7	5-1	12-8	6-2	13-9	7-3	14-10	8-4	15-11	1-12
C	3-12	10-4	4-13	11-5	5-14	12-6	6-15	13-7	7-1	14-8	8-2	15-9	9-3	1-10	2-11
D	4-11	11-3	5-12	12-4	6-13	13-5	7-14	14-6	8-15	15-7	9-1	1-8	10-2	2-9	3-10
E	5-10	12-2	6-11	13-3	7-12	14-4	8-13	15-5	9-14	1-6	10-15	2-7	11-1	3-8	4-9
F	6-9	13-1	7-10	14-2	8-11	15-3	9-12	1-4	10-13	2-5	11-14	3-6	12-15	4-7	5-8
G	7-8	14-15	8-9	15-1	9-10	1-2	10-11	2-3	11-12	3-4	12-13	4-5	13-14	5-6	6-7

16-Team Schedule

Field or Court

A	2-1	14-15	2-7	11-16	13-9	5-12	6-4	10-1	7-8	10-13	14-4	3-10	6-15	11-5	14-12
B	3-16	1-7	4-5	10-2	16-6	4-13	8-2	12-8	1-15	11-12	15-3	4-9	7-14	10-6	2-9
C	4-15	8-6	12-1	12-15	12-10	3-14	7-3	11-9	16-14	4-1	16-2	5-8	8-13	9-7	16-10
D	5-14	10-4	16-8	13-14	2-5	6-11	9-16	13-7	4-11	5-3	1-9	6-7	9-12	8-1	15-11
E	6-13	9-5	13-11	6-1	3-4	7-10	10-15	15-5	3-12	7-16	13-5	16-12	10-11	14-2	3-8
F	7-12	11-3	14-10	7-5	1-11	8-9	11-14	14-6	2-13	6-2	10-8	15-13	1-3	15-16	4-7
G	8-11	12-2	15-9	9-3	15-7	16-1	12-13	16-4	5-10	8-15	12-6	14-1	4-2	13-3	5-6
H	9-10	13-16	3-6	8-4	14-8	2-15	1-5	2-3	6-9	9-14	11-7	2-11	5-16	12-4	1-13

17-Team Schedule

Field or Court

A	1-16	9-7	2-17	10-8	3-1	11-9	4-2	12-10	5-3	13-11	6-4	14-12	7-5	15-13	8-6	16-14	17-15
B	2-15	10-6	3-16	11-7	4-17	12-8	5-1	13-9	6-2	14-10	7-3	15-11	8-4	16-12	9-5	17-13	1-14
C	3-14	11-5	4-15	12-6	5-16	13-7	6-17	14-8	7-1	15-9	8-2	16-10	9-3	17-11	10-4	1-12	2-13
D	4-13	12-4	5-14	13-5	6-15	14-6	7-16	15-7	8-17	16-8	9-1	17-9	10-2	1-10	11-3	2-11	3-12
E	5-12	13-3	6-13	14-4	7-14	15-5	8-15	16-6	9-16	17-7	10-17	1-8	11-1	2-9	12-2	3-10	4-11
F	6-11	14-2	7-12	15-3	8-13	16-4	9-14	17-5	10-15	1-6	11-16	2-7	12-17	3-8	13-1	4-9	5-10
G	7-10	15-1	8-11	16-2	9-12	17-3	10-13	1-4	11-14	2-5	12-15	3-6	13-16	4-7	14-17	5-8	6-9
H	8-9	16-17	9-10	17-1	10-11	1-2	11-12	2-3	12-13	3-4	13-14	4-5	14-15	5-6	15-16	6-7	7-8

18-Team Schedule

Field or Court

A	2-1	15-16	3-4	6-11	9-16	13-5	17-11	7-5	1-11	7-8	10-13	14-2	18-8	5-14	6-4	12-8	16-14
B	3-18	1-7	2-5	8-9	10-15	14-4	5-6	8-4	12-10	16-1	11-12	15-18	2-7	6-13	9-18	17-3	17-13
C	5-16	8-6	12-1	7-10	11-14	15-3	2-9	11-18	13-9	17-15	1-3	16-17	4-5	7-12	10-17	14-6	18-12
D	4-17	9-5	13-11	1-17	12-13	12-6	4-7	10-2	14-8	18-14	4-2	8-1	3-6	9-10	11-16	15-5	2-11
E	6-15	14-17	14-10	18-16	4-1	17-18	3-8	9-3	15-7	2-13	5-18	9-7	1-13	8-11	12-15	16-4	5-8
F	7-14	11-3	15-9	2-15	5-3	10-8	18-10	12-17	16-6	3-12	6-17	11-5	14-12	18-1	13-14	13-7	4-9
G	8-13	12-2	16-8	3-14	7-18	1-9	14-1	13-16	17-5	4-11	7-16	10-6	17-9	4-15	1-5	18-2	3-10
H	9-12	13-18	17-7	4-13	6-2	11-7	15-13	14-15	18-4	5-10	8-15	12-4	16-10	3-16	8-2	10-1	6-7
I	10-11	10-4	18-6	5-12	8-17	16-2	16-12	6-1	2-3	6-9	9-14	13-3	15-11	2-17	7-3	11-9	1-15

AVERAGES & PERCENTAGES

GAMES WON

GAMES PLAYED

	1	2	3	4	5	6	7	8	9	10	11	12	13	14	15	16	17	18	19	20
30	.033	.067	.100	.133	.167	.200	.233	.267	.300	.333	.367	.400	.433	.467	.500	.533	.567	.600	.633	.667
29	.034	.069	.103	.138	.172	.207	.241	.276	.310	.345	.379	.414	.448	.483	.517	.552	.586	.621	.655	.690
28	.036	.071	.107	.143	.179	.214	.250	.286	.321	.357	.393	.429	.464	.500	.536	.571	.607	.643	.679	.714
27	.037	.074	.111	.148	.185	.222	.259	.297	.333	.370	.407	.444	.481	.519	.556	.593	.630	.667	.703	.741
26	.038	.077	.115	.154	.192	.231	.269	.308	.346	.385	.423	.462	.500	.538	.577	.615	.654	.692	.731	.769
25	.040	.080	.120	.160	.200	.240	.280	.320	.360	.400	.440	.480	.520	.560	.600	.640	.680	.720	.760	.800
24	.042	.083	.125	.167	.208	.250	.292	.333	.375	.417	.458	.500	.542	.583	.625	.667	.708	.750	.792	.833
23	.043	.087	.130	.174	.217	.261	.304	.348	.391	.435	.478	.522	.565	.609	.652	.696	.739	.783	.826	.870
22	.045	.091	.136	.182	.227	.273	.318	.364	.409	.455	.500	.545	.591	.636	.682	.727	.773	.818	.864	.909
21	.048	.095	.143	.190	.238	.286	.333	.381	.429	.476	.524	.571	.619	.667	.714	.762	.810	.857	.905	.952
20	.050	.100	.150	.200	.250	.300	.350	.400	.450	.500	.550	.600	.650	.700	.750	.800	.850	.900	.950	1.000
19	.053	.105	.158	.211	.263	.316	.368	.421	.474	.526	.579	.632	.684	.737	.789	.842	.895	.947	1.000	
18	.056	.111	.167	.222	.278	.333	.389	.444	.500	.556	.611	.667	.722	.778	.833	.889	.944	1.000		
17	.059	.118	.176	.235	.294	.353	.412	.471	.529	.588	.647	.706	.765	.824	.882	.941	1.000			
16	.063	.125	.188	.250	.313	.375	.438	.500	.562	.625	.687	.750	.812	.875	.937	1.000				
15	.067	.133	.200	.267	.333	.400	.467	.533	.600	.667	.733	.800	.867	.933	1.000					
14	.071	.143	.214	.286	.357	.429	.500	.571	.643	.714	.786	.857	.929	1.000						
13	.077	.154	.231	.308	.385	.462	.538	.615	.692	.769	.846	.923	1.000							
12	.083	.167	.250	.333	.417	.500	.583	.667	.750	.833	.917	1.000								
11	.091	.182	.273	.364	.455	.545	.636	.727	.818	.909	1.000									
10	.100	.200	.300	.400	.500	.600	.700	.800	.900	1.000										
9	.111	.222	.333	.444	.556	.667	.778	.889	1.000											
8	.125	.250	.375	.500	.625	.750	.875	1.000												
7	.143	.286	.429	.571	.714	.857	1.000													
6	.167	.333	.500	.667	.833	1.000														
5	.200	.400	.600	.800	1.000															
4	.250	.500	.750	1.000																
3	.333	.667	1.000																	
2	.500	1.000																		
1	1.000																			

To use this table enter from the left in the row indicating the number of games played and from the top in the column indicating the number of games won. The intersection will give the appropriate percentage.

GAMES WON

	21	22	23	24	25	26	27	28	29	30
30	.700	.733	.767	.800	.833	.867	.900	.933	.967	1.000
29	.724	.759	.793	.828	.862	.897	.931	.966	1.000	
28	.750	.786	.821	.857	.893	.929	.964	1.000		
27	.778	.815	.852	.889	.926	.963	1.000			
26	.808	.846	.885	.923	.962	1.000				
25	.840	.880	.920	.960	1.000					
24	.875	.917	.958	1.000						
23	.913	.957	1.000							
22	.955	1.000								
21	1.000									

BIBLIOGRAPHY

Alderman, R. B. *Psychological Behavior in Sport.* Philadelphia: W. B. Saunders Company, 1974.

American Association of Health, Physical Education and Recreation Report of a National Conference, *Professional Preparation in Health, Physical Education, Recreation Education.* Washington, D.C.: American Association of Health, Physical Education and Recreation, 1962.

Bell, Mary M. "Are we exploiting high school girl athletes?" *Journal of Health, Physical Education, and Recreation* (February, 1970), p. 53.

Bevan, Bonnie Jo. "The future of interscholastic sports for girls." *Journal of Health, Physical Education and Recreation* (March, 1968), p. 39.

Boyer, John. "Drug use and abuse in athletics." *Amateur Athlete* (May, 1971), pp. 20–23.

Boyle, Robert H. *Sport: Mirror of American Life.* Boston: Little, Brown, 1963.

Counsilman, James. "Easy as taking a stroll." *Sports Illustrated* (July, 1970), pp. 38–43.

Cratty, Bryant J., *Psychology and Physical Activity.* Englewood Cliffs: Prentice-Hall, Inc. 1968.

Dahlem, Glen, "Put the bus ride to work for you." *Scholastic Coach* (April, 1968), p. 48.

Davis, William C. "Football staff organization." *Scholastic Coach* (June, 1970), pp. 36–39.

Dunn, George, J. "Common errors in the discus." *Athletic Journal* (March, 1969), pp. 49–52.

Dvorah, Robert. "Getting the most out of teaching material." *The Coaching Clinic* (May, 1970), p. 31.

Ehrhart, Robert. "The vaulter." *Coach and Athlete* (May, 1970), pp. 14, 40–41.

Farney, Paul. "Improving free-throw averages." *Coach and Athlete* (August, 1966), p. 10.

Farrally, Richard. "Circuit training for soccer." *Athletic Journal* (May, 1969), p. 61.

Fleming, Paul J., and Hainfeld, Harold. "Wrestling coaching aids." *Scholastic Coach* (February, 1970), pp. 48–50.

Forsythe, Charles E., and Keller, Irvin A. *Administration of High School Athletes*. Englewood Cliffs: Prentice-Hall, Inc., 1977.

Freeman, William H. "Training for cross country." *Scholastic Coach* (April, 1968), p. 34.

Friedman, Benny. "Look! See! React!" *Scholastic Coach* (April, 1969), pp. 36–37.

Gaffey, Bill. "Luck — preparation and opportunity." *Scholastic Coach* (November, 1968), p. 50.

Galloway, Charles M. "Teaching is more than words." *Quest* (January, 1971), pp. 67–71.

Gilbert, Bill. "Problems in a turned-on world." *Sports Illustrated* (June 23, 1969), pp. 64–72.

Governali, Paul. "The physical educator as coach." *Quest* (December, 1966), p. 30.

Grieve, Andrew. "Why eligibility regulations." *Athletic Journal* (October, 1968), pp. 64–67.

Hartman, Betty. "Training women to coach." *Journal of Health, Physical Education and Recreation* (January, 1968), pp. 25, 77.

Hayes, Woody. *Hot Line to Victory*. Columbus: Typographic Printing Co., 1969.

Henderson, Joe. "L.S.D. — long slow distance." *Track Technique* (December, 1969), pp. 1196–1199.

Hunter, Joyce. "Defense play in the circle." *Field Hockey and Lacrosse Guide* (August, 1968–1970), pp. 31–36.

Hyman, Mervin D., and White, Gordon S. *Joe Paterno: Football My Way*. New York: The Macmillan Company, 1971.

James, Frank. "Elementary school — not too early for interscholastic sports." *The Physical Educator* (March, 1965), pp. 9–11.

Keating, James W. "Athletics and the pursuit of excellence." *Education* (March, 1965), pp. 428–431.

Keith, Arthur J. "How coaches teach." *The Physical Educator* (December, 1967), p. 162.

Kleinman, Seymour. "The men vs. the women in physical education — a study in non-communication." *The Physical Educator* (May, 1970), pp. 77–78.

Kramer, Jerry. *Farewell to Football*. New York: The World Publishing Company, 1969.

———. *Instant Replay*. New York: The New American Library, 1969.

Landless, Warren R. "Tennis drills to suit your talent." *Coaching Clinic* (March, 1970), p. 28.

Larson, Bob. "Developing the running backs." *Scholastic Coach* (June, 1969), p. 30.

Levine, Howard. "Incentive devices in small school wrestling." *Athletic Journal* (September, 1968), pp. 82–83.

Loy, John W., and Kenyon, Gerald. *Sport, Culture and Society*. New York: The Macmillan Company, 1970.

Martin, Henry C. "Coaching football in junior high school." *Coach and Athlete* (October, 1970), p. 22.

Martin, T. R. "How to improve your swimmers with visual aids." *Swimming Technique* (April, 1968), pp. 5–6.

Massengale, John D. "A certified look at sportsmanship instruction." *The Physical Educator* (October, 1969), pp. 108–109.

Mathews, Donald K., and Fox, Edward L. *The Physiological Basis of Physical Education and Athletics*. Philadelphia: W. B. Saunders Company, 1971.

McCardle, William D. and Magel, John R. "Isometric vs. isotonic strength training." *Scholastic Coach* (January, 1970), pp. 32–34.

McManma, J., and Shondell, D. "Teaching volleyball fundamentals." *Journal of Health, Physical Education and Recreation* (March, 1969), pp. 43–56.

Mitchem, John, and Parkhouse, Bonnie L. "Athletics — the laboratory setting for character development." *The Physical Educator* (March, 1968), pp. 16–17.

Mordy, Margaret, ed., *Quest*. Columbus: The National Association for Physical Education of College Women and The National College Physical Education Association for Men, XIII (January, 1970).

Murphy, Hilton, Kozak, George, and Bolden, Frank. "Crowd control at athletic events." *Journal of Health, Physical Education and Recreation* (April, 1969), pp. 27–31.

Narcotic Education Bureau, 1730 Chicago Avenue, Evanston, Illinois.

Neal, Patsy. *Coaching Methods for Women*. Massachusetts: Addison Wesley Publishing Company, 1969.

Neal, Patsy, and Tutko, Thomas A. *Coaching Girls and Women: Psychological Perspectives*. Boston: Allyn and Bacon, Inc. 1975.

Niemi, Vic. "Give yourself a football clinic." *Scholastic Coach* (May, 1969), pp. 74–75.

Oberteuffer, Delbert. *Physical Education*. New York: Harper and Brothers, 1956.

Obrien, Kenneth. "Developing a finishing kick in middle distance runners." *Athletic Journal* (April, 1969), p. 40.

Ogilvie, Bruce, and Tutko, Thomas. "Sport: if you want to build character, try something else." *Psychology Today* (October, 1971), pp. 61–63.

Pietrofesa, John J., and Rosen, Al. "Interscholastic sports, misdirected? misguided? or misnomer?" *The Clearing House* (November, 1968), pp. 156, 165–169.

Poindexter, Hally B. W., and Mushier, Carole, L. *Coaching Competitive Team Sports for Girls and Women*. Philadelphia: W. B. Saunders Company, 1973.

Prokop, Ludwig. "The problem of doping." *The Journal of Sports Medicine and Physical Fitness* (June, 1965), pp. 88–90.

Rarick, G. L. "Competitive sports for young boys: controversial issues." *Medicine and Science in Sports* (December, 1969), pp. 181–184.

Reeves, Fred J. "Educational leadership of the athletic coach." *Coach and Athlete* (January, 1968), pp. 18–19, 38.

Rousculp, Charles G. *Chalk Dust on My Shoulder.* Columbus: Charles E. Merrill Company, 1969.

Sabock, Ralph J. "A comparative study of high school athletes and non-Athletes concerning ethical decisions in competitive sports situations." Unpublished Master of Arts Thesis, The Ohio State University, 1960.

——. "A history of physical education at the Ohio State University — men's and women's divisions, 1898–1969." Unpublished Ph.D. dissertation, The Ohio State University, 1969.

——. "Current problems and concerns among selected high school coaches in Pennsylvania." *Pennsylvania Journal of Health, Physical Education, and Recreation* (September, 1976), pp. 12–14.

——. "Does your quarterback know how to play the clock?" *Athletic Journal* (October, 1970), pp. 21, 77–79.

——. "Making the most out of pre-season practice." *Scholastic Coach* (May, 1970), pp. 42, 94–95.

——. "Perspiration and inspiration, a five day summer camp experience with the Fellowship of Christian Athletes." *The Ohio High School Athlete* (February, 1969), pp. 139–141.

Sage, George. "Team morale and the problem of intra-squad competition." *Athletic Journal* (November, 1968), p. 44.

——. *Sport and American Society.* Reading: Addison-Wesley Publishing Company, 1970.

Schaafsm, Frances. "Techniques of coaching women." *Fourth National Institute on Girls Sports* (1968), p. 123.

Schmid, Irvin R. "Pointers for the soccer coach." *The Coaching Clinic* (June, 1970), pp. 25–28.

Shillingford, Jenepher P. "The art of goal-keeping." *Field Hockey and Lacrosse Guides* (August 1968–1970), pp. 37–40.

"Should girls play on boys' teams?" *Good Housekeeping* (October, 1969), p. 215.

Simmons, Kenneth. "Track and field clubs for girls." *Journal of Health, Physical Education and Recreation* (April, 1969), pp. 43–44.

Singer, Robert N. "Athletic participation — cause or result of certain personality factors." *The Physical Educator* (December, 1967), p. 169.

Smith, Thomas A., and Brown, Guy. "Hypnosis in track and field coaching." *Track Technique, The Journal of Technical Track and Field Athletics* (December, 1969), pp. 1199–1200.

"The coach's code." *The Physical Educator* (May, 1969), p. 67. *The Pittsburgh Press, Parade.* Theodore Irwin, September, 1970.

Tutko, Thomas A. "The dynamics of a winner." *Letterman* (October/November, 1970), pp. 32–33.

___, and Ogilvie, Bruce. *Problem Athletes and How to Handle Them.* London: Pelham Books, Ltd., 1966.

Twombley, Wells. *Blanda Alive and Kicking.* Los Angeles: Nash Publishing Company, 1972.

Underwood, J. "No goody two-shoes." *Sports Illustrated* (March 10, 1969), pp. 14–23.

Vanek, Miroslav, and Cratty, Bryant J. *Psychology and the Superior Athlete.* London: The Macmillan Company, 1970.

Veller, Don. "The big question—praise or punishment." *Athletic Journal* (February, 1969), pp. 40, 78.

___. "Vital relationships for the coach." *Athletic Journal* (November, 1968), p. 54.

Wade, Nicholas. "Anabolic steroids: doctors denounce them, but athletes aren't listening." *Science* (June, 1972), pp. 1399–1403.

Welch, Edmund. "They called him coach." *Scholastic Coach* (March, 1970), p. 11.

Witthuhn, Bill. "Motivation for winning teams." *Scholastic Coach* (October, 1968), pp. 56–62.

Woods, Sherwyn. "The violent world of the athlete." *Quest* (June, 1971), pp. 55–60.

Zutz, Harold. "Athletics: its holding power in the inner-city school." *Scholastic Coach* (January, 1969), pp. 5, 82–83.

INDEX

Italicized page numbers indicate that the entry contains an illustration or an example of the subject indexed.

Actor, head coach as, 67–68
Acclimitization, 197–199, *197, 198*
Administrators, 6–8, 23, 84, 127, 152, 275
All-star games, 274
All-star teams, 272–274
Appearance, of coaches, 200–201
Assistant coaches, choosing of, 82–84
    roles of, 85–93
Awards, to athletes, 215–217

Band director, coach and, 42–43
Banquets, 178–180
Battle of life, T. Roosevelt, 48
Be the best of whatever you are, 131
Bird dogs, 233–234. Also see *Recruiting*
Booster clubs, 181–182
Budget, preparation of, 175

Captains, tapping ceremony, 179
    team, 178
Checklist, athletes', examples, 154, *155*
    coaches' pre-season, 169, *170*
Cheerleaders, coach and, 45–46
Children, of coaches, 12
Citizen of community, head coach as, 69–70
Citizen of school, head coach as, 70–71
Clinics, attendance at, 90–91
    team, 174–175
    for coaching staff, 151, 190–192, *191, 192*
Coaches, types of, 16–17
Coaches' children, 96
Coaches' families, and social events, 107–108
Coaches' wives, types of, 104
Coaching assignments, 193–195, *194, 195*
Coaching position, applying for, 14
College coaching, as career goal, 13, 21–22, *22*
Conduct, of players and coaches, 200

Consistency, of coach, 145
Courage of convictions, 142–144, *142, 144*
Creed, coaches', 287
Critics, of coaches, 11, 104–105, 48–50
Crowd control, 284–285
Cutting, of players, 206–208

Dear Coach, 40–41
Dedication, of coach, 125–126
Dependability, in assistant coach, 88
Depth chart, 212
Detective, head coach as, 62–63
Dictator, head coach as, 66–67
Dignity, of coaches, 141–142
Diplomat, head coach as, 59
Director, head coach as, 69
Discipline, 57–58, 75, 121, 126, 200, 218, 286
Drills, 128, 201
Drugs, issue of, 261–264

Ego, 71
Emotional tension, 47–48
Emulation, of other coaches, 117
Enthusiasm, 86, 128
Equipment, purchase of, 177–178
Equipment issue, 153, 177
Equipment manager, coach as, 69
Ethics, coaches', 144, 239
    definitions of, 240
    in baseball, 247, 248
    in basketball, 251
    in field hockey, 246, 247–248
    in football, 244, 245–246, 247, 249, 250, 251
    in job application, 13
    in softball, 244–245
    in track, 249–250
    N.E.A. code of, 256–258
    professional. *see* Professional ethics

Ethics (*Continued*)
  in wrestling, 249
  of assistant coach, 89
Evaluation, of player personnel, 127–128, 210–211, *209*
  seniors of program, *184–185*
"Every" concept, 39
Example, teaching by, 61–62, *60, 61*

Face in the Glass, The, 173
Fairness, in coaches, 145
Faith, need for, 6
Fame, for coaches, 4
Family, coaching's effect on, 95–98
  and social events, 196
Female coach, femininity and, 268
  married, 98–99
    survey of, *99–102*
Field general, head coach as, 69
Filming, athletic events and, 180
"Front liners", 233–234. Also see *Recruiting.*
Fundraising, 68–69, 276–277

Gimmicks, 123
Girls' athletics, as issue, 267–268
Glory, for coaches, 4
Goal identification, 126
Good judgement, in coaches, 144–145
Graduate school, 18–19
Great places make great people, 22
Guidance counselor, head coach as, 59
  recruiting role of, 236

Hal Hugemouth—Super Fan, 49–50
Head coach, desire to be, 88
Heat stroke, 197–199, *197, 198*
Honesty, 140–141
  degrees of, 243–244
Human relations, 190
Humor, in coaches, 146

Ideas, from assistant coahces, 92–93
Image, teaching through, 54–55, *55*
Imagination, in coaches, 145–146
Imitation, of other coaches, 117
Indispensable Man, The, 71
Initiative, of assistant coach, 87–88
Inner city, 71–78
  roles of coach, 73–75
Inner-city sports, support for, *77–78*
Insurance, for athletes, 218
Interest in athletes, in head coaches, 119–120
Interview questions, administrators', 15
  for assistant coaches, 83
  for head coaches, 14

Job security, 5–6
Junior high, athletics in, 269

Knowledge of sport, in assistant coaches, 86–87
  in head coaches, 131

Language, use of, 139–140
Leadership, 64–66, *64, 65*
Legal liability, 281–284
Letters, to athletes, *163–166*
  to parents, *167–168*
Liaison, assistant coach and, 92
Like You, 176
Little League athletics, 269–272
Lord of the Flies, 271
Loyalty, *85*
  in assistant coaches, 85–86

Mailing directory, athletes, 162
Male coach, married, 102–109
  survey of, *110–115*
Manager, student, 159
Marriage, athletes and, 285–286
Master schedule, pre-season, 213
Medical considerations, 154
Mediocrity, dislike for, 131–132, *131*
Moral standards, coaches, 140
Moral values, *241*
Morale, 214
Mother figure–father figure, 66
Motivation, 63–64, 121–124, *124*
Mouth guards, 153–154

Non-verbal communication, 57
Notebooks, 168–169

One Day at a Time, 8
Organization, in coaches, 138–139
  staff, 151, 152

Parent involvement, 155–158, *156, 158*
Participation in sport, inner city, 134–135
  reasons for, 132–135
Patton, General G.S., Jr., *4*
Peaks and valleys, emotional, *124*
Pep rallies, 215
Philosophy, 117, 150, 190
  of assistant coaches, 88
Physical, cards from, 218
Physical education, excusing athletes from, 275–276

Physicals, of athletes, 154
Pictures, publicity, 182–183
Plato, *242*
Playing experience, of assistant, 89
Points of decision, 17–25, *19*
Politician, head coach as, 67
Politics, in sport, 266–267
Polls, issue of, 274–275
Positive thinking, 136
Practice plans, 202–206
   during vacations, 170–171
   in field hockey, 203–204
   in tennis, 204–205
   in wrestling, 205
   in baseball, 205
   in football, 205–206
Practice procedures, 196–197
Practice schedule, master, 213
Pre-game–post-game, 214
Pregnancy, in athletes, 285–286
Pre-season, checklist, 169–170, *170*
Pre-season scrimmages, 161, 171
Press, coaches and, 35–37
Pressure, 10
Pride, in coaches, 137–138
Problems in coaching, questionnaire,
   277–280, *277*
Professional ethics, 252–256
Psychologist, head coach as, 63
Public relations, as function of coach, 58
Publicity writer, student, 160–161

Questionnaire, recruiting, *226*

Rapport with athletes, assistant coaches',
   91
Reasoning, in head coach, 118
Recruiting, 223–237
   A.I.A.W. guidelines, 224
   choosing a college, 226–227
   high school coaches and, 228–230
   N.C.A.A. guidelines, 223–224
   policies of head coach, 231–233
   responsibilities of head coach, 224
   role of recruiter, 225
   types of, 233–234
Religion in sport, 267
Respect, in coaches, 120–121

Salary, 5, 10–11
Salesperson, head coach as, 58, 127
Scholarships, athletic, 273–274
Scouting, 206
Scrimmages, pre-season, 161, 171
Secretary, student, 183–184
Senioritis, 172
Sociograms, 211

Son or daughter, problems of coaching,
   284
Special problems, inner city, 76
Special relationships, for coaches, 25–46
   with administrators, 25–30
   with assistant coaches and spouses,
     41–42, *42*
   with athletes, 37
   with band director, 42–43
   with cheerleaders, 45–46
   with community, 44
   with custodians, 43–44
   with equipment sales agents, 44–45
   with faculty, 30–32, *31*
   with guidance office, 43
   with other coaches, 33–45
   with parents, 38–41, *40, 41*
   with press, 35–37
Spirit of the game, 240
Sports, elimination of, 265–266
Sportsmanship, *242*
Statistician, student, 161
Style of play, coach's decision of, 150–
   151
Survey, choosing coaching as a career,
   3–4

Talent, using available, 128
Teacher, head coach as, 54–57, *55*
Teacher-technician, assistant coach as, 86
Team meeting, 217–218
   initial, 171–174, *172, 173*
*Thirty Rules for Getting Things Done
   through People, 218–221*
Trainer, coach as, 69
   student, 161
Training rules, 199, 217
Transparent realism, 118
Travel, team, 202

Understanding, coach's need for, 132–135

Vacations, family, 182
Verbal communication, teaching through,
   55–56

White House Conference on Little
   League, 271
Winning, as issue, 268–269
   coach's ability to win, 146
   coach's desire to win, 129
Winning and losing, 135–137, *136*
Wives, of assistant coaches, 106
Work, willingness to, 130–131
Working day, 46–47, *47*